CHILDREN'S LITERATURE IN SOCIAL STUDIES

TEACHING TO THE STANDARDS

NCSS
Bulletin
95

by DeAn M. Krey

National Council for the Social Studies

Founded 1921

EDITORIAL STAFF ON THIS PUBLICATION: MICHAEL SIMPSON, TERRI ACKERMAN, RICH HANCUFF, RAINEY TISDALE, ERIC L. MILLER
ART DIRECTOR: GENE COWAN   PRODUCTION: ALEXIS BARRERO

LIBRARY OF CONGRESS CATALOG CARD NUMBER 98-068183
ISBN 0-87986-076-6

▶ TABLE OF CONTENTS

▶ ACKNOWLEDGEMENTS

I would like to express my appreciation to the entire staff at the Cooperative Children's Book Center at the University of Wisconsin-Madison. Their enthusiasm for high quality children's literature is catching.

I would also like to acknowledge the consistent help of Michael Simpson, NCSS Director of Publications, and the NCSS publications staff during the preparation of this NCSS Bulletin.

A thank you is also due to Dori Holter. Her cheerful, energetic preparation of the many versions of the manuscript was invaluable.

Finally, I want to thank my husband, Bob, for his unfailing love and support. His attention to "everything else" made it possible for me to focus on and complete this three-year project.

DeAn Krey has always known two things about young learners: that they are enthralled by beauty, and that they possess an acute sense of wonder. Dr. Krey also has a deep understanding of the role of social studies in the school curriculum. In particular, she argues that by nature of its rationale, its epistemology, and its integrative potential, social studies is, or should be, the center of the elementary school program. Other content fields can gain from social studies through an association made with proper meaning and purpose.

Guided by this wisdom, Dr. Krey has constructed a vehicle that now allows us to travel over an important region of the academic landscape. The model that she gives us to navigate this terrain is eloquent and useful, and presents a new way of thinking about the relationship between social studies standards and children's literature. The model represents a wonderful marriage between cultural narratives and content patterns and theories. We have before us the exciting prospect of learning beautiful and important stories about the human condition, as well as systematic ways to understand and apply the lessons in those stories to our lives.

As a professional community, we must be impressed with the way these recommended readings are connected to the instructional patterns presented in the standards. The books listed here are not just any books: they are the most right and powerful set of readings that can be assembled for such a task. And, together with the standards, they offer the opportunity to provide educators and students with a better way to find out who we are, how the social world works, and what is expected of us as citizens, as family members, and as human beings. A reflective journey through these books will lead us to a deeper understanding of our social covenant with one another. The stories will make us cry, make us laugh, and bring us closer together. They will help us in our continuing work to build community, to develop character, and to create content.

On behalf of the social studies community, I want to thank Dr. Krey for this wonderful contribution to our field. It is also proper and right to thank our colleague, Ginny Moore Kruse, of the Cooperative Children's Book Center at the University of Wisconsin in Madison, who has long been a friend of social studies and works tirelessly for the children of our nation.

H. Michael Hartoonian
University of Minnesota
NCSS Past President

Two developments of the 1990s merit special attention by social studies teachers. The first is the widespread adoption of the social studies standards based on ten thematic strands that were published by National Council for the Social Studies in 1994. The second is the significant increase in the number of children's books available for purchase in the United States today. Taken together, these two developments can provide powerful learning experiences for students in social studies classrooms.

The purpose of this Bulletin is to enable teachers to select current children's books whose content specifically incorporates one or more of the ten thematic strands of the social studies. In Chapter One, the ten thematic strands of social studies are presented and the value of the literature-based teaching of social studies is emphasized. The process of selecting children's books with appropriate content for teaching the ten thematic strands of social studies is addressed in Chapter Two. Although the selected books are particularly important for children at the elementary and middle levels, the reader is reminded that they can also be appropriate for use with older students.

Sample social studies literature response activities suitable for use with the books described in this Bulletin are suggested in Chapter Three. The activities have been developed using Gardner's theory of multiple intelligences as a framework. The social studies literature response activities demonstrate that it is possible to teach the major social studies strands and accommodate the various intelligences at the same time.

The remaining chapters contain a collection of 547 recommended children's books published in the 1990s. They have been selected because they are vehicles for delivering the ten thematic strands to children. Each chapter covers one thematic strand. Each title is accompanied by complete annotations. All titles presented in this volume are included in a list at the end. In the annotations, thematic strands are referred to by their number. A fold-out in the back cover allows the reader to identify the strand associated with each number.

8

CHAPTER ONE

LITERATURE-BASED INSTRUCTION IN SOCIAL STUDIES

A fresh era of thought about the teaching of social studies began in 1994 when National Council for the Social Studies (NCSS) identified ten thematic strands of social studies. The ten strands were spawned from a definition that described the social studies as "the integrated study of the social sciences and humanities to promote civic competence."[1] The strands point to a core of fundamental knowledge drawn from many academic disciplines, and most heavily from the social science "disciplines of anthropology, archaeology, economics, geography, history, law, philosophy, political science, psychology, religion and sociology, as well as appropriate content from the humanities, mathematics, and natural sciences."[2]

The Ten Thematic Strands of Social Studies

Each of the ten thematic strands encompasses meanings from one or more of the above disciplines. The ten strands are:

- Ⅰ CULTURE
- Ⅱ TIME, CONTINUITY, AND CHANGE
- Ⅲ PEOPLE, PLACES, AND ENVIRONMENTS
- Ⅳ INDIVIDUAL DEVELOPMENT AND IDENTITY
- Ⅴ INDIVIDUALS, GROUPS, AND INSTITUTIONS
- Ⅵ POWER, AUTHORITY, AND GOVERNANCE
- Ⅶ PRODUCTION, DISTRIBUTION, AND CONSUMPTION
- Ⅷ SCIENCE, TECHNOLOGY, AND SOCIETY
- Ⅸ GLOBAL CONNECTIONS
- Ⅹ CIVIC IDEALS AND PRACTICES[3]

The power of the ten thematic strands lies in their potential to serve as a framework for social studies curricula and stimulate visions of effective classroom learning experiences.

Children's Trade Books and Social Studies: The Research

With increasing frequency, visions of effective social studies learning experiences include literature-based instruction, in which children's books are used as a basis for teaching social studies. McGowan, Erickson and Neufeld make the following observations:

> Literature and social studies teaching have demonstrated a persistent, attractive connection. Educators have long argued that many features of trade books, particularly their de-

tailed descriptions, complex characters, and melodic passages, allow young readers to construct understanding in powerful ways. The potential that these books hold for promoting citizenship learning has made literature-based instruction an appealing option for many social educators.[4]

Studies advocating the teaching of social studies with a literature-based instructional approach have taken many forms.[5] Some articles list appropriate books for teaching social studies, some make rationales for literature-based social studies teaching, and others suggest strategies to be used for literature-based social studies instruction. Very few authors present evidence from research concerning the effects of literature-based instruction.

After reviewing the literature about the relationship between the form of discourse and the formation of time concepts, Downey and Levstik concluded that "the story shape" or "narrative" can provide "temporal scaffolding that makes some degree of historical understanding accessible even to quite young children."[6] This suggests that children's books are appropriate vehicles for carrying the thematic strand of Time, Continuity, and Change, in particular.

In a review of literature that included 59 references advocating literature-based instruction and presenting data-based evidence concerning the effects of literature-based social studies teaching, McGowan, Erickson and Neufeld examined the following questions: "Can literature-based instruction contribute to the teaching and learning of social studies content? In what ways? To what extent?" They sought studies that investigated (a) the extent to which students acquire social studies knowledge through literature-based instruction, (b) whether children are given opportunities to develop a range of skills central to gaining and exercising civic competence through literature-based instruction, and (c) whether teaching with children's books can promote multiple aspects of children's affective growth.[7]

McGowan, Erickson and Neufeld concluded that the research supports, to some degree, the claim that students acquire social studies knowledge through literature-based instruction. Regarding the development of student skills (or competencies) and nurturing values for civic competence, the research was described as thin and lacking, respectively. Nevertheless, they make the following recommendation, which this writer heartily endorses: "We join educators who have advanced the literature-social studies connection and recommend that teachers adopt this potentially productive instructional approach. We also recommend that researchers assemble more evidence so that the effects of literature-based teaching become common knowledge..."[8]

Children's Trade Books:
The Potential for Social Studies

Children's trade books have great potential as social studies teaching tools. They communicate social studies knowledge in an artistic manner. In books of high quality, both the author and illustrator present their subject in aesthetically pleasing forms, making human stories beautiful. The books can stimulate emotional responses in the same way as a great piece of music or a classic painting.

When used to teach social studies, high quality children's literature has the potential to accomplish many goals. First, it expands a learner's knowledge about a particular human event that has not been experienced first hand. Because it is not possible for any student to live in all of the times and places of human experience, literature can be the vehicle to transport learners into other cultures, places and eras. Literature can enable learners to experience the commonplace as well as extraordinary events. Whether reading about traveling on the Underground Railroad, visiting the Inuit, or building cathedrals, such experiences are "new" to most younger readers. For example, in *Birdie's Lighthouse*, by Deborah Hopkinson, the reader vicariously shares a child's life in the year of 1855, learning from Birdie's diary what it was like to spend a year on a tiny, isolated, rock-covered island.[9] The diary entries describe daily events and how ten-year-old Birdie learned to keep the lanterns lit, on her own, in a time of family crisis.

Second, high quality children's literature provides learners with an insider's perspective that includes the emotions of human events. Most young readers have not had enough life experience to be able to imagine what others may be experiencing emotionally as various human events occur. Well-written children's books

take time to explain and even give names to the feelings characters in the stories are experiencing. Good stories address how an immigrant mother of six children feels as she boards a ship bound for America. Good stories have illustrations that can show visually how two African American children felt when they won a cakewalk. Good stories awaken the mind and the heart. For example, in *Sun and Spoon* (1997), Gram has died.[10] Ten-year-old Spoon is struggling mightily with his sadness. He thinks he has found a way to feel better when he takes Gram's favorite deck of playing cards from his grandfather's dining room cabinet. When Grandfather misses the cards, Spoon is not only sad, but also filled with regret and worry. Readers are led to empathize with this moody, middle child as he gradually learns to cope with what is, for him, a new life experience.

Third, high quality children's literature offers a holistic picture of a human event. Good children's books present the reader with much more than "survey" textbooks usually provide. Good stories offer details of the event's setting, often not only in words but in pictures, too. Individual characters become real as their words and actions appear on a book's pages. The specific characters the reader has come to know become involved in plots where problems arise and solutions are sought. All of these elements provide a holistic, vicarious experience for anyone who reads a children's book. For example, in *The Milkman's Boy* (1997), by Donald Hall, both the text and the illustrations show us what it was like to be a part of the Graves Family Dairy in Connecticut.[11] They offer historic details about the era when some families kept cows in their backyards, when bottled milk was delivered to individual doorsteps by horse drawn cart, when small business owners knew their customers by name, and when, once in a while, someone could become gravely ill from drinking raw milk.

Fourth, good books will give readers a balance between the facts of human events and the human characteristics of the people involved. Often, textbooks or reference books provide summary statements that include dates, names of places, names of famous people, statistics of a situation, and events in sequence. The reader, in this case, never becomes familiar with the individual people, their individual aspirations, disappointments, and joys. For example, most elementary textbooks series describe the Great Depression as a time when many people could not find employment.

But in *Potato: A Tale From the Great Depression* (1997, written by Kate Lied when she was eight years old) the reader meets a real family, and each individual family member.[12] The reader is led to empathize with them as they leave Iowa to dig potatoes in Idaho and then trade potatoes for necessities to survive. The reader comes to know the individuals in this story of the Great Depression; they are not lost in summary statements about the era.

Fifth, good books will provide learners with the opportunity to identify with characters, events and emotions that are similar to their own personal experiences. For example, in Megan McDonald's *Insects Are My Life* (1995), Amanda is obsessed with insects.[13] We see her joyfully observing bugs, collecting bugs, and talking about bugs. Readers will identify with Amanda's passion for bugs because most children develop a consuming interest in something, whether it be dinosaurs, horses, soccer, computer games, origami, or beanie babies. This book naturally leads the reader to identify with Amanda and ask the question, What is my obsession? or What is of unending interest to me?

A Connecting Model:
Children's Books and the Strands

If teachers are to move forward by both refining their literature-based social studies instruction and carrying out research to support it, visualizing the relationship between the children's books they choose to use and the ten thematic strands of social studies will be necessary. The five-part model in Figure 1 can assist in the visualization process. It is a representation of the relationships between a thematic teaching unit, focus questions, classroom learning experiences, the ten thematic strands of the social studies, and civic competence. The general thematic model and a specific model are both included.

For purposes of illustration, assume that the curriculum of a school suggests the study of a unit titled "The Places We Call Home," written for children ranging in age from six to nine years old.

Brainstorming what to teach about "The Places We Call Home" could result in the following systematic itemization of knowledge in the form of sets of focus questions. (The focus questions listed here are a suggested partial listing of those that could be used in the development of Thematic Strands I to VII.)

Focus Questions for Developing Thematic Strands in a Social Studies Teaching Unit

1. Culture
   ▶ What leisure activities take place in my home(s)?
   ▶ What is the ethnic background of those who live in my home(s)?
   ▶ What traditions are observed by the people in my home(s)?
   ▶ What religious beliefs are held by people in my home(s)?
   ▶ What language(s) is (are) spoken in my home(s)?

2. Time, Continuity, and Change
   ▶ How has (have) my home(s) changed?
   ▶ When was (were) my present home(s) created?
   ▶ Has my family always lived here?
   ▶ Who else has lived here?
   ▶ What stories exist about events that have occurred in my home(s)?

3. People, Places, and Environments
   ▶ What does (do) my home(s) look like? Inside? Outside?
   ▶ What is the location of my present home(s)? Why?
   ▶ What are the physical and human characteristics of the place(s) I call home?
   ▶ Where else has my family lived?

4. Individual Development and Identity
   ▶ What is special to me about my home(s)?
   ▶ What special events have I experienced in my home(s)?
   ▶ What is my favorite space within my home(s)?

5. Individuals, Groups, and Institutions
   ▶ What family members live in my home(s)? (Each child should be invited to include all persons in the settings they call home.)
   ▶ Who are our neighbors? How are we alike/different?
   ▶ In what groups do my family members and I participate?

6. Power, Authority, and Governance
   ▶ What rules must I observe in my home(s)? Why?
   ▶ Are there rules I must follow in my yard(s) or neighborhood(s)? Why?
   ▶ Who enforces rules and laws in my neighborhood?
   ▶ How can I get help if I need it?

7. Production, Distribution, and Consumption
   ▶ How does the availability of money to the adults in my family affect their decisions about where we live?

- What does it cost to live in different types of homes?
- What personal possessions do I keep in my home(s)?[14]

These groupings of focus questions are directly related to one or more of the ten thematic strands of social studies. For example, Set Three of the question groupings given above, which begins with the question, What does (do) my home(s) look like? develops the meanings contained in Thematic Strand III, People, Places, and Environments. The remaining sets of questions for which homes are a focal point emerge from the other thematic strands creating the "integrated study of the social sciences" called for in the definition of social studies.[15]

The next phase in the teaching process, after brainstorming focus questions for a thematic unit, is to choose learning experiences which enable children to construct knowledge to answer the focus questions. The learning experiences might involve a children's book, a role play, a learning game, an interview, a computer simulation or an infinite variety of other activities. As children are engaged in these experiences, the teacher's role is to guide the children toward constructing the conceptual knowledge (or meanings) of the appropriate thematic strands of social studies. Finally, as children begin to demonstrate acquisition of knowledge related to one or more of the thematic strands, they grow toward civic competence. To summarize the entire teaching process, Figure 1 details this general thematic model for teaching social studies. The phases address (a) a thematic teaching unit, (b) focus questions, (c) classroom learning experiences which will often be literature-based, (d) thematic strands of social studies, and (e) the major purpose of social studies, which is civic competence.[16]

Figure 2 shows the relationship between a children's book and an NCSS thematic strand. It provides a visual representation of the five phases of the thematic model for teaching social studies. Beginning at the bottom of the model, a thematic teaching unit is chosen. Next, major focus questions are identified. At the center of the model, the chosen learning experience is a teacher reading aloud and sharing the illustrations in a children's book coupled with an activity to be used before, during, or after the book is read. The accompanying activity and related discussion questions should be chosen by the teacher to answer the aforementioned focus questions and, in turn, construct the thematic strands of social studies carried by the book. Finally, as children begin to demonstrate acquisition of one or more thematic strands, they grow in the knowledge necessary for civic competence, i.e., the pur-

Figure 1 – General Thematic Model for Teaching Social Studies

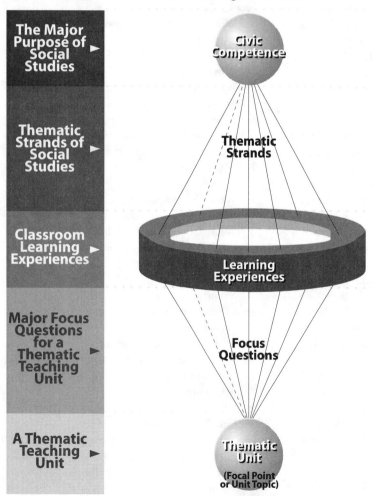

The Major Purpose of Social Studies ▶

Thematic Strands of Social Studies ▶

Classroom Learning Experiences ▶

Major Focus Questions for a Thematic Teaching Unit ▶

A Thematic Teaching Unit ▶

Civic Competence

Thematic Strands

Learning Experiences

Focus Questions

Thematic Unit
(Focal Point or Unit Topic)

Reprinted from *Social Studies and the Young Learner* 8, no. 1 (Sept-Oct 1995), 13.

Figure 2 – Literature-Based Model for Teaching a Theme of the Standards

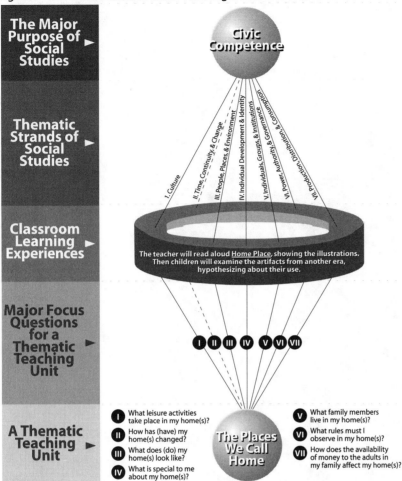

The Major Purpose of Social Studies

Thematic Strands of Social Studies

Classroom Learning Experiences

Major Focus Questions for a Thematic Teaching Unit

A Thematic Teaching Unit

Civic Competence

I. Culture
II. Time, Continuity, & Change
III. People, Places, & Environment
IV. Individual Development & Identity
V. Individuals, Groups, & Institutions
VI. Power, Authority, & Governance
VII. Production, Distribution, & Consumption

The teacher will read aloud Home Place, showing the illustrations. Then children will examine the artifacts from another era, hypothesizing about their use.

I II III IV V VI VII

I What leisure activities take place in my home(s)?
II How has (have) my home(s) changed?
III What does (do) my home(s) look like?
IV What is special to me about my home(s)?

V What family members live in my home(s)?
VI What rules must I observe in my home(s)?
VII How does the availability of money to the adults in my family affect my home(s)?

The Places We Call Home

Notes

1. National Council for the Social Studies (NCSS), *Expectations of Excellence: Curriculum Standards for Social Studies* (Washington, D.C.: National Council for the Social Studies, 1994), 3.

2. *Ibid.*

3. *Op. cit.*, 10-12.

4. Thomas M. McGowan, Lynnette Erickson and Judith A. Neufeld, "With Reason and Rhetoric: Building the Case for the Literature-Social Studies Connection," *Social Education* 60, no. 4 (1996), 203-207.

5. Mary Hammond Bernson, "Beyond Momotaro," *Social Studies and the Young Learner* 10, no. 3 (1998), 24-26; Kathryn Button, "Linking Social Studies and Literacy Development through Children's Books," *Social Studies and the Young Learner* 10, no. 4 (1998), 23-25; Luther B. Clegg and Peggy K. Ford, "Historical Fiction and Fantasy for the Young Learner," *Social Studies and the Young Learner* 9, no. 2 (1996), 24-26; Margaret J. Johnson and Carole Janisch, "Connecting Literacy with Social Studies Content," *Social Studies and the Young Learner* 10, no. 4 (1998), 6-9; Linda D. Labbo, "Off the Shelf: Resources for Celebrating the Lives of African American Women," *Social Studies and the Young Learner* 9, no. 3 (1997), 21-23; Alexa L. Sandmann and John F. Ahern, "More Children's Literature to Promote Citizenship in Upper and Middle Grades," *Social Studies and the Young Learner* 10, no. 2 (1997), 25-28; Loraine M. Stewart, "Reading beyond King, Carver, and Tubman," *Social Studies and the Young Learner* 9, no. 4 (1997), 26-27.

6. Matthew T. Downey and Linda S. Levstik, "Teaching and Learning History," in James P. Shaver (ed.), *Handbook of Research on Social Studies Teaching and Learning* (New York: MacMillan, 1991), 401.

7. McGowan, Erickson and Neufeld, 203-207.

8. McGowan, Erickson and Neufeld, 206.

9. For more details about the book, see p. 81 below.

10. For more details about the book, see pp. 116-17 below.

11. For more details about the book, see p. 148 below.

12. For more details about the book, see p. 148 below.

13. For more details about the book, see p. 111 below.

14. DeAn M. Krey, "Operationalizing the Thematic Strands of Social Studies for Young Learners." *Social Studies and the Young Learner* 8, no. 1 (1995), 12-15, 32.

15. NCSS, *op. cit.*, 3.

16. Krey, *op. cit.*, 12-14.

17. For more details about the book, see p. 64 below.

pose of the social studies, found at the top of the model.

Specifically, Figure 2 shows the relationship between a particular book and a particular NCSS thematic strand. The book is *Home Place* (1990), written by Crescent Dragonwagon and illustrated by Jerry Pinkney.[17] Together, the author and illustrator tell a beautiful story about the passing of time in our lives, about continuity in family life, and about change in rural areas (NCSS Thematic Strand II). A classroom learning activity or a social studies literature response activity is suggested for use after reading *Home Place*, which will engage children in hypothesizing about the use of artifacts from another era, just as the family in the story does. The use of a high quality trade book, along with a social studies literature response activity which focuses on the same thematic strand as the trade book, is an approach which has the potential to refine that strand in the minds of students.

CHAPTER TWO

FINDING THE RIGHT CHILDREN'S LITERATURE

Bibliographic Sources

The 1998 edition of *Children's Books in Print* reported that the number of published children's books available for purchase in the United States at that time was 126,600.[1] This represented an increase of more than 60,000 books since 1990! With this impressive number of children's books on the market, teachers who are choosing books are faced with a complex task. On the one hand, the task might seem to be a luxurious adventure, but on the other, it is an awesome challenge.

How does a teacher choose the "right" children's books for teaching social studies—i.e., the right children's books for developing the ten thematic strands of social studies in the minds of children? It is certainly not efficient for every individual teacher to take the time to browse thoroughly through catalogs, bookstores and libraries to locate the right books. Each year it is estimated that at least 4,500 new books are published in the United States for children and young adults, so the search could be a full-time pursuit![2] How does a teacher begin seeking the books that can serve as vehicles for teaching the thematic strands of social studies?

Consultations with professional librarians when seeking high quality children's books often lead to bibliographic references. Listings like *The Newbery and Caldecott Awards: A Guide to Medal and Honor Books; Children's Books: Awards and Prizes;* and *Children's Choices* are fine starting places.[3] However, these types of lists have been compiled with various literary qualities and criteria in mind as opposed to whether they have the potential to meet the goal of developing the ten thematic strands adopted by National Council for Social Studies.

There are also narrower lists that reflect the social studies content of children's books. McGowan and Powell offer bibliographies of resource books on multicultural education, social issues, and geographic areas of the world.[4] In this case the purpose for including books in these listings was their appropriate topical content as opposed to the potential for developing the ten thematic strands of social studies.

Porter identifies a dozen guides to quality literature. They include bibliographies and activity guides in the areas of history, American history, history-social science, integrated social studies, biographies, geography, cultures, multicultural literature and the *1995 Notable Children's Trade Books in the Field of Social Studies*.[5] All of these are lists that focus on the various thematic strands of social studies. For example, the history bibliographies are good sources for finding books that develop the thematic strand of Time, Continuity, and Change. The geography sources address the thematic strand of People, Places, and Environments and the sources on cultures address the thematic strand of Culture. Three current teachers' guides of this type, which are worthy of mention, are *H is for History: Using Children's Literature to Develop Historical Understandings;*[6] *G is for Geography: Children's Literature and the Five Themes;*[7] and *C is for Citizenship: Children's Literature and Civic Understanding.*[8]

However, even with these types of listings available, Alleman and Brophy point to the trade-offs that are embedded in a literary approach. After examining a K-3 textbook series that incorporates children's literature in its student materials, they identify an emerging problem. Many of the literature selections focus on trivial and peripheral aspects of social studies. They report that even when these literary sources provide appeal and interest, they often distract from the main social education understandings, and in the worst cases they create potential misconceptions or actually contradict social studies goals. One of their examples is a first grade lesson about friendship which utilizes the story of the *Little Red Hen*. They comment:

> This selection is a poor choice for this topic because it conflates personal friendship with prosocial and Golden Rule behavior. In the story, the Little Red Hen calls her friends together to solicit their help in planting and harvesting a field of wheat. Her friends refuse to help her, so when it is time to eat the fruits of her labor, she refuses to share. The story features characters who are unhelpful and spiteful and carries an undertone suggesting that friendship is conditional. These are not values we wish to instill through our social studies teaching.[9]

Alleman and Brophy conclude that the social studies goals and major understandings to be developed can "get lost in the shuffle." The social studies community must address these issues immediately.

Refining the process of selecting children's literature to be used in social studies lessons is a first step. In this first step, new criteria that address social studies goals must be used. The criteria must focus on whether or not the book being selected for use in literature-based instruction has the potential for developing one or more of the ten thematic strands of social studies in the minds of children.

The NCSS thematic strands were adopted as recently as 1994, and few authors who advocate the use of literature-based instruction have analyzed their recommended books for thematic strands, with the exception of a few articles that have appeared in *Social Studies and the Young Learner*.[10] As of fall 1998, only one comprehensive bibliographic source had attempted to identify the specific thematic strands of social studies in each children's book listed—the 1996, 1997 and 1998 *Notable Children's Trade Books in the Field of Social Studies*, published by NCSS itself.[11]

It is obvious that teachers need many more children's books to choose from, in addition to those offered in the above-mentioned sources. In response to this need, the present publication provides a recommended list of children's books published in 1990, 1991, 1992, 1993, 1994, 1995, 1996, and 1997, which are specifically selected for the list because they have the potential to develop one or more of the ten thematic strands of social studies.

Literature for Children and Young Adults

A review of social studies journals from recent years provides numerous examples of how literature can be the "carrier" of knowledge for "young adults" (older than 11) as well as the younger learner (ages 5-11). Examples follow for a variety of social studies classes for young adults, such as history, anthropology, and citizenship.

Banks suggests a literary approach to the study of immigration throughout history. He states that the literary component of social studies units can present "the human element as a balance to the…analysis of political and economic forces."[12] In the same issue of *Social Education*, Connor speaks of teaching United States history thematically. She suggests organizing a course around central ideas rather than chronological periods. In the summer, her future students are

sent lists of books organized under themes such as "Boom or Bust: Economic Development" and "American Cultural Traditions: Religion, Education, and the Arts." Students are encouraged to read at least two books, preferably on the same theme.[13]

Ahern and Sandmann discuss using literature to focus on an historical era such as the Great Depression or World War II. They remind teachers that "literature" provides readers with details of the lives of people from other times and places that go far beyond what a textbook can accomplish. For example, they suggest using *Eleanor Roosevelt: A Life of Discovery* by R. Freedman because it "describes Eleanor's sensitivity to the plight of those who were suffering during the Great Depression and her efforts to help the poor and the unemployed."[14]

Trail and Harvey describe an Advanced Placement U.S. History and English course that they team teach. A glance at their syllabus shows that "literary selections" are the core of the course. They report that "several students remarked on how much better they understood and appreciated" the era being studied because of the literature they read.[15]

Schur, a seventh grade anthropology teacher, states that great literature has the power to dispel myths about another culture by providing students with an insider's point of view. She asks students to read a novel and imagine themselves living among its characters in their time and place. As participant-observers, her students keep a journal of field notes. In this way, students gain "a holistic view of how the material possessions, customary activities and beliefs of people within a culture are interrelated and inseparable."[16]

Lamme identifies children's books for middle level classes that tell stories about child laborers. Examples are *The Bobbin Girl* (1996), *Working Cotton* (1992) and *The Day of Ahmed's Secret* (1990). (All are annotated in this book.)[17]

Trade books for reducing violence have been identified by Ronald A. Banaszak and Mary K. Banaszak. They point out that during reading, students have the opportunity to experience events along with the characters and realize consequences of violent behavior. They recommend books such as *Voices from the Streets: Former Gang Members Tell Their Stories* and Dr. Seuss's *The Butter Battle Book*.[18]

The above citations certainly support the idea that using the books that are annotated in Chapters 5-14 can be a powerful teaching/learning strategy not only for elementary children, but for older students as well. Elleman makes the following comment on using books with text and illustrations as follows:

> Many people still question using picture books with children beyond first or second grade. I wonder why. Television and films rely mostly on pictures to tell their "stories"; a greater quotient of graphics to text is often found in magazines; coffee-table books proliferate; advertisers use images to make their points in ads and commercials; CD-ROMs are filled with graphics; newspapers overflow with full-color photos and diagrams; and computer techies go to great lengths to embed more graphics into new programs. Why, then, do we disparage picture books for older children? But, we answer, older readers consider picture books baby books. If so, then where does that attitude come from? They don't seem to consider the images on the computer screen as "babyish." Do we subconsciously foster and convey this attitude?
>
> Short enough to read aloud in one sitting, picture books are ideal to stimulate classroom discussion; often filled with lyrical prose, they make good writing models; multilayered in story and content, they work in numerous connections across the classroom; and containing a wealth of art styles and mediums, they offer rich aesthetic opportunities. When we ignore picture books as a vehicle to share with children beyond primary grades, we miss a rich opportunity for turning children on to reading, learning, and appreciating art. The potential is there.[19]

The Cooperative Children's Book Center and CCBC Choices

A search for current children's books for teaching social studies was conducted at the Cooperative Children's Book Center (CCBC) at the University of Wisconsin-Madison during the winter of 1996. The CCBC is a noncirculating library of children's and young adult literature. In *CCBC Choices*, 1997, Kathleen T. Horning, Ginny Moore Kruse, and Megan Schliesman describe the CCBC and their role as follows:

As a book examination center and research library, the CCBC receives review copies of almost all of the trade and alternative press books published in English in the U.S.A. for children and young adults during the year. Each week during 1997, we examined newly published books. We subsequently read many of them. We discussed hundreds formally or informally with other librarians and educators in Wisconsin and elsewhere in the nation.[20]

Their work culminates annually with the publication of *CCBC Choices*. In *CCBC Choices* the "excellent" books of the year are recommended. The authors state, "Our criteria are simple: an excellent book is both interesting and accurate. The way in which these criteria are realized is as varied as the books themselves."[21]

During the years 1990 through 1997, 1,615 titles appeared in *Choices*. These books, already judged by the panel of experts at CCBC to be interesting and accurate, form the pool from which the social studies trade books recommended in this bulletin were selected.

The CCBC strongly encourages the use of a "multicultural" collection of children's literature. They state their belief as follows:

> The continued—and increased—publication of a wide range of voices from a wide range of cultural perspectives will help ensure that all children will find validation in the books available to them to read, as well as a stronger understanding of what it means to be a citizen of their community, their nation and the world.[22]

Criteria for Book Selection

Keeping in mind the Cooperative Children's Book Center criteria and the purpose of this publication, the following are the first four criteria used for selecting the books recommended in this publication:

1. The book has the potential for constructing one or more of the ten thematic strands of social studies in the minds of children.
2. The book is interesting. (What this means for each book is as varied as the books themselves.)
3. The book is accurate and free of misconceptions and stereotypes.
4. The collection of books, taken together, will present a multicultural view of the world.

Also taken into careful consideration were the criteria used by the Book Review Committee appointed by NCSS in cooperation with the Children's Book Council (CBC). Their annotated recommended list appears as *Notable Children's Trade Books in the Field of Social Studies* each year in *Social Education*. Their criteria have been described as follows:

> The selection committee looks for books that emphasize human relations, represent a diversity of groups and are sensitive to a broad range of cultural experiences, present an original theme or a fresh slant on a traditional topic, are easily readable and of high literary quality, and have a pleasing format and, when appropriate, illustrations that enrich the text .[23]

From consideration of the NCSS criteria, a fifth and a sixth criterion were developed for selecting the books for this bulletin.

5. The book is of high literary quality.
6. The book has illustrations or photographs that directly support the text.

Criterion six is based on a strong presumption that, for many children and young adults, the images presented in a children's book are as powerful as the text. Too often, books with wonderful illustrations are considered to be only picture books for the very youngest readers in our schools.

The final criterion used for books selected for this publication was:

7. The book is developmentally appropriate for children in the age range indicated in the annotation.

This determination of appropriateness was first made by the panel of experts at CCBC. Each book is listed with a recommended appropriate age range. Some examples are: Ages 3-6, Ages 4-10, Ages 5-8, Ages 6-11, Ages 7-10, Ages 8-12, Ages 9-11 and Ages 9-Adult. Where this author believed a book to be especially appropriate for older readers, the age range has been increased with the words "and older."

Chapter Three presents a number of examples of social studies literature response activities that are appropriate for use with many of the children's books described in the subsequent chapters.

Notes

1. R.R. Bowker, *Children's Books in Print* (New Providence, NJ: Reed Reference Publishing Company, 1998).
2. Kathleen T. Horning, Ginny Moore Kruse and Megan Schliesman, *CCBC Choices*, 1997 (Madison: Cooperative Children's Book Center, School of Education, University of Wisconsin-Madison, 1997).
3. Association for Library Service to Children, *The Newbery and Caldecott Awards: A Guide to the Medal and Honor Books* (Chicago: American Library Association, 1995); Children's Book Council, *Children's Books: Awards and Prizes* (New York: Children's Book Council, 1993); International Reading Association, "Children's Choices," *The Reading Teacher*, annually.
4. Meredith J. McGowan and James H. Powell, "An Annotated Bibliography of Resources for Literature-based Instruction," *Social Education* 60, no. 4 (1996), 231-232.
5. Priscilla H. Porter, editor. "Teacher's Resources: A Story Well Told." *Social Studies and the Young Learner* 8, no. 2 (1995), 23-26.
6. Laurel Singleton, *H is for History: Using Children's Literature to Develop Historical Understandings* (Boulder, Colorado: Social Science Education Consortium, 1995).
7. Laurel Singleton, *G is for Geography: Children's Literature and the Five Themes* (Boulder, Colorado: Social Science Education Consortium, 1993).
8. Laurel Singleton, *C is for Citizenship: Children's Literature and Civic Understanding* (Boulder, Colorado: Social Science Education Consortium, 1997).
9. Janet Alleman and Jere Brophy, "Trade-offs Embedded in the Literary Approach to Early Elementary Social Studies," *Social Studies and the Young Learner* 6, no. 3 (1994), 6-8.
10. Susan Wunder, "Addressing the Curriculum Standards for Social Studies with Children's Literature," *Social Studies and the Young Learner* 8, no. 2 (1995), 4-7; Linda D. Labbo, Sherry L. Field and Diane L. Brook, "Safari Sojourns: Exploring South Africa with the New Geography Standards," *Social Studies and the Young Learner*, 8, no. 2 (1995), 8-12; DeAn M. Krey, "Operationalizing the Thematic Strands of Social Studies," *Social Studies and the Young Learner* 8, no. 1 (1995), 12-15 and 32.
11. National Council for Social Studies, Book Review Committee, "1996 Notable Children's Trade Books in the Field of Social Studies," *Social Education*, 60, no. 4 (1996), Special Supplement; "1997 Notable Children's Trade Books in the Field of Social Studies," *Social Education* 61, no. 4 (1997), Special Supplement; "1998 Notable Children's Trade Books in the Field of Social Studies," *Social Education* 62, no. 4 (1998), Special Supplement.
12. Dennis Banks, "The Debate over Immigration Has a Human Face: A Literary Approach," *Social Education* 61, no. 4 (1997)198.
13. Mary E. Connor, "Teaching United States History Thematically," *Social Education* 61, no. 4 (1997), 203-204.
14. John Ahern, and Alexa Sandmann, "Literature and History—a Focus on the Era of the Great Depression and World War II (1929-1945)," *The Social Studies* 88, no. 6 (1997), 277-282.
15. David Traill, with the assistance of David Harvey, "Team-teaching AP History and English," *Social Education* 62, no. 2 (1998), 77-79.
16. Joean Brodsky Schur, "From Fiction to Field Notes," *Social Education* 61, no. 7 (1997), 380-384.
17. Linda Leonard Lamme, "Child Laborers in Children's Literature," *Social Education* 62, no. 1 (1998), in the *Middle Level Learning* supplement, M15-M16.
18. Ronald A. Banaszak and Mary K. Banaszak, "Trade Books for Reducing Violence," *Social Education* 61, no. 5 (1997), 270-271.
19. Barbara Elleman, editor, "Picture Book Potential," *Book Links* 5, no. 4 (1996), 5.
20. Horning, Kruse and Schliesman, *op. cit.,* 6
21. *Ibid.*
22. *Op. cit.,* 11.
23. "1998 Notable Children's Trade Books in the Field of Social Studies, " *Social Education* 62, no. 4 (1998), special supplement, 2.

SOCIAL STUDIES LITERATURE RESPONSE ACTIVITIES

For an activity to qualify as a social studies literature response activity, it must have two characteristics. First, the activity must focus on the one or more thematic strands of social studies (i.e., Culture or Time, Continuity, and Change) that are developed in the trade book that is being read. Second, the activity must be child-centered and varied to provide for the multiple intelligences possessed by children. Only then will children be able to construct social studies knowledge and to refine and clarify the meaning of a thematic strand in their minds.

Gardner has identified eight learning styles or capacities for learning that he calls multiple intelligences. Concisely defined, they are:

1. *Linguistic.* Children who are strongly linguistic think in words.
2. *Logical-Mathematical.* Children who are strongly logical-mathematical think by reasoning.
3. *Spatial.* Children who are strongly spatial think in images and pictures.
4. *Bodily-Kinesthetic.* Children who are strongly bodily-kinesthetic think through somatic sensations.
5. *Musical.* Children who are strongly musical think via rhythms and melodies.
6. *Interpersonal.* Children who are strongly interpersonal think by bouncing ideas off other people.
7. *Intrapersonal.* Children who are strongly intrapersonal think deeply inside of themselves.[1]
8. *Naturalistic.* Children who are strongly naturalistic think by using sensory input from nature.[2]

No single learning activity can accommodate all eight types of intelligence at once, but most activities can speak to two or three intelligences at the same time. It is therefore important for teachers to keep track of the intelligences each social studies learning experience addresses, so that, over time, all intelligences will be accommodated. Many challenges are posed by the search for a balance that will enable all eight intelligences to be put to use.

Each of the following social studies literature response activities reflects a dimension of multiple intelligence theory, and each is presented in conjunction with one of the trade books annotated later in this book. The social studies thematic strands are identified, along with the intelligences the activity addresses. Most of the sample activities can also be used with many other works of literature recommended in this book.

Linguistic Intelligence

Linguistic learners thrive on the use of words. They excel when they are asked to respond to a story in either oral or written form. For example, a social studies literature response activity to Margaree King Mitchell's *Uncle Jed's Barbershop* would be a teacher-guided, planned class discussion.[3] It would address the economic sacrifices Uncle Jed made while trying to make a living during the depression years in the segregated South. The teacher's role, in this case, would be to plan questions that would draw out student understandings and emotional responses to the story, and develop the social studies strand of Production, Distribution, and Consumption at the same time.

A written, linguistic response might follow the reading of *Snow Day* by Barbara M. Joosse, in which a family observes a day off from school.[4] Learners could write "big books" about what they did on a day off during the school year. They would move through the process of brainstorming, writing, editing, illustrating and publishing. An effective form of publishing is to have authors read their finished books to younger children who have not seen the books in the making. The "big books" could illustrate family traditions and cooperative activities with peer groups, and would thus develop the social studies theme of Individuals, Groups, and Institutions.

Simple, linguistic prompts could be used to stimulate writing after reading James Stevenson's *I Had A Lot of Wishes*.[5] Students could be asked to complete one or both of the following sentence stems, "My wish that came true was . . . ." and "I am still wishing for . . . ." The social studies theme of Individual Development and Identity can be developed through this activity.

Logical-Mathematical Intelligence

Logical-mathematical learners excel in activities that call for reasoning. After reading David Macaulay's *Shortcut*, learners could make cause-effect paper chains that recount the series of events set in motion by the farmer, Albert, and his horse, June, as they made their way to market one sunny day.[6] This activity addresses the social studies strand of Time, Continuity, and Change.

Creating a timeline is another logical-mathematical activity that could follow the reading of Anne Shelby's *Home Place*.[7] Children could choose one of the toys representing each of the six generations in the story, sketch it, and place it appropriately on a class timeline, showing Time, Continuity, and Change.

Having read *Great Grandma Tells of Threshing Day*, by Verda Cross, the teacher could take dictation from the students in order to create a chart to classify the gender-determined working roles of men, women, and children during annual neighborhood threshing bees.[8] The book's setting is on the Great Plains of the mid-twentieth century. The activity illustrates the social studies strand of Individuals, Groups, and Institutions.

Spatial Learners

Bonnie and Arthur Geisert's *Haystack* follows the changes in a haystack, which is presented as a resource throughout the seasons, as it serves people and animals on a Midwestern farm.[9] Since spatial learners rely on images and pictures, a social studies literature response activity to accommodate their needs would be to have students work in groups of four to sketch the haystack in each season. The cycle diagrams could be used to create bulletin board displays. In this case, the learner is acquiring knowledge and understanding of the theme of Production, Consumption, and Distribution.

George Littlechild comments in verse and collage form on his life as a member of the Cree nation in *This Land is My Land*.[10] A spatial social studies literature response would be to have students use their individual class pictures in personal collages that represent their own lives. This art project would reflect the social studies theme of Individual Development and Identity.

In *The Whispering Cloth*, Pegi Dietz Shea presents Hmong story cloths as a record of Hmong migration.[11] For a spatial activity, learners could make simple, sequential drawings that recall a move they have made from one home to another, or a trip they have taken—perhaps even an overnight with a friend. Like the Hmong story cloths, the drawings should tell a story. The social studies theme of Time, Continuity, and Change can be developed in this activity.

Bodily-Kinesthetic Intelligence

The learner with bodily-kinesthetic intelligence tunes in to the world through touch and movement. This learner enjoys sport and physical movement and has a sense of timing when moving the body. Mary D. Lankford's trade book *Hopscotch Around the World* invites readers to actually engage in several versions of the game, as directed by the illustrations and instructions in the book.[12] The book shows children throughout the world playing hopscotch, allowing students to learn the commonality of leisure pursuits and to understand reasons for some of the differences in the way the game is played. Older children can work in small groups to teach one another the games. Younger children will need teacher guidance to learn one game at a time. It is an ideal bodily-kinesthetic activity that demonstrates similarity and differences in culture(s) (strand one).

Chato's Kitchen by Gary Soto is another book that suggests an activity that uses somatic sensations.[13] In the book Chato prepares frijoles (beans), tortillas, salsa, enchiladas, arroz (rice), guacamole, and flan (caramel custard). The teacher and learners might prepare just one of the foods, while help could be enlisted from parents to prepare others. Both the preparation process and the tasting will stimulate the bodily-kinesthetic learner. In this activity, one aspect of Culture emerges.

Diane Hoyt Goldsmith's *Pueblo Storyteller* describes the process of forming the traditional storyteller figure from clay, as seen through the eyes of an eight-year-old Cochiti girl.[14] After reading the steps aloud and clarifying the steps, children can work in pairs with clay to form their own storytellers. One child can form "the grandfather" or "grandmother" and the second child can form the children. The pair should also try to remember a story they have heard their older relatives tell, perhaps about a place they lived in the past and how they worked and had fun with family and friends there. When the figures are complete and the stories recalled, they should be shared with another pair of children. It is clear that this activity accommodates both the bodily-kinesthetic and the linguistic intelligences, while building the social studies theme of Culture.

Musical Intelligence

The musical intelligence is characterized by a sensitivity to patterns of rhythms and tones. *What a Wonderful World*, illustrated by Ashley Bryan, is a children's book that develops the meanings in the song of the same title made famous by Louis Armstrong.[15] The book portrays different environments in the world (deserts, jungles, fiords, mountains, farmlands, etc.). The illustrations use hot, brilliant colors to portray each line of the lyrics. The children in each scene are shown giving a puppet show. Of course this suggests that an appropriate social studies literature response activity might be a puppet show set to the music. Listening to a tape or CD of the song, learning to sing the song, and creating scenery and puppets will catalyze thought about Global Connections.

In George Shannon's *Climbing Kansas Mountains*, a boy and his father view their small prairie town from the top of an elevator. They discuss the patterns formed by the streets, roads, and grain fields.[16] They see the details of a Kansas community from a new perspective. A musical social studies response activity for this story could be writing lyrics to a familiar melody about the learner's own town or city. Children would need to look carefully at their own surroundings to decide what to mention in their song. Songs that repeat themselves, such as "Old McDonald Had a Farm" work well for such an activity. This activity assists in teaching the social studies theme of People, Places, and Environment.

Arnold Adoff's book *Street Music: City Poems* focuses on the sounds of city life.[17] A musical social studies literature response would be choral reading of the poetry. Working in pairs, the children should plan/orchestrate which voices should speak each line of the poem. For example, for the poem "Open Window," they would choose which voices in the class would speak the words "clang," "bang," or "crash," "smash." Then, the whole class could read one another's scripts. Inviting another class to hear the results is exciting for students as they learn about People, Places, and Environments.

The Interpersonal Learner

The learner with interpersonal intelligence possesses the desire and ability to work in situations where things can be talked over and planned with others for mutual benefit. In *The Piñata Maker: El Piñatero*, author George Ancona shows Don Ricardo making a beautiful white swan Piñata.[18] Making a papier-mâché piñata in a trio is an interpersonal activity that children enjoy. From planning through the construction process, this project requires interaction. The interaction allows the learner to develop an understanding of the social studies theme of Culture, in this case, Mexican culture.

Another exciting interpersonal social studies literature response is pantomiming the natural and man-made geographical features found in a children's book.

In Marsha Wilson Chall's *Up North at the Cabin*, the reader experiences a visit to "the cabin" through the eyes of a young girl.[19] After reading the story, learners could work in groups of four or five to pantomime the lake, the loon, the canoe, the dock, the chipmunk, or the woods. The rules for this interpersonal activity are: (1) no sounds can be used during the pantomime, (2) every member of the group must participate in the pantomime, and (3) as each group begins its pantomime, members must announce whether they are acting out a natural or man-made feature. The audience guesses what is being pantomimed. This activity builds the social studies theme of People, Places, and Environments.

Elijah's Angel by Michael J. Rosen is a story about a Jewish boy and his 80-year-old Christian friend, who find a way to share their December holidays.[20] An interpersonal follow-up activity for this book would be to have children interview important persons in their lives about favorite holidays. The teacher should brainstorm with children about questions appropriate to ask in their interviews. Typical questions are: With whom do you usually spend time on that holiday? What do you do on that holiday? What foods do you usually eat on that holiday? Why is it your favorite holiday? Older children can take brief notes; adults should assist younger children with their notes. The teacher should prepare a letter for young children to carry to the interview. This interpersonal activity builds the social studies theme of Individual Development and Identity.

Intrapersonal Intelligence

The learner who possesses intrapersonal intelligence enjoys working alone and feels confident doing it. This learner seeks time to reflect on personal goals, strengths and areas needing improvement. Megan McDonald's book *Insects Are My Life* introduces the reader to a child who is enthralled with learning about insects.[21] An intrapersonal social studies response activity for this book would be the creation of individual silhouettes of each child. Over the course of several days, the teacher makes silhouettes of each child, or, alternatively, older children can trace one another's silhouettes. Then, each child is asked to decide what his or her favorite interest is (i.e., what does he or she like to think about or do often?). A letter can be sent home asking the family to select a variety of objects symbolic of the child's interests, which usually results in an interesting and educational collection.

Children may also be asked to find symbols of their interests in a magazine or on a computer graphics program. The objects can then be placed "inside" the silhouettes of the children, which will be displayed in the classroom. This intrapersonal activity develops the social studies theme of Individual Development and Identity.

In Jo Hoestlandt's *Star of Fear, Star of Hope*, a story set during the Holocaust, a Jewish child gives a homemade gift to her friend, who treasures the gift and the friendship forever.[22] An intrapersonal activity would have the teacher prompt the learners to think of one of their good friends. Then a variety of materials would be provided so that children could make appropriate gifts to give to their friends. In this case, in which a friend disappeared as a result of government persecution and never returned, both the themes of Power, Authority, and Governance and Individual Development and Identity are promoted.

Another intrapersonal activity would begin with listening to the song "Getting to Know You," after which the teacher and children would read *Kodomo* by Susan Kuklin.[23] In this book, individual Japanese children are described in words and photographs. Information is included about their ages, their siblings, their lives at home, their lives at school, and their personal interests. After sharing the book, the teacher can prompt learners to think of the things about themselves that they could share with a child who lives somewhere else in the world. This list could be entered in their journals to be referred to when the teacher provides them with an e-mail, or pen-pal address of a child from another part of the world. The theme of Global Connections would be the social studies focus of this lesson.

Naturalistic Intelligence

Naturalistic intelligence is the ability to use sensory input from nature to gain information and enhance one's ability to adapt and survive in the world. In Kathryn Lasky's book *The Most Beautiful Roof in the World: Exploring the Rainforest Canopy*, the reader is introduced to scientist Meg Lowman and her two sons.[24] In this true story, rock climbing equipment is used to gather specimens from the upper layers of the rainforest in order to learn about its ecosystem. A social studies response activity would be a field trip to a nature center, where guides point out common specimens in an ecosystem and students record their observations in the same manner as Lowman. This naturalistic activity develops the social studies theme of Science, Technology, and Society in the minds of children.

Lynn Reiser's *Beach Feet* uses rhyme to explore human feet and marine life found at a beach.[25] A naturalistic social studies literature response activity would be to listen to a recording of the sounds of the ocean while writing rhyming verse about the activities that humans participate in when they visit a beach: picnicking, building sand castles, sunning, flying kites, playing volleyball or bird watching. The social studies theme of People, Places, and Environments can be developed here.

The book *Seedfolks* by Paul Fleischman is set in an economically disadvantaged urban neighborhood in which some of the residents are relative newcomers to the United States and others have lived there for a lifetime.[26] One by one they claim a spot in a vacant lot and plant gardens. Each one treasures his or her own garden for different reasons and becomes a happier, healthier person. A naturalistic social studies response to this story would be a class community beautification project such as making a small planting in a park or preparing a planter for a senior citizens' center. From fundraising to planting and tending the plants, the activity exemplifies the social studies theme of Civic Ideals and Practices.

Notes

1. Thomas Armstrong, *Multiple Intelligences in the Classroom* (Alexandria, VA: Association for Supervision and Curriculum Development, 1994), 27.
2. Howard Gardner, "Reflections on Multiple Intelligences: Myths and Messages," *Phi Delta Kappan* 77, no. 3 (1995), 200-209.
3. For more details about *Uncle Jed's Barbershop*, see p. 149 below.
4. For more details about *Snow Day*, see p. 132 below.
5. For more details about *I Had A Lot of Wishes*, see p. 110 below.
6. For more details about *Shortcut*, see p. 116 below.
7. For more details about *Home Place*, see p. 64 below.
8. For more details about *Great Grandma Tells of Threshing Day*, see p. 87 below.
9. For more details about *Haystack*, see p. 87 below.
10. For more details about *This Land Is My Land*, see p. 70 below.
11. For more details about *The Whispering Cloth*, see p. 53 below.
12. For more details about *Hopscotch Around the World*, see p. 161 below.
13. For more details about *Chato's Kitchen*, see p. 31 below.
14. For more details about *Pueblo Storyteller*, see p. 46 below.
15. For more details about *What A Wonderful World*, see p. 52 below.
16. For more details about *Climbing Kansas Mountains*, see p. 83 below.
17. For more details about *Street Music: City Poems*, see p. 95 below.
18. For more details about *The Piñata Maker: El Piñatero*, see pp. 45-46 below.
19. For more details about *Up North at the Cabin*, see p. 96 below.
20. For more details about *Elijah's Angel*, see pp. 127-28 below.

21. For more details about *Insects Are My Life*, see p. 111 below.
22. For more details about *Star of Fear, Star of Hope*, see p. 142 below.
23. For more details about *Kodomo*, see p. 39 below.
24. For more details about *The Most Beautiful Roof in the World*, see p. 154 below.
25. For more details about *Beach Feet*, see p. 80 below.
26. For more details about *Seedfolks*, see pp. 169-70 below.

CHAPTER FOUR

SELECTION CRITERIA

The ten chapters that follow contain annotated lists of children's books published in the 1990s that offer particularly valuable support for standards-based social studies teaching. Each chapter includes books that represent one of the ten thematic standards of social studies. The collection includes the following literary genres: (a) historical fiction; (b) contemporary realistic fiction; (c) picture books; (d) biographies and autobiographies; (e) poetry and song books; (f) informational books; and (g) folklore.

The books lend themselves to a variety of reading strategies. Many would be wonderful for teachers to read aloud. Some could be used with small groups of children in literature circles. Others could be read independently by children. And still others could be offered in sets for children to select as resources for project work. Teachers will need to guide students toward books which meet their particular reading skills.

The Screening Process

No claim is made here that the recommended collection contains the "best" or the "only" books written in the 1990s for teaching social studies. But the collection presented has undergone a double screening process, first by the panel of experts at the Cooperative Children's Book Center in Madison, Wisconsin, and secondly, by the author. However, not every book in the collection is for every child, every classroom setting or every family. Teachers must engage in a third reading or screening which focuses on the appropriateness of the book for their particular classroom and school community.

It is intended that the books in this collection will (a) serve as models of the types of books that incorporate the thematic strands of social studies and (b) exemplify the high quality of children's literature that is currently available for classroom use in social studies. Most importantly, this collection is presented to assist teachers in the process of locating the children's books they need for teaching social studies in their classrooms.

The criteria for selecting the books in this recommended collection were:

1. The book has the potential to develop one or more of the ten thematic strands of social studies in the minds of children.
2. The book is interesting. (The way this is accomplished in each book is as varied as the books themselves.)
3. The book is accurate and free of misconceptions and stereotypes.
4. The collection of books, taken together, will present a multicultural view of the world.
5. The book is of high literary quality.
6. The book has illustrations or photographs which support the text.
7. The book is developmentally appropriate for young readers.

Classification by the Ten Thematic Strands of Social Studies

To reiterate, the ten thematic strands of social studies sought in the books were:

- **Ⅰ CULTURE**
- **Ⅱ TIME, CONTINUITY, AND CHANGE**
- **Ⅲ PEOPLE, PLACES, AND ENVIRONMENTS**
- **Ⅳ INDIVIDUAL DEVELOPMENT AND IDENTITY**
- **Ⅴ INDIVIDUALS, GROUPS, AND INSTITUTIONS**
- **Ⅵ POWER, AUTHORITY, AND GOVERNANCE**
- **Ⅶ PRODUCTION, DISTRIBUTION, AND CONSUMPTION**
- **Ⅷ SCIENCE, TECHNOLOGY, AND SOCIETY**
- **Ⅸ GLOBAL CONNECTIONS**
- **Ⅹ CIVIC IDEALS AND PRACTICES**[1]

In the chapters that follow, each book has been classified according to the principal thematic strand of social studies that is represented in its text and illustrations. Many books incorporate more than one social studies thematic strand, and in these cases the annotation records the second and third most important strands represented in the book. Although each book is listed and annotated according to the strand with which it is most strongly connected, at the end of each chapter is a list of books whose second or third most important thematic strand is the same as the theme of the chapter.

To take an example, Paula Kurzband's *The Feather-Bed Journey* is classified under the theme of Time, Continuity, and Change in Chapter 6 because the feather bed was made in another era by a Jewish great-grandmother in Poland and later sent to a grandmother in America.[2] A secondary theme in the book is Power, Authority, and Governance because the story deals with German government actions that forced Jewish people into ghettos in Poland. Third, Global Connections are apparent in the book as a Jewish family hears how the feather bed was sent to America by a Polish farmer who helped save grandma's life.

The reader will observe, upon examination of the list, that some thematic strands are more frequently developed in the content of the books than others. This reflects the current coverage of the strands by trade books of the kind presented here. Part of the reason for this disproportionality is that a number of strands in the social studies standards are broader than others—for example, those dealing with Culture (strand I), Time, Continuity and Change (II), or People, Places and Environments (III). It is predictable that more titles will appear under these themes than, say, under the more limited and focused theme of Science, Technology, and Society (VIII). In this author's opinion, the infrequently represented strands in this collection—strands VI-X—are probably also not being given enough attention by publishers of trade books at the present time.

About the Annotations

The following is a model of the annotation system similar in style, though different in text, to the model that appears on page 2 of the *Notable Children's Trade Books* pull-out. Each annotation contains the following information:

① Title: Subtitle

② Author

③ Illustrator/Photographer

④ Publisher and Year

⑤ Number of pages

⑥ International Standard Book Number (ISBN)

⑦ Age Level

⑧ Descriptive annotation

⑨ Thematic strands of the curriculum standards for social studies (see list above) by first, second, and third choice

LAURA LOVES HORSES

Joan Hewett. Photographs by Richard Hewett. (Clarion, 1990) 40 pages. ISBN: 0-89919-844-9. Level: Ages 4-9.
Eight-year-old Laura Santana grew up surrounded by the activities at the southern California boarding and riding stable where her father is employed and near which the family lives. To this Mexican-American child's long-time pleasure in riding Sugar Baby bareback down to the creek are now added riding lessons which prepare her to compete in her first horse show. Thirty-five full-color photographs well placed on the pages picture Laura enjoying both kinds of riding, while the short text in a large typeface echoes this spirit.

The descriptive annotations for each book were prepared for *CCBC Choices* by the panel of experts at the Cooperative Children's Book Center, on the campus of the University of Wisconsin-Madison.[3] The author of this book has selected the 547 books from CCBC Choices because of their applicability to social studies themes and classified each book according to its major, second, and third thematic strands.

Educators interested in the use of trade books to support their social studies teaching can find up-to-date information on publishers in *Children's Books in Print*.[4] For easier ordering by libraries, media centers or bookstores, the ISBN (International Standard Book Number) of each book has been included in the annotation in addition to the standard information on the title, author, illustrator, publisher and year of publication.

Notes

1. National Council for the Social Studies (NCSS), *Expectations of Excellence: Curriculum Standards for Social Studies* (Washington, D.C.: National Council for the Social Studies, 1994), x-xii.
2. For more details about *The Feather-Bed Journey*, see p. 62 below.
3. *CCBC Choices* is published in Madison, WI, by the Cooperative Children's Book Center annually. This book has benefited specifically from the selections and annotations in Kathleen T. Horning, Ginny Moore Kruse and Merri V. Lindgren, *CCBC Choices* 1990; *CCBC Choices* 1991; and *CCBC Choices* 1992; Kathleen T. Horning, Ginny Moore Kruse, Megan Schliesman, with Merri V. Lindgren, *CCBC Choices* 1993; and Kathleen T. Horning, Ginny Moore Kruse and Megan Schliesman, *CCBC Choices* 1994; *CCBC Choices* 1995; *CCBC Choices* 1996; and *CCBC Choices* 1997.
4. R.R. Bowker. *Children's Books in Print*. New Providence, NJ: Reed Reference Publishing Company, 1998.

CHAPTER FIVE

CHILDREN'S TRADE BOOKS WITH CULTURE AS THE MAJOR THEMATIC STRAND

ABUELA'S WEAVE

Omar S. Castaneda. Illustrated by Enrique O. Sanchez. (Lee & Low, 1993) 32 pages. ISBN: 1-880000-00-8. Level: Ages 6-9.

When it comes to weaving, young Esperanza couldn't have a better teacher than her grandmother, a Mayan elder who is well known for her beautiful tapestries in the rural area of Guatemala where they live. But when it comes to taking the weavings into town to sell at market, her grandmother insists on staying behind. She is afraid that the birthmark on her face will discourage customers from buying their work, and she is especially anxious for the elaborate weaving she and Esperanza worked on together to get the attention it deserves. Abuela's reluctance to enter the marketplace makes Esperanza feel self-conscious about the items she has for sale, until she sees customers walking past the commercial stalls to look at her weavings. Brightly colored, distinctive illustrations by a talented new artist add to the overall appeal. Authentic cultural details enrich both the text and the pictures in this unusual story of a child's first steps toward pride and self-sufficiency.

AHYOKA AND THE TALKING LEAVES

Peter and Connie Roop. Illustrated by Yoshi Miyake. (Lothrop, Lee & Shepard, 1992) 60 pages. ISBN: 0-688-10697-8. Level: Ages 7-10 and older.

By developing a writing system for use by the Cherokee people, the Cherokee leader Sequoyah did after twelve years "what no one person had ever done before—he had created a written language from a spoken language." Sequoyah's accomplishments come to life throughout this original story featuring Sequoyah's young daughter, Ahyoka. The easy-to-read, six-chapter book is illustrated with eighteen black-and-white drawings. The 86-symbol Cherokee syllabary appears at the beginning of the story. A short bibliography follows the authors' epilogue which provides facts about the famous American Indian leader, in whose honor the "towering majestic redwoods" were named, Sequoia National Park was created, and the annual Sequoyah Children's Book Award is given by Oklahoma children.

ALL NIGHT, ALL DAY: A CHILD'S FIRST BOOK OF AFRICAN-AMERICAN SPIRITUALS

Ashley Bryan. (Atheneum Publishers, 1991) 48 pages. ISBN: 0-689-31662-3. Level: All ages.

The words and music to twenty spirituals are accompanied by luminous full-color paintings. Bryan's art provides a lush, visual interpretation of well-known songs such as "I'm Going to Eat at the Welcome Table," "Peter, Go Ring the Bells," and the title song, "All Night, All Day." This is a welcome addition to Bryan's earlier children's books that interpret this distinctive, African American contribution to music.

ALPHABET CITY

Stephen T. Johnson. (Viking, 1995) 32 pages. ISBN: 0-670-85631-2. Level: Ages 3-6.

Paintings that resound with the realism of photographs offer an enticing array of hidden (and not-so-hidden) treasures in a book that finds letters of the alphabet in cityscapes and city objects. Johnson's vision invites readers to look—and then look again—at the world around them.

THE AMAZING PAPER CUTTINGS OF HANS CHRISTIAN ANDERSEN

Beth Wagner Brust. (Ticknor & Fields, 1994) 80 pages. ISBN: 0-395-66787-9. Level: Ages 8-12 and older.

During a visit to the Hans Christian Andersen Museum in Odense, Denmark, the author learned about the paper cuttings often created by Andersen as gifts to young people. In an amazing book illustrated with thirty-three black-and-white paper cuttings, Brust shares her admiration for this dimension of the Danish writer whose world fame stems from autobiographical writings based on his harsh early years. The bibliography and source notes are organized according to the six short chapters.

THE AMERICAN EYE: ELEVEN ARTISTS OF THE TWENTIETH CENTURY

Jana Greenberg and Sandra Jordan. (Delacorte, 1995) 120 pages. ISBN: 0-385-32173-2. Level: Ages 10-18 and older.

The authors profile pioneering contemporary artists, giving examples of their art reproduced in full color, analyzing what makes each great, and suggesting why each artist is distinctively American. At the end of the text, readers will find a sixty-six term glossary offering a virtual course in art appreciation, data about each artwork pictured, a list of where to see works by the artists, a general bibliography as well as one for each artist, and a standard index. The artists are Arthur Dove, Georgia O'Keeffe, Edward Hopper, Thomas Hart Benton, Stuart Davis, Romare Bearden, Isamu Noguchi, David Smith, Jackson Pollock, Andy Warhol, and Eva Hesse. A fine companion to the authors' earlier works, THE PAINTER'S EYE: LEARNING TO LOOK AT CONTEMPORARY AMERICAN ART (Delacorte, 1991) and THE SCULPTOR'S EYE: LOOKING AT CONTEMPORARY AMERICAN ART (Delacorte, 1993).

ANGEL'S KITE / LA ESTRELLA DE ANGEL

Alberto Blanco. Illustrated by Rodolfo Morales. (Children's Book Press, 1994) 32 pages. ISBN: 0-89239-121-9. Level: Ages 4-7.

An enchanting picture book featuring lively, colorful collage art and an engaging, original story about Angel, a young man who consoles himself over the disappearance of the church bell in his Mexican town by making beautiful kites. His "comets" and "stars," as the kites are called, cheer everyone but Angel himself, until he creates one particular kite that is not only beautiful, but magical as well. Originally written in Spanish, the text is presented in English and Spanish. The singular illustrations are alive with detail created from items that the artist in every child will recognize: string, foil stars, tissue paper, fabric, and other art box treasures.

ANTHONY REYNOSO: BORN TO ROPE

Martha Cooper and Ginger Gordon. (Clarion, 1996) 32 pages. ISBN: 0-395-71690-X. Level: Ages 7-10.

Anthony Reynoso is nine years old and lives with his parents in Guadalupe, Arizona. Like his father and grandfather before him, Anthony is practicing to become a charro, or Mexican cowboy. He is a skilled rider and roper, but there is always more to learn from his father, with whom he also performs in exhibitions. Anthony's first-person voice provides the narrative for this engaging photoessay in which readers get a glimpse into other aspects of Anthony's life and community as well, from his interest in basketball, to the importance of extended family gatherings, to his excitement at the pending arrival of a new baby brother or sister.

ANY KIND OF DOG

Lynn Reiser. (Greenwillow, 1992) 24 pages. ISBN: 0-688-10915-2. Level: Ages 3-6.

"Richard wanted a dog, any kind of dog. But his mother said a dog was too much trouble . . ." Each of the substitutes that Richard's mother offers in place of a dog (caterpillar, mouse, alligator, lamb, etc.) has a feature in common with one breed of dog shown in the illustration on the facing page (an alligator, for example, is long like a dachshund), but Richard only wants a dog. The patterned language of the text balances the exaggerated humor of the illustrations in this delightful picture book.

ARCTIC MEMORIES

Normee Ekoomiak. (Henry Holt, 1990) 32 pages. ISBN: 0-8050-1254-0. Level: Age 5 and older.

Seventeen extraordinary full-color reproductions of fabric art works composed of felt applique and embroidery show Inuit ice fishing, "Iglu" life, blanket tossing, and other games, legends, and seasonal events, including an Inuit Nativity. The artist's written interpretations of specific Inuit traditions integrate his personal worldview with times and events almost totally past in James Bay in Arctic Quebec. The parallel, bilingual Inuit-English texts are visually striking. Important background information at the end describes the Inuit people and language as well as contemporary Inuit art and artists. Ekoomiak's own words explain how permanent damage to his hearing in childhood never keeps him from hearing the language of the earth's creatures. Ekoomiak's artistic tribute to his people combined with his expressions of natural unity result in a one-of-a-kind book offering multiple levels of information and insight.

ASHLEY BRYAN'S ABC OF AFRICAN AMERICAN POETRY

Ashley Bryan. (Jean Karl/Atheneum, 1997) 32 pages. ISBN: 0-689-81209-4. Level: Ages 6-12.

Lines and images from African American poetry form

the foundation of this unusual alphabet book in which Bryan lets form and content inspire one another. Rather than trying to arrange the names of twenty-six poets so that each corresponds to a single letter of the alphabet, or finding poems in which the first letter of the first word would do the same, Bryan was moved to create tempera and gouache images inspired by individual poems and then "use only the lines of each poem that inspired the image, and . . . capitalize the alphabet letter wherever it occurred in those lines." The result is an alphabet book for older children that offers a world of cultural richness and is not bound by traditional rules (though all twenty-six letters do make an appearance, in their usual order). Each dazzling page of this $12\frac{1}{2}$ x $9\frac{1}{2}$ in. volume features a full-page image in Bryan's vibrant color scheme. In the upper left-hand corner of the page is the alphabet letter; in the lower left-hand corner is the short poem or excerpted lines that relate directly to the art, with the featured letter emphasized. At the bottom of the page is the name of the African American poet who wrote the words. An acknowledgments page is arranged by each letter of the alphabet and provides the full bibliographic citation for each poem or excerpt in this bold, dynamic book.

AT THE BEACH

Huy Voun Lee. (Henry Holt, 1994) 24 pages. ISBN: 0-8050-2768-8. Level: Ages 6-10.

There's no better place for Xiao Ming to practice his Chinese character writing than in the sand at the beach, where real people and objects mirror the images of the characters he is writing. Cut-paper collages work beautifully to convey abstract symbols through simple, concrete images, from "big" (a man stretched out on the beach) to "good" (mother and child together).

BIG MEETING

Dee Parmer Woodtor. Illustrated by Dolores Johnson. (Atheneum, 1996) 32 pages. ISBN: 0-689-31933-9. Level: Ages 3-8.

"It happens the third week of August, in some places the second, when people get together Down Home." Extended families from most heritages hold regular family gatherings, but reunions have particular significance for many African American families. Readers are reminded of or introduced to this special experience through one family's visit Down Home, "a place to run free," according to the young narrator. Grandma Bessie's place and

the Little Bethel A.M.E. Church serve as the geographic locales for Down Home family events rich in emotion and memory. Johnson's characters have distinctive faces and great body language. Her etchings and aquatints with watercolor and colored pencil are wonderfully effective in this warm story celebrating and elevating small, happy moments in a conscious echo of the mid-twentieth century.

BLESSED ARE YOU: TRADITIONAL EVERYDAY HEBREW PRAYERS

Michelle Edwards. (Lothrop, Lee & Shepard, 1993) 32 pages. ISBN: 0-688-10760-5. Level: Ages 3-6.

Brief traditional Hebrew prayers suggest opportunities for opening and closing the day, asking for comfort, and offering expressions of thanksgiving and wonder. Thirteen texts are decorated with small paintings and borders and printed in Hebrew and English with transliterations of the Hebrew on the left side of each double page spread. Each full-page picture on the right side suggest a contemporary family—most often a brother and sister with their baby brother—engaged in ordinary activities: camping in the backyard, baking bread, watching a thunderstorm, playing on an ocean beach, burying a tiny dead pet in the woods, enjoying a book together on the sofa. The children are not pictured praying "because remembering God is part of their everyday lives." The distinctive full-color paintings and decorations were created for the $9\frac{1}{4}$ by 11 in. book in watercolor, gouache, and colored pencil.

A BLUE BUTTERFLY: A STORY ABOUT CLAUDE MONET

Bijou Le Tord. (Doubleday, 1995) 32 pages. ISBN: 0-385-31102-8. Level: Ages 5-8.

The beauty and heart of Monet's artistry is the subject of this graceful picture book that touches upon the passion of the painter and his exquisite work. In a text that is fewer than two hundred words, Le Tord describes Monet's painting in language that is as carefully chosen and placed as brushstrokes on a canvas. Words placed in a deliberate vertical arrangement on the page encourage readers—and listeners—to savor the images they create. Le Tord's illustrations are inspired by Monet's work. A loving, carefully crafted introduction to an artist who amazed and inspired, and to the wonder of nature that amazed and inspired him.

BOODIL MY DOG

Pija Lindenbaum. (Henry Holt, 1992) 48 pages. ISBN: 0-8050-2444-1. Level: Ages 3-7.

According to the narrator of this story, Boodil the bullterrier is the most amazing dog in the world—only her remarkable self-control keeps her from tearing the dreaded vacuum cleaner to pieces, for example. While Boodil's adoring owner describes all of her dog's endearing and impressive qualities, viewers get quite a different picture from the illustrations of an ordinary, slightly lethargic, pink-tummied, overstuffed sausage of a dog who is, indeed, everything her enthusiastic owner imagines her to be—and more!

BROWN ANGELS: AN ALBUM OF PICTURES AND VERSE

Walter Dean Myers. (HarperCollins, 1993) 40 pages. ISBN: 0-06-022917-9. Level: All ages.

Original rhymes and poems accompany old photographs of young African American children collected by Myers. Myers comments in his brief opening statement that these were children both loved in their time by the adults who prepared them for a photograph and valued by the person behind the camera. By immortalizing these Brown Angels, Myers implies the importance of all children. In writing about them, he emphasizes their beauty and worth. Preschoolers will enjoy paging through the album to see other children in photographs. Older children might make up stories about them and their families or wonder about photographs kept by their own families. Adults can reflect upon what can be understood by seeing the faces, little suits and dresses, ribbons and ties, bare feet and toys. This exquisitely designed and printed album of brown-toned photos is wonderfully decorated with the recurring image of a full-color bird in flight. Elegant bookmaking expresses Myers' tender respect for these children of yesterday.

CANTO FAMILIAR

Gary Soto. Illustrated by Annika Nelson. (Harcourt Brace, 1995) 79 pages. ISBN: 0-15-200067-4. Level: Ages 9-12.

Gary Soto offers twenty-five original poems in a collection that is rich with the sounds and images of Mexican American culture and brims with experiences of childhood. Little brothers, serapes, lost eyeglasses, tortillas, dish washing, math tests, and other familiar events and objects are depicted in poems that weave Spanish words, like touchstones, into their fabric. Colorful full-page prints by Annika Nelson accompany some poems.

THE CAROLERS

Georgia Guback. (Greenwillow, 1992) 32 pages. ISBN: 0-688-09772-3. Level: Ages 2-8.

A group of young carolers bearing a star enters a picturesque village decorated with Christmas lights. When the carolers are outside a home singing "O Little Town of Bethlehem," the landscape of Christmas Bethlehem can be seen near them and music for the carol runs along the bottom of both pages. The next double page picture shows a white family inside the home decorating cookies amidst other holiday preparations. The family joins the carolers to sing "The First Noel" at the next house where, once again, readers see both outside (the scene of an angel appearing to shepherds) and inside (a black family involved in holiday activity). At each stop the carolers make, another part of the Christmas Story unfolds in a new carol, outdoor scene, and indoor family life. One family seems to be grandparents while another is a woman and two children. The six families have visibly distinctive ways of observing Christmas: some customs are religious, some are ethnic, and some are secular. Each family joins in the spontaneous outdoor community celebration. Reading the pictures as this cumulative, wordless story evolves invites singing along. The artist developed a fresh concept by creating full-color art done in cut-paper collage.

CELEBRATING KWANZAA

Diane Hoyt-Goldsmith. Photographs by Lawrence Migdale. (Holiday House, 1993) 32 pages. ISBN: 0-8234-1048-X. Level: Ages 5-12.

Eighth-grader Andiey Barnes tells how her five-generation Chicago-area family celebrates the seven-day African American festival that begins on December 26th. The origin of this celebration and its founder, Dr. Maulana Karenga, are introduced, as are the Seven Principles. Expressions of cultural pride from present and past African American leaders are quoted to underscore the Kwanzaa values expressed throughout the book, which will appeal to older children as well as families. Sections showing Chicago's Ujamaa market and the family's Kwanzaa Karaamu, or feast, are two of several distinctive features of this striking 9¼ by 10¼ in. color photodocumentary account.

CHAMPIONS: STORIES OF TEN REMARKABLE ATHLETES

Bill Littlefield. Illustrated by Bernie Fuchs. (Little, Brown, 1993) 132 pages. ISBN: 0-316-52805-6. Level: Ages 7-12.

Ten athletes presented in this 11½ by 8½ in. volume are introduced briefly, then quoted, and finally pictured in chapters laced with dialogue. The athletes are Satchel Paige (baseball player), Julie Krone (jockey), "Pele" (soccer player), Joan Benoit Samuelson (runner), Nate Archibald (basketball player), Susan Butcher (dogsled racer), Muhammad Ali (boxer), Billie Jean King (tennis player), Diana Golder (skier), and Roberto Clemente (baseball player). Paintings of the athletes are each reproduced on a full page in full color, contributing another unique dimension to an absorbing book.

CHATO'S KITCHEN

Gary Soto. Illustrated by Susan Guevara. (Putnam, 1995) 32 pages. ISBN: 0-399-22658-3. Level: Ages 4-8.

Chato and his best friend Novio Boy are streetwise cool cats from "East Los" who are thrilled when a family of mice moves in next door. When Chato invites his new neighbors over for dinner, they innocently accept, not realizing that their host plans to serve them as the main course. Gary Soto skillfully integrates Spanish into the text of this wry cat-and-mouse tale. While surprising plot twists and amusing turns of phrase will delight monolingual English-speaking readers, there will be double the fun for those who understand Spanish as well, as Soto plays with both languages simultaneously. Equally playful is artist Susan Guevara, who fills her illustrations with cultural references: a calendar page open to May 5 (Cinco de Mayo); an elegant birds' wedding taking place in a mailbox; and tiny letters on a banana label reading sangre de Honduras. Small visual details such as these add an extra layer of meaning for observant readers without detracting from the overall fun of the story. Guevara's style suits the broad humor perfectly, as she is especially gifted at expressing subtleties of character through controlled exaggeration. ¡Delicioso!

CHICKEN SOUP BOOTS

Maria Kalman. (Viking, 1993) 36 pages. ISBN: 0-670-85201-5. Level: Ages 4-8.

Kalman's highly original artistic and literary perspectives distinguish a picture book about people at work. A traveling salesman, composer, doorman, artist, short-order cook, and fire-fighter are just a few of the occupations described. Each of them is connected by a child-narrator's voice as she talks about the various workers she encounters in her neighborhood. Her witty stream-of-consciousness description reveals as much about herself, her family, and her neighborhood as it does about the world of work.

CHRISTMAS IN THE BIG HOUSE, CHRISTMAS IN THE QUARTERS

Patricia C. and Fredrick L. McKissack. Illustrated by John Thompson. (Scholastic, 1994) 68 pages. ISBN: 0-590-43027-0. Level: Ages 8-13 and older.

To depict daily life for the two communities living in parallel realities on a Virginia plantation during December 1859, the authors gained access to primary source materials from Tidewater plantation records and held interviews there to find out more family histories. Wisely setting their text immediately before the outbreak of the Civil War, the McKissacks offer an amazing balance of perspectives while they report the distinctive culture of the Quarters. Showing the misery as well as the dignity of families in captivity, they allow readers to draw their own conclusions. Thompson's detailed paintings rendered in acrylic and reproduced in full-color recreate the season and the buildings as well as some of the distinctive Afro-centric head-wraps of enslaved women and holiday decorations in the Big House. Both the text and the illustrations move far beyond conventional media-induced images of plantation life. Incomparable in scope, content, and emotional impact, this well-designed, easy-to-read account furnishes provocative information and offers dynamic year-round reading.

CHRISTMAS TREE MEMORIES

Aliki. (HarperCollins, 1991) 32 pages. ISBN: 0-06-020007-3. Level: Ages 3-6.

Two lively children and their parents settle down for a snack in front of their lighted tree on Christmas Eve. "Some of the ornaments were older than the children. But most of them the family had made, some together with friends." Scraps of conversation and accompanying double-page spreads picture the origin of familiar decorations: a walnut cradle from Granny's, stained glass cookies shaped in kindergarten, the late Aunt Eunice's lion and lamb, museum origami, spool figures made during recovery from chicken pox, and a starfish Santa. Seasonal mementos and the anecdotes they evoke suggest a family's shared experiences as well as the anticipation of Christmas Day. Ink, watercolors, and pencil crayons were used by the artist to create the images for this lovely book.

THE CIRCLE OF THANKS: NATIVE AMERICAN POEMS AND SONGS OF THANKSGIVING

Joseph Bruchac. Illustrated by Murv Jacob. (Bridge Water, 1996) 32 pages. ISBN: 0-8167-4012-7. Level: Ages 7-11 and older.

American Indian peoples from across the country recite poems and songs of thanks to acknowledge their gratitude for creation and the bounty of the natural world. Abenaki storyteller and writer Joseph Bruchac retells some of these thanksgiving poems in a collection illustrated with Cherokee painter Murv Jacob's singular full-color art, which reflects the heritage of the people from which each poem or song originated. Reader-friendly notes at the end of the text provide additional information on the importance of each poem's subject.

CLEAN YOUR ROOM, HARVEY MOON!

Pat Cummings. (Bradbury Press, 1991) 32 pages. ISBN: 0-02-725511-5. Level: Ages 3-6.

The Voice of Doom that Harvey Moon hears when he has has settled down to watch Saturday morning cartoons is that of his mother, reminding him to clean his room. A humorous, rhyming text lists the ordinary and the extraordinary items for which poor Harvey has to find a place while the colorful, angular illustrations amusingly depict the child's archetypal problem bedroom.

COME HOME WITH ME: A MULTICULTURAL TREASURE HUNT

Aylette Jenness. Illustrated by Laura DeSantis. Photographs by Max Belcher. (The New Press, 1993) 48 pages. ISBN: 1-56584-064-X. Level: Ages 7-12 and older.

Abdus is African American, Annie is Irish American, Marcos is Puerto Rican, and Terri is Cambodian. These four friendly, appealing tour guides take readers on an exploration of the ethnically diverse Boston neighborhoods in which they live in a different kind of adventure story that combines lively, informative text with photographs and colorful graphics. Readers must turn back and forth through the pages as they make decisions about where to go and what to see next, accompanied each step of the way by one of the four children. Facts about the African American, Irish American, Latino, and Cambodian cultures are provided in stimulating asides that

will challenge children to consider the people and world around them. Inspired readers will want to follow some of the tips at the end of the text for exploring new neighborhoods and making a video like the one on which this book is based.

COMING HOME: FROM THE LIFE OF LANGSTON HUGHES

Floyd Cooper. (Philomel, 1994) 32 pages. ISBN: 0-399-22682-6. Level: Ages 4-12.

Cooper's lyrical prose and striking full-color paintings are combined in this brief, moving portrait about a prominent writer of the Harlem Renaissance. His grandma took care of young Langston Hughes in Kansas; she had once worked on the Underground Railroad, and so he heard those stories, along with ones she told him about John Brown, the Buffalo soldiers, and his own grandfather. Although Hughes apparently felt emotionally homeless as a youth, his life and works continue to offer both hope and home to many. A tour de force by Floyd Cooper.

CONFETTI: POEMS FOR CHILDREN

Pat Mora. Illustrated by Enrique O. Sanchez. (Lee & Low, 1996) 28 pages. ISBN: 1-880000-25-3. Level: Ages 5-8.

"Red shouts a loud, balloon-round sound . . ." (from "Colors Crackle, Colors Roar"). Children will delight in the imagery and rhythm of these thirteen lively, evocative poems from writer Pat Mora. Spanish words are used throughout and are defined in a glossary at the end of the book. Sanchez illustrates each verse with colorful acrylic art that is filled with energy and joy.

CUCKOO: A MEXICAN FOLKTALE/ CUCÚ: UN CUENTO FOLKLÓRICO MEXICANO

Translated into Spanish by Gloria de Aragón Andújar. (Harcourt Brace, 1997) 36 pages. ISBN: 0-15-200274-X. Level: Ages 3-9.

Even though Cuckoo was admired for her lovely voice and bright feathers, a little goes a long way when one is also vain and lazy. "Even the sweetest song can turn sour = *Pero aun la canción más dulce se puede amargar*." One day while the other birds are asleep, Cuckoo notices flames threatening to destroy a season's supply of seeds. Flying with one seed at a time in her beak, Cuckoo carries seeds "from the fiery fields to the cool woods" and drops them into Mole's tunnel. The next day a raspy cry, "Cuckoo," is the only sound Cuckoo can muster, and her feathers are scorched black. All of the creatures agree, "You can't tell much about a bird by looking at its feathers = *Todos estaban de acuerdo al final que no se puede juzgar a un pájaro por su plumaje.*" The type-face for both languages is large, and the brief text is easy to read. Ehlert's stunning Pre-Columbian palette has a strikingly contemporary appearance. In short notes written at the end of the tale for interested older readers, Ehlert writes that "the illustrations were inspired by a variety of Mexican crafts and folk art, including cut-paper fiesta banners, tin work, textiles, metal milagros, clay 'tree of life' candelabrum, and wooden toys and sculptures." Her mixed media assemblages are skillfully photographed, giving the illusion of three dimensions.

CUTTERS, CARVERS & THE CATHEDRAL

George Ancona. (Lothrop, Lee & Shepard, 1995) 32 pages. ISBN: 0-688-12056-3. Level: Ages 8-12.

Daily visitors to the Cathedral of St. John the Divine in New York City see a working cathedral where worship, festivals, concerts, art exhibits, and lectures are held, and where homeless and otherwise helpless people are befriended. This unfinished cathedral has a hidden story—one about people. Ancona traveled to a fossil-rich Indiana limestone quarry mill to photograph 11½ in. ton blocks of stone being cut for transport across five states to the Cathedral. He found the chief masonry draftsman using a computer to produce templates. He talked to carvers in the stone-yard and on scaffolds. Ancona's images and interviews reveal the diverse cultural and national backgrounds of individuals who take pride in making a cathedral during this century and the next. Color photos show the high tech work, hard labor, and artistry involved in creating a classic structure in contemporary times. A marvelous companion to materials about the Middle Ages.

THE DANCING FOX: ARCTIC FOLKTALES

John Bierhorst, editor. Illustrated by Mary K. Okheena. (Morrow, 1997) 142 pages. ISBN: 0-688-14406-3. Level: Ages 9-14 and older.

Eighteen tales retold in rich language and set in a large, easy-to-read typeface include "The Woman under the Sea," "Worms and Lice," and "The Blind Boy and the Loon." Bierhorst is known as a scholar of traditional literature with a gift for communicating old tales to today's young readers. In a splendid introduction, he explains

that traditional values remain essential to the modern Inuit community. These values are expressed many ways: in the continued use of the Inuit language; in the harvesting of Arctic foods; in music, graphic art, and the recollection of old stories. Bierhorst interprets the role of storytellers, the presence of the natural world, the "art of living," the connection of the supernatural, story sources, and "basic themes that link this distinctive literature to the world community." The tales in this handsome volume are accompanied by Inuit printmaker Mary K. Okheena's black-and-white illustrations and are followed by source notes and references.

DAY OF DELIGHT: A JEWISH SABBATH IN ETHIOPIA

Maxine Rose Schur. Illustrated by Brian Pinkney. (Dial, 1994) 32 pages. ISBN: 0-8037-1414-9. Level: Ages 5-9.

For more than one thousand years, Jews have inhabited the high mountains of Ethiopia. Using the narrative voice of a young boy, Menelik, Schur describes the hardworking inhabitants of one of these Jewish communities. The villagers make pottery, prepare raw cotton or weave, work the soil they sharecrop, grind grain into flour, and forge the iron for which they are known. Children help by collecting cow dung for fuel or harvesting honey. The work and worries of the week are set aside for the Sabbath. Menelik tells how his mother bakes dabo (white Sabbath bread) and makes wat (peppery chicken stew). Families bathe and don clean shammas before the Sabbath eating, singing, rest, and worship begin. Pinkney's full-color artwork contains important cultural details and was prepared using scratchboard, black ink, oil pastels, oil paints, and gouache.

DE COLORÉS AND OTHER LATIN-AMERICAN FOLK SONGS FOR CHILDREN

Jose-Luis Orozco, compiler. (Dutton, 1994) 56 pages. ISBN: 0-525-45260-5. Level: Ages 5-10.

Each of the twenty-seven Latin American songs, chants, and rhymes chosen by performer/songwriter Jose-Luis Orozco for inclusion in this text are presented with lyrics in Spanish and English, simple musical arrangement, and explanatory notes about the song's subject and how it is traditionally sung. Elisa Kleven's brightly colored collage illustrations are lively, joyous accompaniments to the music.

DID YOU HEAR WIND SING YOUR NAME? AN ONEIDA SONG OF SPRING

Sandra De Coteau Orie. Illustrated by Christopher Canyon. (Walker, 1995) 32 pages. ISBN: 0-8027-8350-3. Level: Ages 4-9.

A lyrical poem from Oneida writer Sandra De Coteau Orie celebrates the coming of spring with keen, gentle questions that invite children to observe and appreciate nature's gifts. "Did you see / the White Birch standing tall among the Darkwoods / and the greening of the Aspen saplings?" Orie, who grew up and still resides in Wisconsin, uses elements of nature significant to her Oneida culture to mark spring's arrival, explaining their meaning in an author's note. Canyon's rich, detailed paintings are filled with the small wonders of nature, as well as its expansive beauty.

DIEGO

Jonah Winter. Illustrated by Jeanette Winter. (Alfred A. Knopf, 1991) 32 pages. ISBN: 0-679-81987-8. Level: Ages 5-9.

A poetic, easy-to-read account of the childhood and early adulthood of Mexican muralist Diego Rivera is presented in bilingual texts (English / Spanish). Rivera is characterized as a visionary and dreamer who liked to draw the colors, people, and events he witnessed in his native land. The brief text of the $9\frac{1}{4}$ x $7\frac{1}{4}$ in. volume is accompanied throughout by bordered 3 x $3\frac{1}{2}$ in. exquisitely stylized paintings that dramatically lead up to a wordless double-page spread of Rivera at work on a mural, effectively communicating the magnitude of his art form.

DREAMCATCHER

Audrey Osofsky. Illustrated by Ed Young. (Orchard, 1992) 32 pages. ISBN: 0-531-08588-0. Level: Ages 4-9.

"A dream net for baby / like a small spiderweb / spun of nettle-stalk twine / stained dark red with the bark of wild plum" hung by the Ojibway people of centuries ago on babies' cradleboards. Such a net might serve as a charm to catch "dark dreams . . . like flies in a spider's web" before a bad dream could reach a slumbering infant. Good dreams "drift through the hole in the center of the web; dreams of . . . white shells tinkling in the breeze / pheasant feathers ruffling / sucking maple sugar in a birchbark cone." Young's decorative page borders pay tribute to the floral patterns of Ojibway artists, and his images of clothing and other objects allude to this cultural history. Ojibway language references and names are accurate. The full-color illustrations were created in pastel for this $9\frac{3}{4}$ x $10\frac{1}{2}$ in. picture book.

DREAM CATCHER: THE LEGEND AND THE LADY

Karen Hartman. Illustrated by Julie Cuccia-Watts. (Weeping Heart Publications, 1992) 56 pages. Level: Ages 6-13.

There were two books published in 1992 about the Ojibway dream catcher (or dream web, as it is sometimes called). While Osofsky's picture book describes earlier uses of the dream catcher in a work of realistic historical fiction for younger children, Hartman's book gives background information about the artistic tradition itself. She describes how she herself learned to make dream catchers from an Ojibway elder years ago and relates a story the woman told her, passed down through the generations, of how dream catchers came to be made by the Ojibway people. She then provides a step-by-step account of how she makes a dream catcher, including explanations of what each part symbolizes. This treasure trove of hard-to-find information will be a welcome addition to school and public libraries.

DRUMBEAT ... HEARTBEAT: A CELEBRATION OF THE POWWOW

Susan Braine. (We Are Still Here) (Lerner, 1995) 48 pages. ISBN: 0-8225-2656-5. Level: Ages 7-11.

Braine shares her own anticipation and excitement for the powwow with readers in an inviting, informative photoessay. Braine, a member of the Assiniboine Tribe in Montana, talks about the importance of the powwow to American Indian culture, and its significance in uniting Native and non-Native peoples. Her enthusiasm is infectious as she takes readers through a typical day at a powwow, which might include a parade, a rodeo, and many related activities, in addition to the steps and spins of the dancers and the rhythm of the drum. Engaging color photographs capture both the high energy and the reflective, quiet moments of a powwow gathering.

EAGLE DRUM: ON THE POWWOW TRAIL WITH A YOUNG GRASS DANCER

Robert Crum. (Four Winds Press, 1994) 48 pages. ISBN: 0-02-725515-8. Level: Ages 7-11.

"I almost can't remember a time when I wasn't a dancer," says nine-year-old Louis Pierre. Louis, a Pend Oreille Indian, lives on the Flathead Reservation in Montana. Louis's knowledge of traditional dance has been passed on to him from his grandfather, along with an understanding of the importance of dance to the history and culture of his people. This photodocumentary shows Louis as he learns a new dance—the grass dance—and dances it in a powwow for the first time.

END OF WINTER

Sharon Chmielarz. Illustrated by Annette Cable. (Crown, 1992) 32 pages. ISBN: 0-517-58745-9. Level: Ages 6-9.

Because the villagers are tired of cold, dark days, Hans and his friends parade in masks to drive winter away. After that fails, Hans suggests filling a wheel with straw to create a fiery sun with warmth enough to frighten the frigid weather. For one reason or another, the long nights become shorter and the air warmer. Detailed illustrations reproduced in full color suggest folk art in this $10\frac{1}{4}$ x $8\frac{3}{4}$ in. picture story. The original folktale featuring personified elements is based on medieval Germanic rituals in which masks were worn to scare Winter and flaming wheels were rolled down mountainsides to celebrate light. The author's note suggests that contemporary observances in several world religions feature light during the year's "shortest" days and may be continuations of those medieval traditions, as are contemporary Mardi Gras masks.

FAITH RINGGOLD

Robyn Montana Turner. (Little, Brown, 1993) 32 pages. ISBN: 0-316-85652-5. Level: Ages 7-12. (Also see FRIDA KAHLO in this list of annotations, another book in this series.)

This addition to a fine series involves the African American artist Faith Ringgold. Ringgold's children's books TAR BEACH (Crown, 1991) and AUNT HARRIET'S UNDERGROUND RAILROAD IN THE SKY (Crown, 1992) originated from her three-dimensional story quilts and thrust other works based on her African American heritage into the spotlight as well. Like the other $11\frac{1}{4}$ by 8 in. books in the series, this concise biography contains material documented from sources typically not tapped in children's books about artists. Each book in the series is generously illustrated with reproductions of artwork in full color.

FAMILY PICTURES/CUADROS DE FAMILIA

Carmen Lomas Garza. (Children's Book Press, 1990) 32 pages. ISBN: 0-89239-050-6. Level: Age 7 and older.

Brilliantly colored oil, acrylic, and gouache paintings illustrate scenes from the Chicano artist's childhood in Kingsville, Texas. Details from traditional Hispanic family and community life abound in the naïve-style illustrations, as well as in the accompanying explanatory passages printed in both English and Spanish.

FOUR SEASONS OF CORN: A WINNEBAGO TRADITION

Sally M. Hunter. Photographs by Joe Allen. (We Are Still Here) (Lerner, 1996) 40 pages. ISBN: 0-8225-2658-I. Level: Ages 7-11.

Planting in the spring; tending in the summer; harvesting, storing, and giving thanks in the fall; food throughout the winter. These are the four seasons of corn for the Winnebago, or Hochunk, people. Twelve-year-old Russell, a member of Hochunk Nation who lives in St. Paul, is learning about the importance of corn from his grandfather, who takes Russell, his brothers, sisters, and cousins to the country each year to plant and care for a field. But the corn is more than food for the Hochunk; it is also considered a gift from the spirits. As Russell and his family give attention to the corn every season in the midst of their busy city lives, they reaffirm ties to their heritage and knowledge of the ways of their people. Text and color photographs constitute another welcome portrayal of contemporary American Indian lives.

FRIDA KAHLO

Robyn Montana Turner. (Little, Brown, 1993) 32 pages. ISBN: 0-316-85651-7. Level: Ages 7-12. (Also see FAITH RINGGOLD in this list of annotations, another book in the series.)

This addition to a fine series involves the Mexican artist Frida Kahlo. Books about Kahlo for adults, as well as media and commercial attention, have resulted in new visibility for this Mexican artist. Like the other $11\frac{1}{4}$ by 8 in. books in the series, this concise biography contains material documented from sources typically not tapped in children's books about artists. Each book in the series is generously illustrated with reproductions of artwork in full color.

FROZEN MAN

David Getz. Illustrated by Peter McCarty. (A Redfeather Book/ Henry Holt, 1994) 68 pages. ISBN: 0-8050-3261-4. Level: Ages 8-16 and older.

Hiking across the Alpine Similaun Glacier between Austria and Italy during 1991, two tourists discovered a frozen body. This hiking victim carried a tool from the Stone Age. The probable identity of the well-preserved corpse was unraveled through the combined efforts of scientists and scholars of life more than five thousand years ago in that region. As riveting as a modern thriller, the high interest, easy-to-read text is interspersed with color photos, black-and-white sketches, and maps.

GATHERING THE SUN: AN ALPHABET IN SPANISH AND ENGLISH

Alma Flor Ada. English translation by Rosa Zubizarreta. Illustrated by Simón Silva. (Lothrop, Lee & Shepard, 1997) 40 pages. ISBN: 0-688-13903-5. Level: Ages 5-10.

Ada celebrates the lives and work of Latino farm laborers in this singular bilingual alphabet book that pays welcome tribute to the hardworking people who harvest the bounty of the land. Each double-page spread features a short poem about some aspect of field workers' lives in both Spanish and English. The featured alphabet letter is taken from the first letter of the Spanish-language titles to poems such as Árboles (Trees), Lluvia (Rain), and Orgullo (Pride). The poem for the letter C is titled César Chávez, in whose memory Ada dedicated this book that is illustrated with the glowing, expansive artwork of Simón Silva, which spans each two-page spread of this 11½ x 9½ in. volume. Silva's deeply hued gouache paintings of the laborers and the land are infused with the heat of the sun and the dignity of the people.

GOING BACK HOME: AN ARTIST RETURNS TO THE SOUTH

Michelle Wood with Igus Toyomi. (Children's Book Press, 1996) 32 pages. ISBN: 0-89239-137-5. Level: Ages 9-12.

Wood's paintings are based on her family's early twentieth century sharecropping experiences in the southern United States. Containing patterns reminiscent of African textiles, Wood's works are distinctive and intriguing. Igus's interpretations of Wood's reflections on her journey home accompany eighteen works reproduced in full color. Igus's comments serve as invitations to look closely at Wood's paintings. Both have appeal for and are accessible to children.

GONNA SING MY HEAD OFF!: AMERICAN FOLK SONGS FOR CHILDREN

Kathleen Krull. Illustrated by Allen Garns. (Alfred A. Knopf, 1992) 145 pages. ISBN: 0-394-81991-8. Level: All ages, especially ages 8-12.

A collection of sixty-two folk songs particularly appealing to older children balances regional and topical music popular for different reasons during various times. The range of songs includes "Down In The Valley," "Follow The Drinking Gourd," "If I Had A Hammer," "Joe Hill," "John Henry," "The Motorcycle Song," "Shall We Gather At The River," "Shenandoah," "Tell Me Why," "What Have They Done To The Rain?", and "Yankee Doodle." Easy piano and guitar arrangements, a first-line index,

and an index of song types facilitate use of this book of alphabetically arranged songs.

THE GREEN FROGS: A KOREAN FOLKTALE

Yumi Heo, reteller and illustrator. (Houghton Mifflin, 1996) 32 pages. ISBN: 0-395-68378-5. Level: Ages 3-8.

"Long ago when tigers still smoked pipes … " a pair of naughty frogs always did the opposite of what their mother told them to do. This pourquoi tale explains why frogs always cry "Gaegul! Gaegul! Gaegul!" whenever it rains and why—in Korea—"children who don't listen to their mother are called chung-gaeguri or green frogs." Heo remembers hearing the story of the green frogs when she was a little girl in Korea. Her humorous illustrations suggest swampy, underwater, and under-the-microscope images. They were created with oil paint and pencil and are reproduced in full color—mostly shades of green.

HABARI GANI? / WHAT'S THE NEWS?: A KWANZAA STORY

Sundaira Morninghouse. Illustrated by Jody Kim. (Open Hand, 1992) 32 pages. ISBN: 0-940880-39-3. Level: Ages 4-9.

A seven-chapter illustrated story about a contemporary family interprets information about the "only nationally celebrated, indigenous, non-heroic African-American holiday in the U.S." One full-color painting accompanies each chapter, along with a symbol representing the candles for each day. The Seven Principles and a twenty-eight item glossary for Swahili words and Kwanzaa terms are appended at the end of this well-designed book.

HALMONI AND THE PICNIC

Sook Nyul Choi. Illustrated by Karen M. Dugan. (Houghton Mifflin, 1993) 32 pages. ISBN: 0-395-61626-3. Level: Ages 5-8.

Yunmi's Korean grandmother has lived with her U.S. family in New York City for two months but is still reluctant to use English words when she sees Yunmi's school friends, even though she was a teacher in Korea. Rather than proving to be the embarrassing situation Yunmi expects, a school picnic provides Yunmi and her classmates with an opportunity to encourage this very smart, exceedingly gracious woman to enjoy herself in a social setting. The picnic features Halmoni's kimbap, which she has made as a treat for them all, as well as a chance for her to turn the jump rope. The children find out that it is polite to call her Halmoni (grandmother) but rude to address an elder by her name. A contemporary story by the Korean-born author of YEAR OF IMPOSSIBLE GOODBYES (Houghton Mifflin, 1991) specifies ways to understand how someone new to a language might feel. Korean language words are used in context within this cheerful 10¼ by 7½ in. picture story illustrated in full color.

THE HANDMADE ALPHABET

Laura Rankin. (Dial Books for Young Readers, 1991) 32 pages. ISBN: 0-8037-0975-7. Level: Ages 4-12.

The manual alphabet is used as the basis for this original and artistic concept book. Realistic drawings of hand signs for each letter are shown with an object beginning with that letter—a cup dangling from the thumb forming a "c"; the hand forming "m" reflected in a mirror; a ribbon wrapped around the hand forming "r." This imaginative approach to the alphabet could serve as an introduction to finger spelling, as well as an aesthetic experience.

HANUKKAH!

Roni Schotter. Illustrated by Marylin Hafner. (Joy Street/Little, Brown, 1990) 32 pages. ISBN: 0-316-77466-9. Level: Ages 2-5.

"In darkest December/Night steals in early/And whisks away the light./But warm inside,/Mama, Papa and Grandma Rose/Light the sun … " So opens a full-color picture book rendering of the way each person in a family with five children contributes to a contented Hanukkah evening together somewhere and sometime in the mid-twentieth century. A half-page explanation of Hanukkah follows the picture story noteworthy for the language of its text and for the depiction of intergenerational activity during a ritual celebration.

HARLEM: A POEM

Walter Dean Myers. Illustrated by Christopher Myers. (Scholastic, 1997) 32 pages. ISBN: 0-590-54340-7. Level: Age 12 and older).

Walter Dean Myers has written a riveting, richly textured poem that traces the history of Harlem in a cascade of freewheeling, carefully chosen words. Harlem was the gathering place. Harlem was the welcoming place. Harlem was Black faces, Black voices, Black energy. Harlem was Black without apology, "… a promise/Of a better life, of a place where a man didn't/Have to know his place/Simply because he was/Black." Myers's rhythmic free-verse text vibrates with joy and pain and pulses with the people and places, the sights and sounds of Harlem throughout the twentieth century: Langston Hughes, Countee Cullen and W.E.B. DuBois, Marcus

Garvey, and Malcolm X. The Apollo Theater and the Cotton Club. A capella on the street corners, Sunday night gospel, a soprano saxophone, rent parties, checker games, funerals, children "living out their own slam-dunk dreams/Listen/for the coming of the blues." The images are touchstones of history and emotional experience, inviting readers to dive deeply into the history of Black experience in America, to know the facts, but also the feelings of both triumph and despair. To accompany his father's poem, Christopher Myers has used ink and gouache over torn paper to create bold, dramatic collage art that is as richly layered as the words, giving face and form to the soul of Harlem.

HER STORIES: AFRICAN AMERICAN FOLKTALES, FAIRY TALES, AND TRUE TALES

Virginia Hamilton, reteller and author. Illustrated by Leo and Diane Dillon. (Blue Sky/Scholastic, 1995) 109 pages. ISBN: 0-590-47370-0. Level: Ages 7-14 and older.

In a companion volume to THE PEOPLE COULD FLY: AMERICAN BLACK FOLKTALES (Knopf, 1985), Hamilton retells nineteen tales with female protagonists that have been passed down from generation to generation by African American women. The tales are divided into five sections: animal stories, fairy tales, the supernatural, folkways and legends, and true tales. Each section is introduced by an author's note and includes three or four stories. Each tale is told in a distinctive voice and followed by commentary that places the story in a historical and cultural context. The Dillons' distinguished color paintings add to the overall elegance of this beautifully designed volume.

HOANG ANH: A VIETNAMESE-AMERICAN BOY

Diane Hoyt-Goldsmith. Photographs by Lawrence Migdale. (Holiday House, 1992) 32 pages. ISBN: 0-8234-0948-1. Level: Ages 8-12.

A photo-essay uses color photographs and a short first-person text to describe the day-to-day life of a young Vietnamese-American boy living in San Rafael, California. Hoang Anh briefly recounts the circumstances of his family's escape from Vietnam in 1978, their life in a refugee camp, and details of his family's bicultural life style in the United States. Roughly one-half of the book is devoted to Hoang Anh's observances of the New Year (TET), making this a useful source for information about the Vietnamese holiday.

THE HOKEY POKEY

Larry LaPrise, Charles P. Macak, and Taftt Baker. Illustrated by Sheila Hamanaka (Simon & Schuster, 1997) 32 pages. ISBN: 0-689-80519-5. Level: Ages 2-6.

Beginning with a spirited young girl in red high-top tennis shoes and blond pigtails, Hamanaka illustrates the Hokey Pokey by adding a new character to the dance with each verse and double-page spread. The effect is that the song becomes a cumulative tale on a visual level, and young children looking at the book will delight in finding the character who has joined the dance on each page, especially the dancing dog, cat, and mouse. Hamanaka also varies the perspective on each page so that sometimes we are looking at the dancers in profile, sometimes we see them from above, and sometimes from below. By the time we get to the "left hip" page, we see the dancers from such a distance that it appears as though the entire world population has joined the dance line. This fact may escape the youngest readers—they'll be looking for that mouse! And they'll find him, wiping his brow, seated atop the barcode on the back cover of the book.

HOLD THE ANCHOVIES! A BOOK ABOUT PIZZA

Shelley Rotner and Julia Pemberton Hellums. Photographs by Shelley Rotner. (Orchard, 1996) 24 pages. ISBN: 0-531-09507-X. Level: Ages 3-6.

Young pizza lovers will learn how a pizza is made in this mouth-watering photo-essay. Simple text and bold color photographs show where the ingredients for each part of the pizza—dough, sauce, cheese, and toppings—come from, and how they are combined to make the delicious treat. A basic pizza recipe is included.

HOME LOVELY

Lynne Rae Perkins. (Greenwillow, 1995) 32 pages. ISBN: 0-688-13688-5. Level: Ages 4-7.

Tiffany must stay home alone in the trailer during afternoons while her mother is at work. With no neighbors, it's a lonely time. Then she finds and plants some seedlings next to the driveway in the hopes of brightening up their new home, and they draw the attention of the mailman, Bob, on his daily rounds. With the help of Bob and her mother, Janelle, Tiffany nurtures a bountiful garden of vegetables, flowers, and friendship. A warm, realistic picture book shows a financially struggling, single-parent family filled with creativity and love. Full-color illustrations of pen and ink and watercolor shine with caring moments and tender details.

HOORAY, A PIÑATA!

Elisa Kleven. (Dutton, 1996) 32 pages. ISBN: 0-525-45605-8. Level: Ages 4-7.

Clara and her friend Samson go shopping for a special piñata for Clara's birthday party and they find just the one Clara wants. Trouble is, she likes it so well she can't bear the thought of breaking it! Filled with lots of intriguing visual details, Kleven's bright picture story about a young Latina girl and her African American friend is a true celebratory delight from beginning to end.

HOW SWEET THE SOUND: AFRICAN-AMERICAN SONGS FOR CHILDREN

Wade Hudson & Cheryl Willis Hudson. Illustrated by Floyd Cooper. (Scholastic, 1995) 48 pages. ISBN: 0-590-48030-8. Level: Ages 5-12.

The lyrics for twenty-three songs from African American traditions or perspectives are printed to be read or sung with pictures of present and past African American life for inspiration. This inviting picture book meshes the words of spirituals and modern music with other songs. Cooper's full-color illustrations were rendered in oil wash. Easy musical notations at the end take into account the African American component of improvisation. Huddie Ledbeter, Billy Strayhorn, James Brown, Stevie Wonder, James Weldon Johnson, J. Rosamund Johnson, and Thomas A. Dorsey are among the musicians and poets represented. A brief history is provided for each song, along with an eight-item list of related resources and an index.

THE HUNTERMAN AND THE CROCODILE: A WEST AFRICAN FOLKTALE

Baba Wagué Diakité. (Scholastic, 1997) 32 pages. ISBN: 0-590-89828-0. Level: Ages 5-9.

A marvelous storytelling voice with a playful tone relates the circular tale of Bamba the Crocodile who is on his way to Mecca with his family. After Bamba begs Donso, a passing hunter, for help, the hunter finds himself in precarious waters, both literally and figuratively. Because Donso and other humans have not lived in harmony with nature, the hunter receives little sympathy from a cow ("dingi-donga"), an old horse ("ke-te-ba"), and a chicken ("ko, ko, ko"). A nearby mango tree also declines to help Donso. Rabbit gives sound advice, however, and even Bamba agrees to help when Donso has a second crisis. This volume offers a perfect example of a text completely unified with its visual elements. Growing up in a village in Mali, West Africa, Diakité is close to his storytelling heritage. As an artist using the clay surfaces of pottery for his canvas, Diakité created the artwork here on hand-painted ceramic tiles.

"I HAVE A SONG TO SING, O!": AN INTRODUCTION TO THE SONGS OF GILBERT AND SULLIVAN

John Langstaff, editor. Illustrated by Emma Chichester-Clark. (Margaret K. McElderry Books, 1994) 74 pages. ISBN: 0-689-50591-4. Level: Ages 8-12 and older.

In his introductory note to young readers, Langstaff writes that when he was a child, his entire family sang—and even acted out—Gilbert and Sullivan songs. "There were solos, duets, and trios we performed together, with everyone joining in the rousing chorus refrains." Whether this collection is used to add to the repertoire for family sing-alongs and classroom choruses, or to prepare young theater-goers for a Gilbert and Sullivan experience, the sixteen songs chosen from eight operettas will undoubtedly please, as will Chichester-Clark's full-page illustrations—in both color and black-and-white—that perfectly embody the zany Gilbert and Sullivan style. Even Brian Holmes's musical arrangements are a delight, with directions such as "pompous but bold," "jaunty and boastful," and "with matter of fact haughtiness" to help young singers cast just the right mood to the song. Preparing for a long car trip? This is a book to bring, O!

THE INDIAN WAY: LEARNING TO COMMUNICATE WITH MOTHER EARTH

Gary McLain. Illustrated by Gary McLain and Michael Taylor. (John Muir Publications, 1990) 103 pages. ISBN: 0-945465-73-4. Level: Ages 7-11.

Two contemporary Arapaho children always look forward to times when there is a full moon because on those evenings their Grandpa Iron tells them a Full Moon Story. Each of Grandpa Iron's stories teaches reverence for nature and respect for Mother Earth. The book includes suggestions for creative activities that children can undertake to help them remember the ecological lesson inherent in each of the thirteen stories.

IT'S KWANZAA TIME!

Lynda Goss and Clay Goss. Illustrated by award-winning artists. (Putnam, 1995) 71 pages. ISBN: 0-399-22505-6. Level: Ages 5-12.

This introduction to Kwanzaa includes suggestions for home decorations and a ceremony, a variety of stories and tales to read aloud, a play to dramatize, a poem, directions for making Kwanzaa cards and celebrative clothing, a game to play, three songs to sing, and eight recipes to cook. Seven full-color illustrations feature some of the leading African American artists of children's books: Ashley Bryan, Carole Byard, Floyd Cooper, Leo and Diane Dillon, Jan Spivey Gilchrist, Jonathan Green, and Jerry Pinkney. Many of the readings can be used all year, such as Eloise Greenfield's previously published biographical prose about Rosa Parks. A resource list completes an engaging, attractive do-it-yourself family book. A many-faceted exploration of this holiday that celebrates the richness of traditional African heritage offers something for everyone.

K IS FOR KWANZAA: A KWANZAA ALPHABET BOOK

Juwanda G. Ford. Illustrated by Ken Wilson-Max. (Cartwheel/ Scholastic, 1997) 32 pages. ISBN: 0-590-92200-9. Level: Ages 3-8.

A child-friendly ABC book about Kwanzaa features words such as Africa, Bendera, Candle, and Dashiki, with short written definitions and brightly colored illustrations depicting the main idea. A brief history of Kwanzaa opens the book.

KODOMO: CHILDREN OF JAPAN

Susan Kuklin. (Putnam, 1995) 48 pages. ISBN: 0-399-22613-3. Level: Ages 5-11.

An engaging photoessay provides a colorful portrait of children in modern Japan. Divided into two parts, the first, titled "A Way of Life," introduces U.S. children to three of their counterparts living in Hiroshima: eight-year-old Eri and nine-year-old Nozomi both describe their day-to-day lives at school and at home, while fourteen-year-old Ai tells readers about the tradition of dressing in a special kimono on New Year's Day. Part Two presents readers with "traditional activities" as they are observed by four children in Kyoto. These traditions include martial arts, calligraphy, and the tea ceremony.

KWANZAA

A. P. Porter. Illustrated by Janet Lee Porter. (Carolrhoda, 1991) 56 pages. ISBN: 0-87614-688-X. Level: Ages 5-9.

An easy reader briefly traces the origin of the African American holiday created by Maulana Karenga in 1966 and then describes how it is observed by families today. Special attention is given to the historical significance of each of Kwanzaa's seven principles and to the meanings and uses of Kwanzaa symbols. Full-color illustrations appear on each double-page spread, adding appeal and accessibility to the text. A glossary of the Kiswahili words used throughout the book provides English definitions and a pronunciation guide.

KWANZAA: A FAMILY AFFAIR

Mildred Pitts Walter. (Lothrop, Lee & Shepard, 1995) 95 pages. ISBN: 0-688-11553-5. Level: Age 9 and older.

The author of HAVE A HAPPY … (Lothrop, 1989), a novel about a boy and his family celebrating Kwanzaa, has been observing Kwanzaa for thirty years. In this user-friendly handbook, she interprets the background, seven principles, and the symbols of Kwanzaa, a special African American holiday that takes place between December 26 and January 1. Daily activities are described, and a helpful crafts section contains directions for making games, gifts, and other items needed during Kwanzaa. Four recipes are included along with a glossary, pronunciation key, and a list of related books. Most of these activities can be undertaken by a reliable older child or teenager, although Walter encourages readers to secure a parent's permission. Walter is the author of many children's books, including JUSTIN AND THE BEST BISCUITS IN THE WORLD (Lothrop, 1986), MARIAH LOVES ROCK (Bradbury, 1988), MARIAH KEEPS COOL (Bradbury, 1990), and TROUBLE'S CHILD (Lothrop, 1985), a novel for young teenagers.

LA BODA: A MEXICAN WEDDING CELEBRATION

Nancy Van Laan. Illustrated by Andrea Arroyo. (Little, Brown, 1996) 32 pages. ISBN: 0-316-89626-8. Level: Ages 4-7.

The traditional Zapotec wedding ceremony borrows elements from both Native and Catholic traditions. Here a young girl learns about them by asking her patient abuela countless questions as the two participate in the wedding ceremony of Alfonso and Luisa. The curved lines of Arroyo's stylized illustrations suggest sweeping movement as the entire town participates in this joyous community event. Even the typography helps to tell the story.

LAUGHING TOMATOES, AND OTHER SPRING POEMS / JITOMATES RISUEÑOS, Y OTROS POEMAS DE PRIMAVERA

Francisco X. Alarcón. Illustrated by Maya Christina Gonzalez. (Children's Book Press, 1997) 32 pages. ISBN: 0-89239-139-1. Level: Ages 7-10.

"A poem makes us see everything for the first time." Francisco Alarcón's epigraph to his vibrant picture book col-

lection of twenty original poems holds the promise of discovery, and young readers will not be disappointed at what they find—poems that reminisce, delight, and surprise. Some of the poems, like "Other Voices," "Strawberries," and "Chile," are a mere handful of words, drops of water forming a small pool that reflects everyday items and occurrences in new and exciting ways. Other poems, like "My Grandmother's Songs," are a cascade of memories and observations as seen through the poet's passionate and exacting eye: "My grandmother's songs / … consoling / the chairs placed / upside down / delighting / the family portraits / on the walls." Some of the poems were written originally in Spanish and others in English. All are presented in both languages and paired with Gonzalez's colorful artwork—imaginative, interpretive paintings that will conjure up a laugh, a smile, a moment (or more) of contemplation, just as the poems do.

LAURA LOVES HORSES

Joan Hewett. Photographs by Richard Hewett. (Clarion, 1990) 40 pages. ISBN: 0-89919-844-9. Level: Ages 4-9.

Eight-year-old Laura Santana grew up surrounded by the activities at the southern California boarding and riding stable where her father is employed and near which the family lives. To this Mexican American child's long-time pleasure in riding Sugar Baby bareback down to the creek are now added riding lessons that prepare her to compete in her first horse show. Thirty-five full-color photographs well placed on the pages picture Laura enjoying both kinds of riding, while the short text in a large typeface echoes this spirit.

LIFE AROUND THE LAKE: EMBROIDERIES BY THE WOMEN OF LAKE PATZCUARO

Maricel E. Presilla and Gloria Soto. (Henry Holt, 1996) 32 pages. ISBN: 0-8050-3800-0. Level: Ages 9-12 and older.

Some of the Tarascan women of central Mexico create traditional needlework for sale at the market as one way to support themselves while the local fishing economy dwindles. A guild organized more than fourteen years ago equips local women to become master embroiderers. Most of their embroideries reflect a happier time. The women honor their heritage by stitching images of life before Lake Patzcuaro became polluted, before soil run-offs from mountains bare of trees filled the lake, before the fish began to die, before the wild ducks disappeared. Their dazzling stitchery shows an abundance of fish in Lake Patzcuaro. It recreates Tarascan mythology and seasonal observances often still enjoyed. Full-color photographs of the women's intricately designed embroideries grace each page of this beautiful 10¼ in. square book about culture, economy, environment, and the art of resilient, hard working Tarascan women.

LIFT EV'RY VOICE AND SING

James Weldon Johnson. Illustrated by Jan Spivey Gilchrist. (Scholastic, 1995) 32 pages. ISBN: 0-590-46982-7. Level: Age 3 and older.

Gilchrist's powerful Afro-centric images offer an emotional match for the classic words of Johnson's famous anthem. Her watercolor paintings suggest a painful history and the pride of heritage while celebrating African American struggle and survival. The jacket art features children looking forward and up, while the title page offers a personified image of continental Africa, weeping into the ocean. Water becomes a life force in illustrations picturing elders from past centuries next to their descendants today. Hope is offered through images of a rooted tree and liberation by flying. Although the artistic concepts are sophisticated, all family members can appreciate this important 12¼ x 9¼ in. book in one or more ways.

LION DANCER: ERNIE WAN'S CHINESE NEW YEAR

Kate Waters and Madeline Slovenz-Low. Photographs by Martha Cooper. (Scholastic/Hardcover, 1990) 32 pages. ISBN: 0-590-4306-7. Level: Ages 4-11.

Clear color photographs illustrate a short photoessay focusing on two days in the life of a young Chinese American boy living in New York City. Readers see Ernie Wan preparing for his role as a lion dancer in a New Year's celebration in Chinatown. Both family and community celebrations of the Chinese New Year are detailed.

LIVES OF THE ARTISTS: MASTERPIECES, MESSES (AND WHAT THE NEIGHBORS THOUGHT)

Kathleen Krull. Illustrated by Kathryn Hewitt. (Harcourt Brace, 1995) 96 pages. ISBN: 0-15-200103-4. Level: Ages 7-14 and older.

Twenty artists are featured in these brief, breezy biographical sketches accompanied by an iconographic painting containing visual clues to that person's works and quirks. Krull and Hewitt begin where encyclopedias typically stop, just as they did in LIVES OF THE MUSICIANS (Harcourt, 1993) and LIVES OF THE WRITERS (Harcourt, 1994). They create somewhat unconventional portraits of each artist, leaving readers with a sense of

him/her as an actual person and a zest to know more. The artists are da Vinci, Michelangelo, Bruegel, Anguissola, Rembrandt, Hokusai, Cassatt, van Gogh, Kollwitz, Matisse, Picasso, Chagall, Duchamp, O'Keeffe, W. H. Johnson, Dali, Noguchi, Rivera, Kahlo, and Warhol.

LIVES OF THE MUSICIANS

Kathleen Krull. Illustrated by Kathryn Hewitt. (Harcourt Brace Jovanovich, 1993) 96 pages. ISBN: 0-15-248010-2. Level: Ages 7-14 and older.

Tidbit-filled sketches of the famous reveal infamous habits and quirks for a generation accustomed to thumbnail glimpses of celebrity personalities. Brief selected musical "notes" add other facts. Twenty musicians are thus introduced to young readers who may not have heard of most or all of them: Vivaldi, Bach, Mozart, Beethoven, Chopin, Verdi, Schumann, Foster, Brahms, Tchaikovsky, Gilbert & Sullivan, Satie, S. Joplin, Ives, Stravinsky, Boulanger, Prokofiev, Gershwin, and W. Guthrie. Personal details and anecdotes are linked to the unconventional full-color art accompanying each two-page account. Material typically unavailable in encyclopedias brings European and American musicians to life. By their unconventional approach, Krull and Hewitt may just have revolutionized the generally dull form of collective biography for young readers.

LOOK TO THE NORTH: A WOLF PUP'S DIARY

Jean Craighead George. Illustrated by Lucia Washburn. (HarperCollins, 1997) 32 pages. ISBN: 0-06-023641-8. Level: Ages 3-7.

The author of JULIE OF THE WOLVES (HarperCollins, 1972) shares her expertise and fascination for wolves in an engaging volume for young readers. Written in second person, the narrative sets the mood by asking young readers to "look to the north" at various times of the year and to think about wolf pups. When dandelions begin to turn white, wolf pups are being born. When you see baby robins, wolf pups are being weaned. When you're out trick-or-treating, young wolves are learning to hunt for themselves. Each double-page spread ingeniously links a common occurrence in our temperate climate with the growth of a wolf from birth to adulthood, and to put the information in context, realistic acrylic paintings and a second strand of third-person narrative follow a specific litter through its growth cycle.

LUKA'S QUILT

Georgia Guback. (Greenwillow, 1994) 32 pages. ISBN: 0-688-12155-1. Level: Ages 4-8.

The traditional Hawaiian quilt Luka's tutu (grandmother) makes for her looks nothing like the elaborate, brightly colored quilt Luka had pictured in her head, and she cannot hide her disappointment when Tutu presents it to her. When the two attend a Lei Day celebration, Luka's nontraditional approach to lei-making gives Tutu an idea about enhancing the quilt to suit both generations. Charming cut-paper collages reveal a surprising amount of cultural detail through the folk-art-style illustrations.

MAKE A JOYFUL SOUND: POEMS FOR CHILDREN BY AFRICAN-AMERICAN POETS

Deborah Slier, editor. Illustrated by Cornelius Van Wright and Ying-Hwa Hu. (Checkerboard Press, 1991) 97 pages. ISBN: 1-56288-000-4. Level: Ages 4-12.

A thick volume, generously illustrated, pulls together seventy-five poems from diverse sources by well-known poets (Lucille Clifton, Countee Cullen, Eloise Greenfield, Langston Hughes), as well as others who rarely appear in children's poetry anthologies (Kali Grosvenor, Nanette Mellage, Useni Eugene Perkins, Quincy Troupe). These poems for young children touch on such topics as family, friends, playing outside and school, in addition to cultural pride and African American heritage. The overall effect of this marvelously rich anthology is best expressed by one of the selections by Mari Evans: "Who/can be born black/and not/sing/the wonder of it/the joy/the challenge . . ."

MANY THOUSAND GONE: AFRICAN AMERICANS FROM SLAVERY TO FREEDOM

Virginia Hamilton. Illustrated by Leo and Diane Dillon. (Alfred A. Knopf, 1993) 151 pages. ISBN: 0-304-82873-9. Level: All ages.

Here are Sojourner Truth, Harriet Tubman, and Frederick Douglas. Here, too, are Chloe Cooley, Addison White, and Jackson of Alabama. Hamilton has gathered together stories of individuals living in the time of slavery and laid them out in a powerful presentation that chronicles this chilling era in American history and the endurance of a people. Some of the names may be familiar to children, many others will not be, but each vignette—each life—is compelling and lends itself to a greater understanding of the whole, such as how laws to protect free African Americans were often ignored while others were passed to strengthen the grip of owners in the south. In some cases, the vignettes are only fragments,

pieces of a life, as if this is all that is known, and these serve as striking, painful reminders of how much has been lost, the "many thousand gone." Modifying her usual descriptive prose style, Hamilton pares language to a minimum here, writing in short, explosive sentences that propel people and events to the forefront, while the Dillons' moody black-and-white illustrations give shape to sorrow, grief, anger, bravery and pride, and expression to the overwhelming desire to be free.

MARVIN'S BEST: CHRISTMAS PRESENT EVER

Katherine Paterson. Illustrated by Jane Clark Brown. (An I Can Read Book, HarperCollins, 1997) 48 pages. ISBN: 0-06-027159-0. Level: Ages 4-7.

Young Marvin wants to think of a gift to make for his mother all by himself. He's determined to do this without any help from his older sister, May, maker of ideal family gifts. Everyone loves the wreath Marvin makes to hang on the trailer. Marvin loves it so much himself that he refuses to let the wreath be taken down on New Year's Day. Time passes, and so does winter. A gentle resolution to a small family drama maintains Marvin's self-respect while sustaining the interest of new readers. Brown's full-color illustrations complement Paterson's skillfully crafted, minimal words.

MAY'NAISE SANDWICHES & SUNSHINE TEA

Sandra Belton. Illustrated by Gail Gordon. (Four Winds Press, 1994) 32 pages. ISBN: 0-02-709035-3. Level: Ages 5-8.

Belton's child narrator remembers her grandmother's stories, especially the one about her friendship with Bette Jean and the fun they had with imaginary play. One family was working class and the other was not. Belton handles an important theme seldom approached in books for the young.

THE MEAN HYENA: A FOLKTALE FROM MALAWI

Judy Sierra. Illustrated by Michael Bryant. (Lodestar/Dutton, 1997) 32 pages. ISBN: 0-525-67510-8. Level: Ages 6-10.

"Tell me, Who is this? He thinks his vest is so fine he never takes it off, even when he sleeps." A riddle opens this tale of revenge through art, telling how Kamba the tortoise finally fools Fisi, the tricky hyena who is always playing mean tricks on jungle creatures. After Kamba "paints" new coats for Mbanda the zebra and Nyalugwe the leopard, other creatures from miles around come to get new coats; even "night-skulking Fisi" wants a new coat. "Don't play a trick on someone unless you want a bigger trick played on you." According to Sierra's note at the back, Kamba and Fisi appear in nearly all the trick-ster tales of Malawi: "Kamba is the slow, steady trickster who is never outwitted, whereas Fisi is the eternal dupe, always tricked and always shamed." Bryant's full-color paintings successfully picture the creatures, the natural setting, and the very dramatic action.

MIMI'S TUTU

Tynia Thomassie. Illustrated by Jan Spivey Gilchrist. (Scholastic, 1996). 32 pages. ISBN: 0-590-44020-9. Level: Ages 3-5.

As the first daughter born into her extended African American family in many years, little Mimi is lavished with attention from all her female elders. More than any-thing, Mimi likes to observe her family's tradition of Af-rican dance by attending classes with her mother and by wearing the beautiful lapa (Guinean wrap-around) made by Gramma M'bewe. Boldly colored pastel and water-color paintings deftly capture a young child's enthusiasm for dance, movement, and participating in the social and cultural world of grown-ups.

MOON FESTIVAL

Ching Yeung Russell. Illustrated by Christopher Zhong-Yuan Zhang. (Boyds Mills, 1997) 32 pages. ISBN: 1-56397-596-3. Level: Ages 6-9.

Many Chinese people celebrate the Moon Festival, also called Mid-Autumn Festival, at the time of the full moon. Family reunions and celebratory foods such as "golden brown moon cakes filled with bean paste and salty duck egg yolks" are central to the Moon Festival celebration. Parades display handmade paper lanterns pasted with smashed, freshly cooked rice that are "shaped like fish, star fruits, and rabbits." Zhang's luminous full-color oil paintings picture elements of the celebration and show images of the legendary goddess Chang O who is be-seeched for blessings. Wise language choices and rich words express the delight of children preparing, parad-ing, eating, and listening to ghost stories.

MUSICIANS OF THE SUN

Gerald McDermott. (Simon & Schuster, 1997) 40 pages. ISBN: 0-689-80706-6. Level: Ages 6-10.

"Out of the starry night he came, invisible, untouchable. Lord of the Night. King of the Gods. Soul of the World." Dramatic language introduces the principle Aztec deity whose name means "Smoking Mirror." Even more dra-matic visual images rendered in blues and purples domi-nate these pages to launch the large presentation of a formerly lost fragment of the mythological tradition of the Aztecs. "'Children do not laugh. Women do not dance. Men do not sing. The people spend their lives in darkness and silence. I will change all this,' declared the Lord of the Night." And he did. McDermott's bold shapes and colors were created using acrylic fabric paint, opaque ink, and oil pastel on paper handmade in Mexico. He pro-vides helpful background information on the final page.

MY FIRST KWANZAA BOOK

Deborah M. Newton Chocolate. Illustrated by Cal Massey. (Cartwheel/Scholastic, 1992) 24 pages. ISBN: 0-590-45762-4. Level: Ages 2-7.

Easy-to-read short sentences relay basic information about Kwanzaa and are paired with brightly colored il-lustrations picturing a little boy, his father, and his mother each preparing for the celebration with their extended family. The full-color pictures are filled with cultural in-formation. A brief history of Kwanzaa, its Seven Prin-ciples, definitions of symbols and words used during Kwanzaa, and a citation for an adult resource are listed at the back of this high-spirited, helpful 8¼ x 10¼ in. picture book.

MY MEXICO / MEXICO MIO

Tony Johnston. Illustrated by F. John Sierra. (Putnam, 1996). 36 pages. ISBN: 0-399-22275-8. Level: Ages 5-8.

Johnston creates moments of exciting activity and quiet contemplation in eighteen poems that evoke some of the sights and sounds of Mexico. Sierra's illustrations, which span each double-page spread, are washed with color and inflected with light—soft, warm depictions of each poetic scene. The poems appear in English and Span-ish, and a glossary is included for some of the Spanish words.

MY PAINTED HOUSE, MY FRIENDLY CHICKEN, AND ME

Maya Angelou. Photographs by Margaret Courtney-Clarke. (Clarkson Potter, 1994) 40 pages. ISBN: 0-517-59667-9. Level: Ages 5-8.

In Angelou's engaging first-person narrative, young read-ers meet Thandi, an eight-year-old Ndebele girl in South Africa. Thandi relates details of her own life and of Ndebele culture, and these details are brought into focus through Courtney-Clark's shining, colorful photographs of Ndebele people. The Ndebele custom of painting houses with intricate, colorful patterns forms the inspiration for the design of this vibrant book that is an invitation to friendship.

MY TWO UNCLES

Judith Vigna. (Albert Whitman, 1995) 32 pages. ISBN: 0-8075-5507-X. Level: Ages 4-8 and older.

Elly loves her two uncles—her father's brother Ned and his partner Phil. Together the three of them work on a special handmade gift for her grandparents' fiftieth wedding anniversary, but then Elly is saddened to learn that Uncle Phil has not been invited to the anniversary party and Uncle Ned refuses to go without him. An unusually realistic account of a young child's struggle to understand the complexities of homophobia within her extended family ends not with happiness but with hope.

THE MYSTERIOUS VISITOR: STORIES OF THE PROPHET ELIJAH

Nina Jaffe. Illustrated by Elivia Savadier. (Scholastic, 1997) 112 pages. ISBN: 0-590-48422-2. Level: Age 4 and older.

Hundreds of tales can be found in Jewish folklore about the prophet Elijah, a messenger from heaven to earth. Jewish children begin to learn about this popular prophet when the door is opened for Elijah to attend the Passover Seder meal. All children, however, can enjoy the eight tales Jaffe chose for this handsome volume, including "The Dream," "The Bear in the Forest," and "Elijah and the Fisher Boy." Jaffe's helpful introduction precedes the tales, and there is also a glossary, notes about the stories, a bibliography, and a list of other books containing Elijah stories. The collection is beautifully designed, and eight of Savadier's marvelous paintings are reproduced in full color and placed opposite the opening page of each tale.

NEIGHBORHOOD ODES

Gary Soto. Illustrated by David Diaz. (Harcourt Brace Jovanovich, 1992) 68 pages. ISBN: 0-15-256879-4. Level: Age 8 and older.

Twenty-one poems reflect pleasures, loves, joys, regrets, and fears experienced growing up in a Chicano neighborhood in California. The poet hones in on the small details of ordinary places (the park, the library) and ordinary things (a sprinkler, Pablo's tennis shoes) with such extraordinary clarity of vision that each ode packs an emotional punch, taking the reader by surprise. The poems are accompanied by striking black-and-white illustrations.

ON PASSOVER

Cathy Goldberg Fishman. Illustrated by Melanie W. Hall. (Atheneum, 1997) 32 pages. ISBN: 0-689-80528-4. Level: Ages 4-8. (Also see ON ROSH HASHANAH AND YOM KIPPUR in this list of annotations, another book in this series.)

In this book, a young girl describes the observance of Passover. She tells readers that she doesn't even need to use a calendar to know when Passover is near because her home is filled with memorable activities. Hall's slightly offbeat illustrations rendered in collagraph and mixed media will grab the attention of young readers familiar with the meaning and import of these Jewish holidays and inform those who aren't. A one-page glossary defines words important to know.

ON ROSH HASHANAH AND YOM KIPPUR

Cathy Goldberg Fishman. Illustrated by Melanie W. Hall. (Atheneum, 1997) 32 pages. ISBN: 0-689-80526-8. Level: Ages 4-8. (Also see ON PASSOVER in this list of annotations, another book in this series.)

A young girl's first-person narration graces this book. She tells readers of her family activities and the traditional foods of Rosh Hashanah and Yom Kippur. As in the companion volume, ON PASSOVER, Hall's slightly offbeat illustrations rendered in collagraph and mixed media will grab the attention of young readers familiar with the meaning and import of these Jewish holidays and inform those who aren't.

ONE NATION, MANY TRIBES: HOW KIDS LIVE IN MILWAUKEE'S INDIAN COMMUNITY

Kathleen Krull. Photographs by David Hautzig. (Lodestar, 1995) 48 pages. ISBN: 0-525-67440-3. Level: Ages 8-12.

Eleven-year-old Thirza and twelve-year-old Shawnee are students at the Milwaukee Community Indian School, which is distinctive for a number of reasons discussed in the text: its urban location, its funding through

Potawatomi bingo hall profits, and its inclusion of five Wisconsin tribes in the student body. Within this context, both children are presented as unique individuals: Shawnee dreams of becoming an architect and returning to the reservation, while Thirza, an aspiring actress, is headed for Broadway or Hollywood. An upbeat text and appealing color photographs show the two children in their day-to-day activities in and out of school.

THE OTHER SIDE: HOW KIDS LIVE IN A CALIFORNIA LATINO NEIGHBORHOOD

Kathleen Krull. Photographs by David Hautzig. (Lodestar, 1994) 48 pages. ISBN: 0-525-67438-1. Level: Ages 7-11.

Twelve-year-old Cinthya Guzman and brothers Francisco and Pedro Tapia, ages eight and twelve, all were born in Mexico and are living now in Castle Park, a Latino neighborhood in Chula Vista, California. For all three, moving to the United States meant making many adjustments, but because Chula Vista is only seven miles from Tijuana, Mexico, they have also been able to remain grounded in their birth culture, regularly returning to visit family. Text and photographs examine the similarities and differences between the children's lives and communities on both sides of the border.

PABLO REMEMBERS: THE FIESTA OF THE DAY OF THE DEAD

George Ancona. (Lothrop, Lee & Shepard, 1993) 48 pages. ISBN: 0-688-11250-1. Level: Ages 5-9.

A color photodocumentary explanation of El Dia de Los Muertos features a Mexican family's observances of The Day of The Dead beginning October 31, All Hallow's Eve. Bakers make special bread, candy makers create sugar skulls, marigolds are harvested, women prepare special foods, and children cut out cardboard skeletons in anticipation of the fiesta. Family altars are readied in advance of the bell-ringing that signals the spirits' return and heralds the activities and visits that are part of the three-day family and community event. Ancona's camera and text feature Pablo, his three sisters, and his parents as they honor the memory of their ancestors, especially their grandmother who died two years ago. Spanish words used in context or defined as necessary amplify Ancona's interpretation in a book measuring $8\frac{1}{4}$ x $10\frac{1}{8}$ in. in size and larger in importance.

PASS IT ON: AFRICAN-AMERICAN POETRY FOR CHILDREN

Wade Hudson, selector. Illustrated by Floyd Cooper. (Scholastic, 1993) 32 pages. ISBN: 0-590-45770-5. Level: Ages 4-9.

A $10\frac{3}{4}$ by $8\frac{5}{8}$ in. picture-book poetry anthology ranges in theme and mood from Eloise Greenfield's light-hearted "To Catch a Fish" to the sobering "Incident" by Countee Cullen. A line from "Listen Children" by Louise Clifton was the inspiration for the title of the collection. Other poets represented by the nineteen selections are Gwendolyn Brooks, Henry Dumas, Paul Laurence Dunbar, James A. Emanuel, Mari Evans, Nikki Giovanni, Nikki Grimes, Langston Hughes, Lessie Jones Little, Linda Michelle Baron, and Naomi Long Madgett. The title also represents the compiler's hope that a fine heritage will be introduced to a generation for whom this African American poetry and some of these poets are unfamiliar. Cooper's illustrations painted in oil wash appear in full color on every page. Brief information is provided about each poet.

PATRICK DESJARLAIT: CONVERSATIONS WITH A NATIVE AMERICAN ARTIST

Neva Williams. (Runestone / Lerner, 1995) 56 pages. ISBN: 0-8225-3151-8. Level: Ages 8-14 and older.

Patrick DesJarlait was an artist who belonged to the Red Lake Chippewa Band (Anishinabe) of northern Minnesota. More than twenty years ago, Williams tape-recorded the interviews that form the basis for this book and feature DesJarlait's life and art, along with his comments about reservation life in the 1920s, boarding school, and his development as an artist. During World War II, he worked as a film animator for the U.S. Navy and had a short stint as the art director at a relocation camp where Japanese Americans were held. His paintings employ bright, rich tones to portray the many traditions of his people. Although DesJarlait did not receive wide recognition or acclaim while alive, his career has inspired younger American Indian artists, and his paintings were pivotal in the development of contemporary American Indian art.

THE PIÑATA MAKER / EL PIÑATERO

George Ancona. (Harcourt, Brace, 1994) 40 pages. ISBN: 0-15-261875-9. Level: Ages 8-10.

In Ejutla de Crespo, a village in southern Mexico, seventy-seven-year-old Don Ricardo makes piñatas for all the festive occasions. Tio Rico, as the children call him, is clearly valued among children and adults alike in the community. Color photographs and text show how Tio Rico makes both traditional and unusual piñatas for parties and holiday celebrations. A brief author's note at the end of this bilingual book provides suggestions for making simple piñatas.

POWWOW

George Ancona. (Harcourt Brace Jovanovich, 1993) 48 pages. ISBN: 0-15-263268-9. Level: Ages 5-11.

Dynamic color photographs underscore Ancona's explanation of the Crow Fair in Montana, the biggest powwow in North America. Readers see how people gather on the prairie to renew acquaintances and celebrate the shared heritage of Lakota, Ojibwa, Cheyenne, Crow, Cree, Blackfoot, Fox, and other Native peoples. The opening parade, role of the drum, and main types of dancing are explained and pictured. Whether a dancer wears Traditional, Fancy, Grass, or Jingle-dress clothing, each one has practiced long before donning his specific celebratory garments at this event. Occasionally Ancona details the enjoyment and excitement of Anthony Standing Rock, a young Traditional dancer, and other children at this annual reaffirmation of shared American Indian heritage and tradition. This striking 8¼ x 11¼ in. account pictures a community created in one place annually for a celebration of carefully prepared tributes to its common history.

POWWOW SUMMER: A FAMILY CELEBRATES THE CIRCLE OF LIFE

Marcie R. Rendon. Photographs by Cheryl Walsh Bellville. (Carolrhoda, 1996) 48 pages. ISBN: 0-87614-986-7. Level: Ages 7-11.

"According to Native tradition, the circle of life is endless. It has no beginning. There is no end." Rendon's text and Bellville's many color photographs look at some of the ways in which one Anishinabe family celebrates the circle of life: by opening their arms and their hearts to welcome foster children into their family, by keeping close ties among the generations, by grieving together in the aftermath of a death. The Downwind family—parents, children, foster children—is profiled over the course of a summer, during which time they go on the powwow trail, attending two gatherings where they become part of a larger community, thus entering the circle of life in yet another way. At powwows, ceremonies and dances also mark the continuous cycle of connections and changes important in Anishinabe culture. The open, engaging narrative explains the importance of the rituals and traditions at the powwows by using comparisons that will resonate for many non-Native readers. The book also discusses how, by emphasizing the importance of family and community, the Downwinds are maintaining ties to traditional Anishinabe ways, ties that keep them strong in the wake of many challenges that Native peoples face in contemporary times.

PUEBLO STORYTELLER

Diane Hoyt-Goldsmith. Photographs by Lawrence Migdale (Holiday House, 1991) 26 pages. ISBN: 0-8234-0864-7. Level: Ages 6-10.

A concise first-person text and color photographs document the day-to-day life of April Trujillo, a ten-year-old Cochiti girl who lives with her grandparents near Santa Fe, New Mexico. April is a member of a gifted family—both of her grandparents are potters and her uncle is a drum maker. She describes the step-by-step process her grandparents go through to make clay storyteller sculptures, from going out to dig up the clay they will use; to kneading and shaping it and sculpting the figure; to sanding, polishing, and painting it before firing it in a kiln. A deep respect for elders and cultural traditions is apparent in April's young voice, as she places every-day activities in a cultural context.

RAMADAN

Suhaib Hamid Ghazi. Illustrated by Omar Rayyan. (Holiday House, 1996) 32 pages. ISBN: 0-8234-1254-7. Level: Ages 6-9.

Hakeem is a Muslim who will fast all day long with his family during the month of Ramadan, the holiest month of the Islamic calendar. Like Muslims all over the world and throughout the United States, Hakeem and his family do not eat or drink anything during the day until the sun has set. Hakeem's mother makes a variety of foods for them to eat until the break of dawn "when there is enough light to see the difference between black thread and a white thread." They then perform the first of five daily prayers, do good deeds, and repair broken relationships. Rayyan's color illustrations succeed in differentiating between contemporary and historic times.

RAPUNZEL

Paul O. Zelinsky. (Dutton, 1997) 40 pages. ISBN: 0-525-45607-4. Level: Ages 7-11.

An elegant edition unfolds the classic tale of the dire outcomes of a bargain made in desperation with a sorceress by a father-to-be. The sorceress raises the child she names Rapunzel until age twelve and then imprisons her in a tower. Known to the girl as a stepmother, the sorceress visits Rapunzel by hoisting herself on the girl's rope-like braid. One day a prince hears the girl singing and begins secret visits to her in the same manner. Their liaison turns into marriage after they hold a private ceremony in Rapunzel's tower dwelling, and soon her dress grows "tight around her waist." After cutting Rapunzel's hair, the sorceress casts her from the tower, and soon disaster befalls the prince. Years later, the two lovers meet in the countryside where Rapunzel is raising twin children. Zelinsky drew upon the Italian Renaissance to create a detailed visual environment conveying a great depth of feeling and turmoil. Even within his patterned, formal gardens, it is clear that nothing in life can be completely predictable. Here an herb known in German as "rapunzel"—a bellflower seen throughout the book—becomes the object of the pregnant woman's craving. Details of architecture, furnishings, clothing, and flowers are beautifully rendered in oil paintings illustrating a book also notable for its splendid design and complete background notes.

THE RETURN OF THE BUFFALOES: A PLAINS INDIAN STORY ABOUT FAMINE AND RENEWAL OF THE EARTH

Paul Goble, reteller and illustrator. (National Geographic Society, 1996) 32 pages. ISBN: 0-7922-2714-X. Level: Ages 8-12.

The winter food supplies of the Lakota people are depleted. The children are too weak from hunger to play. Even though spring has already arrived, the buffalo have not returned to the Great Plains. Two young men are dispatched to go far into the hills and find the buffaloes for their starving people. They meet a mysterious and wonderful woman who leads them into a cave, addresses each as Grandson, and causes the famine to end. Extensive author's notes and the details about both parfleches and buffalo hunting make this volume especially valuable to anyone wanting information about the Lakota people. Goble's illustrations were created in India ink and watercolor. His earlier book BUFFALO WOMAN (Bradbury, 1984) featured a tale about a different visitation of this holy Mother Earth figure.

SAM AND THE LUCKY MONEY

Karen Chinn. Illustrated by Cornelius Van Wright & Ying-Hwa Hu. (Lee & Low, 1995) 32 pages. ISBN: 1-880000-13-X. Level: Ages 4-7.

When Sam goes to Chinatown with his mother to shop for New Year's Day, he carries the four dollar bills his grandparents gave him in bright red leisees, just in case he should find something to buy with his newly acquired wealth. Four dollars seems like a lot of money to him until he sees the prices on things he wants in the toy shop. But the money turns out to be lucky for Sam after all when he finds just the right way to spend it. Karen Chinn's charming story of a young boy's first understanding of value is accompanied by expressive watercolors which capture the bustling excitement of Chinatown on New Year's Day, as well as Sam's many moods.

SEÑOR CAT'S ROMANCE, AND OTHER FAVORITE STORIES FROM LATIN AMERICA

Lucia M. González. Illustrated by Lulu Delacre. (Scholastic, 1997) 40 pages. ISBN: 0-590-48537-7. Level: Ages 4-11.

The six tales in this colorfully illustrated handsome collection are: "The Little Half-Chick," "Juan Bobo and the Three-Legged Pot," "Martina, the Little Cockroach," "The Billy Goat and the Vegetable Garden," "How Uncle Rabbit Tricked Uncle Tiger," and the title story. González provides a two-page foreword explaining how she became familiar with these tales herself as a child in Cuba and why they are "cuentos favoritos," or favorite tales of children across Latin America. According to González, the dominant themes of these tales are "universal to childhood experience. Their characters learn the power of sharing, they learn the value of wit and cleverness." A note about each story, along with a brief glossary and pronunciation guide, is included. Artist Delacre also provides a two-page note in which she relates how she recalls the stories from her Puerto Rican childhood and discusses some of her design and illustration decisions.

SEVEN CANDLES FOR KWANZAA

Andrea Davis Pinkney. Illustrated by Brian Pinkney. (Dial, 1993) 32 pages. ISBN: 0-8037-1293-6. Level: Ages 3-9.

An easy-to-read and understand explanation of Kwanzaa features images of a contemporary U.S. family observing each of the seven days in activities recognizable to today's children. Emphasis is placed on Kwanzaa as "an American holiday inspired by African traditions . . . not intended as a religious, political, or heroic holiday, nor is it a substitute for Christmas." The striking full-color artwork for this 9¼ by 11¼ in. picture book was prepared using scratchboard and oil pastels.

SEVEN DAYS OF KWANZAA

Ella Grier. Illustrated by John Ward. (A Holiday Step Book) (Viking, 1997) 18 pages. ISBN: 0-670-87327-6. Level: Ages 3-8 and older.

A lively book containing short readings for each day of Kwanzaa begins with the words of a Kwanzaa song: "Call your father! Call your mother! Call your sister! Call your brother! It's Kwanzaa time. Family time . . . Seven candles we will light." Although the small volume is meant to reinforce information, four recipes at the end (popcorn nut crunch, date and peanut salad, muhindi, and jambalaya salad) will require adult supervision.

SHANNON: AN OJIBWAY DANCER

Sandra King. Photographs by Catherine Whipple. (Lerner, 1993) 48 pages. ISBN: 0-8225-9643-1. Level: Ages 7-11.

This marvelous book uses photographs and text to depict the life of a thirteen-year-old Ojibway girl, Shannon Anderson, who lives with her grandmother, sisters, and cousins in Minneapolis. Shannon's life is firmly rooted in her cultural heritage. A fancy dancer belonging to two drum and dance groups, Shannon goes through detailed preparations to get her intricate costumes ready for performances, but she is proud of her skills in the traditional ways of her people. "It's a good thing I'm Indian," she says to her grandmother, and her grandmother replies, "always remember to be glad. Remember that wherever you go, all that you are goes with you."

SHOES FROM GRANDPA

Mem Fox. Illustrated by Patricia Mullins. (Orchard Books, 1990) 32 pages. ISBN: 0-531-08448-5. Level: Ages 3-7.

An up-to-date cumulative variation on THE HOUSE THAT JACK BUILT features Jessie and rings with lines such as "And her mom said, / 'I'll buy you a skirt that won't show the dirt, / to go with the socks from the local shops, / to go with the shoes from Grandpa' " The final, full-color collage shows high-spirited Jessie's preference for jeans as she dashes away on her skateboard. The 11½ x 9½ in. format is perfect for group use.

SIMPLE SIGNS

Cindy Wheeler. (Viking, 1995) 32 pages. ISBN: 0-670-86282-7. Level: Ages 5-8.

An astonishingly effective presentation of the American Sign Language signs for twenty-eight simple words. The sign or action for each word is illustrated with a black-and-white line drawing showing a child completing the sign. A written hint for making the sign accompanies the drawing (e.g., for "ball," like holding a ball.) Each word is illustrated in full color next to the drawing.

SNAPSHOTS FROM THE WEDDING

Gary Soto. Illustrated by Stephanie Garcia. (G. P. Putnam's Sons, 1997) 32 pages. ISBN: 0-399-22808-X. Level: Ages 4-8 and older.

The flower girl at a Mexican American wedding describes all the highlights of the event—from her perspective. We notice the yawning altar boy with dirty tennis shoes and Uncle Juan in his itchy new suit during the ceremony. At the banquet, we see how perfectly black olives fit onto each of the narrator's fingertips. Soto aptly captures the child's view of an adult occasion. Garcia's distinctive three-dimensional illustrations are equally appealing. Each one uses human figures sculpted in clay, painted and dressed in clothes made from fabric, and placed in small boxes that have been created to look like stage sets. The overall effect is a pleasing mixture of fantasy and reality, rather like a real wedding ceremony.

SOLO GIRL

Andrea Davis Pinkney. Illustrated by Nneka Bennett. (Hyperion Chapters, Hyperion, 1997) 51 pages. ISBN: 0-7868-2265-1. PBK: 0-7868-1216-8. Level: Ages 6-8.

Cass is a whiz at math, but that's little consolation to this young African American girl when she wants to learn double Dutch. Her feet can't keep even one rope from getting tangled. Her brothers, Jackson and Bud, write a rhyme to help Cass keep the rhythm when she jumps. When Cass blows the beat of the rhyme on the whistle she won in a school math contest, she learns how to jump a single rope. But will she ever learn double Dutch? To Cass's pleasure and surprise, her math skills play an unexpected role in helping her master the difficult footwork in this satisfying story about a young girl adjusting to life in her new city neighborhood.

SONGS FROM THE LOOM: A NAVAJO GIRL LEARNS TO WEAVE

Monty Roessel. (Lerner, 1995) 48 pages. ISBN: 0-8225-2657-3. Level: Ages 7-11.

Jaclyn Roessel is learning how to weave in the traditional Navajo way. Her grandmother, Ruth, is teaching her how to shear the sheep, dye the wool, and work the loom. At the same time, she is teaching her the stories and songs of weaving that are part of her Navajo culture. Without them, her grandmother makes clear, Jaclyn's education as a Navajo weaver will be incomplete. Monty Roessel, Jaclyn's father, documents Jaclyn's education in photographs taken when she was between the ages of ten and twelve. In accompanying text, he shares Jaclyn's experience, as well as the stories and songs that she learns.

THE SPIRIT OF TIO FERNANDO: A DAY OF THE DEAD STORY / EL ESPIRITU DE TIO FERNANDO: UNA HISTORIA DEL DIA DE LOS MUERTOS

Janice Levy. Illustrated by Morella Fuenmayor. (Albert Whitman, 1995) 32 pages. ISBN: 0-8075-7585-2. Level: Ages 6-9.

When he goes to the market, a little Mexican boy is reminded of the ways he can honor his uncle's spirit during All Souls' Day or El Dia de Los Muertos. Venezuelan artist Morella Fuenmayor's watercolors illustrating this sweet bilingual picture story suggest important cultural details rarely seen in U.S. books. In real life, a child Nando's age would not require as many explanations about the special activities in which he and his mother engage while they remember the people they love who have died. Outsiders to these observances will enjoy learning about them in this way.

STORIES FROM THE CLASSICAL BALLET

Belinda Hollyer. Illustrated by Sophy Williams. (Viking, 1995) 127 pages. ISBN: 0-670-86605-9. Level: Ages 6-11 and older.

Each of Hollyer's eight fictionalized versions of classical ballets is accompanied by three other distinctive elements: a brief history of the ballet, three pastel paintings reproduced in full color, and Irina Baronova's one-page reminiscence of her experience as a ballerina in that particular ballet. An autobiographical chapter by Baronova, whose childhood training led her to the Russian Ballet, precedes this unique material. This absorbing reading for beginning or advanced dancers and for others, as well, features "La Bayadere," "Coppelia," "The Firebird," "Giselle," "The Nutcracker," "Petroushka," "The Sleeping Beauty," and "Swan Lake."

TAKE ME OUT TO THE BALLGAME

Jack Norworth. Illustrated by Alec Gillman. (Four Winds Press, 1992) 32 pages. ISBN: 0-02-735991-3. Level: Age 3 and older.

Typically seen as electronic sing-along signs when sung at Big League baseball games, lilting words dance across pages picturing a game, but not one played during the late twentieth century. The illustrations replicate images of the former Brooklyn Dodgers at Ebbets Field during the 1947 World Series. The pictures were drawn in pen, painted with watercolor, and highlighted with colored pencil. Background information about the song, original verses, and a musical arrangement follow the almost wordless story of a famous strikeout. Considerable Dodger history appears on the last double-page spread of this picture book tribute to baseball in general, "the" baseball song, and especially to a specific team and time.

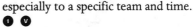

TALKING WITH ARTISTS

Pat Cummings, editor. (Simon & Schuster, 1995) 96 pages. ISBN: 0-689-80310-9. Level: Ages 6-14 and older.

Cummings has illustrated many books for children, including C.L.O.U.D.S. (Lothrop, 1986), STORM IN THE NIGHT (Harper, 1988), and C IS FOR CITY (HarperCollins, 1995). She also realizes that although she shares things in common with other illustrators, her studio work on each picture book is unique. In her popular TALKING WITH ARTISTS (Harper, 1992), she provided a vehicle for fourteen picture book creators to respond to frequently asked questions. This second volume featuring thirteen artists includes each one's explanation of personal technique and a photo of his/her studio. The artists are Thomas B. Allen, Mary Jane Begin, Floyd Cooper, Julie Downing, Denise Fleming, Sheila Hamanaka, Kervin Henkes, William Joyce, Maira Kalman, Deborah Nourse Lattimore, Brian Pinkney, Vera B. Williams, and David Wisniewski. Their published books are listed, and readers can see a childhood and an adult photo of each, a reproduction of one piece of childhood art, and a published illustration. Terrific organization and compelling subject matter mark these glimpses into artists' careers that offer realistic encouragement within excellent reading.

THE TIE MAN'S MIRACLE

Steven Schnur. Illustrated by Stephen T. Johnson. (Morrow, 1995) ISBN: 0-688-13464-5. Level: Ages 5-8.

A tie salesman comes to the door on the snowy eighth night of Hanukkah. He's been colder, Mr. Hoffman responds to an inquiry. No, he has no family waiting for him. Dad invites him to join them while they light the menorah. Baby Hannah reminds Mr. Hoffman of his own Hannalah and his family lost in the war. Seth, the narrator, has not yet heard about that time, a time when someone could lose an entire family. Changing moods, Mr. Hoffman tells how as a child, he believed that if all eight Hanukkah candles went out at once, his wishes would be carried straight to the ear of God. Although Seth and Hannah never see Mr. Hoffman again, every year they wish on the eight candles. Dramatic watercolor paintings illustrate a gentle story hinting at the history about which Seth and Hannah will some day learn.

TREE OF CRANES

Allen Say. (Houghton Mifflin, 1991) 32 pages. ISBN: 0-395-52024-X. Level: Ages 5-7.

A Japanese boy "not yet old enough to wear long pants" catches a cold playing at a neighbor's carp pond and is put to bed by his mother after a hot bath. The mother seems unusually preoccupied and even severe as she folds origami figures; she then, inexplicably, digs up and brings inside the little pine tree belonging to her son. As she hangs tiny origami birds on the tree, the mother reminisces about Christmas during her own childhood in warm California, long before she came to Japan and met the boy's father. Two stories about promising and giving overlap in an unusual full-color $11\frac{1}{4}$ x $10\frac{1}{4}$ in. book evoking two past generations, two cultures, and early twentieth century traditional Japanese domestic life.

THE TWELVE DAYS OF CHRISTMAS: A SONG REBUS

Emily Bolam, illustrator. U.S. edition. (Anne Schwartz/Atheneum, 1997) 30 pages. ISBN: 0-689-81101-2. Level: Age 3-adult.

A unique method of visualizing the traditional English game song uses a rebus or picture to help young singing readers and their adults keep track of an ever-growing number of gifts. For example, an early page reads "On the second day of Christmas, my true love sent to me two turtle doves and a [picture of a partridge] in a pear tree." On the opposite page is Bolam's acrylic painting of the two turtle doves constituting the gift during the second day. The pattern continues until the twelfth day when singers begin "On the twelfth day of Christmas, my true love sent to me, 12 lords a-leaping, 11 [ladies dancing], 10 [pipers piping]," etc. The music is printed at the end of this lively, lovely, colorful volume.

UNCERTAIN ROADS: SEARCHING FOR THE GYPSIES

Yale Strom. (Four Winds, 1993) 112 pages. ISBN: 0-02-788531-3. Level: Ages 9-14 and older.

Strom's opening paragraph states that "with the collapse of communism, the fall of the Berlin Wall and the reunification of Germany, Pandora's box has been opened, and its contents—nationalism, pan-Slavism, tribalism, and anti-Semitism—have created an atmosphere of intolerance" for which the "most easily identifiable targets" are the approximately ten million to eleven million Rom living in Europe. Strom presents the people typically called "gypsies" by outsiders through interviews with individuals, most of whom are young. He provides background information about the origin of the Rom in India and some of the reasons for their historic movement across Europe. Casual discrimination against the Rom as well as intentional acts of prejudice, including those during the Holocaust, are discussed. Strom's many superb full-color photos alternate with others reproduced in black and white to extend the interviews. The book is organized by contemporary nation: Romania, which has thirteen distinct Rom tribes; Hungary; Ukraine; and Sweden. A bibliography, glossary, and notations for several songs add valuable elements to this important book.

THE UGLY MENORAH

Marissa Moss. (Farrar Straus Giroux, 1996). 32 pages. ISBN: 0-374-38027-9. Level: Ages 5-8.

Spending the eight days of Hanukkah with her widowed grandmother, Rachel is surprised and disappointed to discover Grandma's menorah is a plain wood board with tin cylinders. But when Grandma tells her about the menorah's origins in the days when she and Grandpa were young and poor, Rachel is able to see its sweet and shining beauty. Full-color, full-page illustrations accompany a tender family story.

THE UNINVITED GUEST AND OTHER JEWISH HOLIDAY TALES

Nina Jaffe. Illustrated by Elivia. (Scholastic, 1993) 72 pages. ISBN: 0-590-44653-3. Level: Ages 5-10 and older.

Beginning with Rosh Hashanah and "The Never-Ending Song," the meaning of six more Jewish holidays are briefly explained and accompanied by a story: "Miracles on the Sea" by Peretz (Yom Kippur); "The Magician's Spell" (Sukkot); "Hannah the Joyful" (Hanukkah); "The Purim Trunk" (Purim); "The Two Brothers" (Passover); and "The Uninvited Guest" (Shabbat). The final ten pages include sections containing information about each story, an explanation of the Jewish calendar, a glossary, a bibliography, and a list of recommended readings about Jewish folklore and the holidays. A distinctive full-page painting done with watercolors and crayon and reproduced in full color accompanies each story in an $11\frac{1}{4}$ by $8\frac{1}{4}$ in. book full of interest for all readers.

VEJIGANTE MASQUERADER

Lulu Delacre. (Scholastic, 1993) 40 pages. ISBN: 0-590-45776-4. Level: Ages 5-9.

Since 1858, boys and men in Ponce, Puerto Rico, have celebrated Carnival for the entire month of February. These masqueraders or vejigantes wear clown-like costumes and papier mache masks resembling animals. Delacre's English/Spanish story based on this local custom features young Ramon, who has found ways to create his first vejigante costume and work in exchange for a mask so that he can participate in the merriment with the older boys. During the opening festivities, Ramon's foolhardy actions gain the boys' respect but also ruin his costume. Bilingual information about three masqueraders from Mexico, Spain, and Venezuela; directions for making a vejigante mask; several vejigante chants; a glossary; and a bibliography support the story. All portions of this unique $9\frac{1}{2}$ by $10\frac{1}{4}$ in. picture book are illustrated in full color with art created in watercolor, colored pencils, and pastels.

VISIONS: STORIES ABOUT WOMEN ARTISTS

Leslie Sills. (Albert Whitman, 1993) 64 pages. ISBN: 0-8075-8491-6. Level: Ages 9-14 and older.

In a compact volume measuring 9 by 11 in., Sills showcases the life and art of four women: Mary Cassatt, Leonorra Carrington, Betye Saar, and Mary Frank. The handsome volume contains photographs of selected works and of the artists, while the text engages interest in their progressive and distinctive spirits. Cassatt is an artist whose life and work are familiar to many readers. Among the other artists, Carrington's origins in northern England exposed her to Celtic legends, Christian stories about miracles and Catholic saints, and family suggestions that she raise fox terriers rather than attend art school. After learning about surrealism in art, Carrington ultimately emigrated to Mexico where she continued to "see the invisible" and create "fantasies with other worldly creatures." Saar's early fascination with found objects extended into a career involving three-dimensional assemblages, a famous one being "The Liberation of Aunt Jemima," her response as an African American artist to outsider notions about kitchen slaves. In recent years Saar continues to transform ordinary objects, including circuit boards, into artistic statements. Born in England, Frank was sent to the United States in 1940 to live with grandparents. Throughout her career sculpting and, more recently, creating monoprints, Frank explores universals: life and life experience. Detailed picture credits and bibliographies conclude Sills's second fine work about women artists; the first was INSPIRATIONS (Albert Whitman, 1989).

VOICES FROM THE FIELDS: CHILDREN OF MIGRANT FARM WORKERS TELL THEIR STORIES

S. Beth Atkin. Illustrated by Will Clay. (Joy Street/Little Brown, 1993) 96 pages. ISBN: 0-316-05633-2. Level: Ages 9-14 and older.

First-person narratives and/or poems introduce ten voices representative of Latino migrant children and teenagers working in the Salinas Valley of California. This unparalleled photodocumentary children's book originated in migrant programs and in the fields where some of the children and teenagers agreed to tell their stories and be photographed. Atkin's brief introductory passages establish a context for each commentary. These children of Mexican heritage speak about work, family, fitting in, the gang, and teen parents. Spanish was used in most of the interviews; the English translations offer an urgent witness and testimony to certain realities and experiences and, sometimes, to hopes, as well.

WAITING FOR CHRISTMAS

Monica Greenfield. Illustrated by Jan Spivey Gilchrist. (Scholastic, 1996) 32 pages. ISBN: 0-590-52700-2. Level: Ages 3-6.

On Christmas Eve an African American brother and sister anxiously await the end of the day and the beginning of Christmas morning. Gilchrist's wintery acrylic paintings aptly capture the children's anticipatory mood, heightened by the short, lyrical lines of the text.

WEAVING A CALIFORNIA TRADITION: A NATIVE AMERICAN BASKETMAKER

Linda Yamane. Photographs by Dugan Aguilar (We Are Still Here) (Lerner, 1996) 48 pages. ISBN: 0-8225-2660-3. Level: Ages 7-11.

Eleven-year-old Carly Tex, a member of the Western Mono tribe in California, is continuing the tradition of basketweaving that has been part of her family and her culture for generations. Carly enjoys learning from her aunt and mother about gathering and preparing grasses, branches, and other materials required for weaving, and about the various methods for creating baskets. With her entire family, which includes her father, a younger sister, and an older sister home from college, Carly also attends a California Indian Basketweavers Gathering, where she displays her work and continues to learn. Aguilar's color photographs accompany Yamane's sensitive, informative text that also discusses the beliefs that go hand-in-hand with the Western Mono weaving tradition.

WHAT A WONDERFUL WORLD

Ashley Bryan, illustrator. (Atheneum, 1995) 24 pages. ISBN: 0-689-80087-8. Level: Ages 2-8.

Six children paint scenery: flowers, trees, sun, moon, stars, and a rainbow. They draw, cut, and mount animal, bird, and reptile shapes. Hand puppets are costumed. Lettered signs proclaim "Puppet Show Today" and "Satchmo the Great!" The performance begins, "I see trees of green, red roses too, I see them bloom/for me and you, and I think to myself, 'What a wonderful world!' " Backstage, children hold up set pieces picturing flora, fauna, and puppet people indigenous to each hemisphere. "The bright, blessed day, the dark, sacred night;" the hands lifting the sun and moon onto the stage vary in skin color. Bryan's inspired vision for a hopeful future is also a tribute to Louis Armstrong, whose performances of this song composed three decades ago are legendary. By addressing the young in love ("They'll know much more/than I'll ever know"), Armstrong sang a personal testimony to goodness. That Bryan understands this song on a deep level is evident in his tempera and gouache paintings incorporating bright borders and stylized patterned shapes while expanding the meanings of the lyrics and music in this $12\frac{1}{4}$ x $10\frac{1}{4}$ in. book.

WHAT INSTRUMENT IS THIS?

Rosmarie Hausherr. (Scholastic Hardcover, 1992) 38 pages. ISBN: 0-590-44644-4. Level: Ages 4-8.

Sixteen musical instruments are introduced one at a time, first with a color photograph of a boy or girl playing an instrument paired with the question forming the book's title. Upon turning the page, a photograph of someone playing it corresponds with brief information about the instrument. The instruments include a recorder, saxophone, bagpipes, electric guitar, pipe organ, and trumpet. A visual symbol and phrase designate to which instrument group each one belongs. Brief details about instruments, lessons, teaching methods, practice time, joining an orchestra or band, and recitals appear at the book's end to respond to adults' questions. The diversity of the children showing an interest in the instruments can encourage the natural curiosity of readers from varying backgrounds.

WHEN BIRDS COULD TALK AND BATS COULD SING: THE ADVENTURES OF BRUH SPARROW, SIS WREN, AND THEIR FRIENDS.

Virginia Hamilton, reteller. Illustrated by Barry Moser. (Blue Sky/Scholastic, 1996) 63 pages. ISBN: 0-590-47372-7. Level: Ages 7-12 and older.

Unforgettable winged creatures practically fly off the pages of this elegant volume. Virginia Hamilton has selected and retold eight African American folktales first written down in authentic dialect by folklorist Martha Young, who collected the stories from former slaves on her father's plantation in Alabama. In each of the brief stories, the creatures behave like humans with human weaknesses: pride, selfishness, and just plain nosiness. The stories are written in a prose style known as cante fable, meaning that songs and verses are woven into the story and each one ends with a moral. The characters themselves are brilliantly characterized by a combination of Hamilton's perfectly crafted dialogue and Moser's stunning watercolor paintings. Despite the human attributes Moser gives Miss Bat and the birds through the facial expressions and the hats they wear, we never forget that they are creatures of the sky, thanks largely to a page design that causes viewers' eyes to sweep upward as they follow the characters' antics, making an inevitable fall from grace all the more dramatic.

THE WHISPERING CLOTH

Pegi Deitz Shea. Illustrated by Anita Riggio. (Boyds Mills, 1995) 32 pages. ISBN: 1-56397-134-8. Level: Ages 7-11.

Mai, a young Hmong girl living in a refugee camp in Thailand, waits for the day she might join her cousins in the United States. To pass time, Mai listens to the women tell stories of their Laotian homeland, and she watches the stories take shape inside the beautiful borders of the pa'ndau, the story cloth they sew. Wanting to stitch her own pa'ndau, Mai finds herself remembering the death of her parents and her flight from Laos to the refugee camp with her grandmother. An important narrative about the experience of Hmong refugee people is illustrated with full-color paintings and an actual pa'ndau stitched for the text to tell Mai's story. An author's note provides information on Ban Vinai, the refugee camp where the story is set.

WITH NEEDLE AND THREAD: A BOOK ABOUT QUILTS

Raymond Bial. (Houghton Mifflin, 1996) 48 pages. ISBN: 0-395-73568-8. Level: Ages 9-16 and older.

For centuries people from many cultures have made quilts for comfort. In recent years a resurgence of quiltmaking and a growing interest in art quilts and quilt exhibitions has occurred in this nation. Bial writes about heirloom quilts, commemorative quilts, art quilts, the AIDS quilt, quilts made for charitable causes, a Hmong quilt, an Amish quilt, and others. Color photographs show some of the remarkable designs and details. They show quilters at work, too, even a young girl stitching her first block. The author's intent is to write about the many connections people have with quilts, and the anecdotes included attest to this. A list of further reading concludes the book.

Children's Trade Books with Culture as a Second Thematic Strand

The title index on pp. 173-180 lists the number of the page on which each book is annotated.

TITLE	AUTHOR	DATE	AGE LEVEL
A Bellbird in a Flame Tree	Kilmeny Niland	1991	All ages
A Is for Africa	Ifeoma Onyefulu	1993	Ages 3-7
Angela Weaves a Dream: The Story of a Young Maya Artist	Michelle Solá	1997	Ages 8-11
Appalachia: The Voices of Sleeping Birds	Cynthia Rylant	1991	Ages 7-11
Arctic Son	Jean Craighead George	1997	Ages 5-9
At Christmastime	Valerie Worth	1992	Ages 5 and older
Bill Pickett: Rodeo-Ridin' Cowboy	Andrea D. Pinkney	1996	Ages 7-10 and older
The Birthday Swap	Loretta Lopez	1997	Ages 5-8
The Block	Langston Hughes	1995	Age 11 and older
Buffalo Days	Diane Hoyt-Goldsmith	1997	Ages 7-11
Building an Igloo	Ulli Steltzer	1995	Ages 7-11
C Is for City	Nikki Grimes	1995	Ages 3-6
Calvin's Christmas Wish	Calvin Miles	1993	Ages 5-8
Chibi: A True Story from Japan	Barbara Brenner and Julia Takaya	1996	Ages 7-10
Children of Clay: A Family of Pueblo Potters	Rina Swentzell	1992	Ages 7-13
Children of Promise: African-American Literature and Art for Young People	Charles Sullivan, editor	1991	Age 5 and older
The Christmas Tree / El Árbol de Navidad: A Christmas Rhyme in English and Spanish	Alma Flor Ada	1997	Ages 2-5
The Christmas Tree Ship	Jeanette Winter	1994	Ages 5-9
Clambake: A Wampanoag Tradition	Russell M. Peters	1992	Ages 7-13
Country Fair	Elisha Cooper	1997	Ages 3-8
The Day of Ahmed's Secret	Florence Parry Heide and Judith Heide Gilliland	1990	Ages 5-9
Emeka's Gift: An African Counting Story	Ifeoma Onyefulu	1995	Ages 4-7
Families: A Celebration of Diversity, Commitment and Love	Aylette Jenness	1990	Ages 5-12

Fort Chipewyan Homecoming: A Journey to Native Canada	Morningstar Mercredi	1997	Ages 8-11
Fun—No Fun	James Stevenson	1994	Ages 4-8
Fun with 9umbers	Massin	1995	Ages 7-11
Gabriella's Song	Candace Fleming	1997	Ages 4-7
Georgia O'Keefe	Robyn Montana Turner	1991	Ages 7-12
Gingerbread Days	Joyce Carol Thomas	1995	Ages 3-7
Good-bye, Curtis	Kevin Henkes	1995	Ages 3-6
A Great Miracle Happened There: A Chanukah Story	Karla Kuskin	1993	Ages 5-10
Great Women in the Struggle	Toyomi Igus, editor	1991	Age 7 and older
The Hired Hand	Robert D. San Souci	1997	Ages 8-11
Home Field	David Spohn	1993	Ages 3-7
Houses of Adobe: The Southwest	Bonnie Shemie	1995	Ages 9-11
Houses of Bark: Tipi, Wigwam and Longhouse	Bonnie Shemie	1990	Ages 6-9
How My Family Lives in America	Susan Kuklin	1992	Ages 4-7
Hush! A Thai Lullaby	Minfong Ho	1996	Ages 2-5
I Am a Jesse White Tumbler	Diane Schmidt	1990	Ages 7-12
In My Family / En Mi Familia	Carmen Lomas Garza with Harriet Rohmer	1996	Age 5 and older
The Inner City Mother Goose	Eve Merriam	1996	Age 14 and older
In the Heart of the Village: The World of the Indian Banyan Tree	Barbara Bash	1996	Ages 8-11
In the Street of the Temple Cloth Printers	Dorothy Field	1996	Ages 9-14
I Was a Teenage Professional Wrestler	Ted Lewin	1993	Ages 8-14
Imani's Gift at Kwanzaa	Denise Burden-Patmon	1992	Ages 3-8
John Henry	Julius Lester	1994	Ages 4-12
June 29, 1999	David Wiesner	1992	Ages 4-9
Kinaalda: A Navajo Girl Grows Up	Monty Roessel	1993	Ages 7-11 and older
Little White Cabin	Ferguson Plain	1992	Ages 5-8

Lives of the Athletes: Thrills, Spills and What the Neighbors Thought	Kathleen Krull	1997	Ages 11-14 and older
The Magic Moonberry Jump Ropes	Dakari Hru	1997	Ages 4-7
Mayeros: A Yucatec Maya Family	George Ancona	1996	Ages 7-11
A Million Fish …More or Less	Patricia C. McKissaack	1992	Ages 4-7
Morning, Noon, and Night: Poems to Fill Your Day	Sharon Taberski	1996	Ages 5-8
Mother Gave a Shout: Poems by Women and Girls	Susanna Steele and Morag Styles, editors	1991	Ages 9-13 and older
My Buddy	Audrey Osofsky	1992	Ages 4-9
My Fellow Americans: A Family Album	Alice Provensen	1995	Ages 5-14 and older
My Name Is Maria Isabel	Alma Flor Ada	1993	Ages 7-9
Neve Shalom/Wahat A-Salam: Oasis of Peace	Laurie Dolphin	1993	Ages 7-10
Night Tree	Eve Bunting	1991	Ages 3-7
Ogbo: Sharing Life in an African Village	Ifeoma Onyefulu	1996	Ages 7-10
On the Pampas	Maria Cristina Brusca	1991	Ages 4-8
A Picture Book of Jesse Owens	David A. Adler	1992	Ages 5-9
The Red Comb	Fernando Pico	1994	Ages 7-11
Remember That	Leslea Newman	1996	Ages 4-8
Samuel Todd's Book of Great Inventions	E. L. Konigsburg	1991	Ages 3-6
The Seasons Sewn: A Year in Patchwork	Ann Whitford Paul	1996	Ages 9-12
Six Words, Many Turtles, and Three Days in Hong Kong	Patricia McMahon	1997	Ages 8-11
Snow Day!	Barbara M. Joosse	1995	Ages 3-6
Stories in Stone: Rock Art Pictures by Early Americans	Caroline Arnold	1996	Ages 9-12 and older
Street Music: City Poems	Arnold Adoff	1995	Ages 7-11
Sunflakes: Poems for Children	Lilian Moore	1992	Ages 2-7
Sweet Words so Brave: The Story of African American Literature	Barbara K. Curry and James Michael Brodie	1996	Ages 9-16 and older
Talking with Artists: Conversations with Victoria Chess, Pat Cummings, Leo and Diane Dillon, Richard Egielski, Lois Ehlert, Lisa Campbell Ernst, Tom Feelings, Steven Kellogg, Jerry Pinkney, Amy Schwartz, Lane Smith, Chris Van Allsburg and David Wiesner	Pat Cummings, compiler	1992	Ages 6-14 and older

Tanya and Emily in a Dance for Two	Patricia Lee Gauch	1994	Ages 3-7
Tar Beach	Faith Ringgold	1991	Ages 5-11
Tonight Is Carnival	Arthur Dorros	1991	Ages 4-8
Totem Pole	Diane Hoyt-Goldsmith	1990	Ages 5-10
Treemonisha	Angela Shelf Medearis	1995	Ages 9-12 and older
When I Am Old with You	Angela Johnson	1990	Ages 3-6
A Young Painter: The Life and Paintings of Wang Yani— China's Extraordinary Young Artist	Zheng Zhensun and Alice Low	1991	Age 8 and older
The Zebra-Riding Cowboy: A Folk Song from the Old West	Angela Medearis	1992	Ages 5-9

Children's Trade Books with Culture as a Third Thematic Strand

The title index on pp. 173-180 lists the number of the page on which each book is annotated.

Afro-Bets First Book about Africa	Veronica Freeman Ellis	1990	Ages 6-12
Arctic Hunter	Diane Hoyt-Goldsmith	1992	Ages 9-13
Artist in Overalls: The Life of Grant Wood	John Duggleby	1996	Ages 9-14 and older
Brown Honey in Broomwheat Tea	Joyce Carol Thomas	1993	Ages 5-10
Clouds for Dinner	Lynne Rae Perkins	1997	Ages 4-8
Cynthia Gregory Dances Swan Lake	Cynthia Gregory	1990	Ages 5-11
Dia's Story Cloth: The Hmong People's Journey to Freedom	Dia Cha	1996	Ages 8-11 and older
Eagle Song	Joseph Bruchac	1997	Ages 9-11 and older
Elijah's Angel: A Story for Chanukah and Christmas	Michael J. Rosen	1992	Ages 7-11
Everglades; Buffalo Tiger and the River of Grass	Peter Lourie	1994	Ages 9-11 and older
Girls and Young Women Inventing: Twenty True Stories about Inventors, Plus How You Can Be One Yourself	Frances A. Karnes and Suzanne M. Bean	1995	Ages 10-14 and older
Gus and Grandpa and the Christmas Cookies	Claudia Mills	1997	Ages 4-6
Hattie and the Wild Waves: A Story from Brooklyn	Barbara Cooney	1990	Ages 6-9
The Heart of the Wood	Marguerite W. Davol	1992	Ages 3-8
Hiawatha: Messenger of Peace	Dennis Brindell Fradin	1992	Ages 7-11 and older
How I Was Adopted	Joanna Cole	1995	Ages 3-7

L'chaim: The Story of a Russian Emigre Boy	Tricia Brown	1994	Ages 8-11
The Little Lama of Tibet	Lois Raimondo	1994	Ages 7-10
Look Alive: Behind the Scenes of an Animated Film	Elaine Scott	1992	Ages 7-11 and older
Meet Danitra Brown	Nikki Grimes	1994	Ages 7-10
Mom Can't See Me	Sally Hobart Alexander	1990	Ages 6-11
Night on Neighborhood Street	Eloise Greenfield	1991	Ages 3-9
Red Dog, Blue Fly: Football Poems	Sharon Bell Mathis	1991	Ages 7-11
The Sacred Harvest: Ojibway Wild Rice Gathering	Sharon Bell Mathis	1991	Ages 7-11
Teammates	Peter Golenbock	1990	Ages 5-10
This Land Is My Land	George Littlechild	1993	Ages 9-14 and older
What Zeesie Saw on Delancey Sreet	Elsa Okon Rael	1996	Ages 5-8
The Window	Michael Dorris	1997	Ages 10-13 and older
Zora Hurston and the Chinaberry Tree	William Miller	1994	Ages 6-9

CHILDREN'S TRADE BOOKS WITH TIME, CONTINUITY, AND CHANGE AS THE MAJOR THEMATIC STRAND

AT CHRISTMASTIME

Valerie Worth. Illustrated by Antonio Frasconi. (Michael di Capua Books/HarperCollins, 1992) 32 pages. ISBN: 0-06-205020-6. Level: Age 5 and older.

Original short poems with titles such as "Winter Dusk," "Tree Lot," and "Twelfth Night" embrace a wide range of impressions—secular and religious—about an observance stretching longer than a month. "Creche" is an example of the insight to discover in every poem: "The angel/is lacking/A wing;/Even the/Baby looks/Shabby—/So that/It's hard/To explain/Their sturdy/Abiding/Beauty." A final poem, "Spring," suggests a memory: "By the muddy path/Glints a single/Crumpled strand/Of Christmas tinsel." Frasconi's striking full-color images in woodcuts and mixed media give visual power to this handsome 11¼ x 9½ in. edition of superb poetry.

BETSY ROSS: PATRIOT OF PHILADELPHIA

Judith St. George. Illustrated by Sasha Meret. (Henry Holt, 1997) 118 pages. ISBN: 0-8050-5439-1. Level: Ages 9-11 and older.

Children who have heard of Betsy Ross know of her as the patriot who sewed the first "stars and stripes" flag for our country. What they may not know is that Betsy Ross was also a brave, independent, compassionate woman. They probably never heard that she eloped when her parents wouldn't consent to her marrying outside her religion, or that she was widowed three times, raised seven children, and ran her own business for fifty years. It was because of Betsy's upholstery business that George Washington is believed to have sought her out during the Revolutionary War to ask her to sew the first flag. In an author's note at the end of the text, St. George explains that there is no definitive proof that Betsy did sew the first flag, but there is much evidence to suggest that she did, including signed affidavits from her daughter and granddaughters swearing Betsy told them about her meeting with General Washington, and, most moving of all, a signed paper pattern for a five-pointed star kept in safe-keeping by her family. This engaging biography casts light on a beloved figure from history who is too often referenced without really being seen.

BILL PICKETT: RODEO-RIDIN' COWBOY

Andrea D. Pinkney. Illustrated by Brian Pinkney. (Gulliver/Harcourt Brace, 1996) 32 pages. ISBN: 0-15-200100-X. Level: Ages 7-10 and older.

The child of former slaves, Bill Pickett grew up on the wide open Texas prairie. "He was quick as a jackrabbit, more wide-eyed than a hooty owl—and curious." The eager boy developed his own unique style of cow wrestling in which he sank his teeth into the animal's lip to keep it under control. Observer's called it bulldogging, and it was to become Bill's trademark in a distinguished career as a cowboy and rodeo rider. Almost one in four cowboys who rode the western states in the nineteenth century was black, author Andrea Pinkney notes in historical information that follows the text of this lively biography. Bill Pickett was among the most famous of them all. Brian Pinkney's scratchboard illustrations capture the expansive feeling of the western landscape and the energy of humans and animals in motion on the pages of this 11 x 9 in. book.

BLACK HEROES OF THE WILD WEST

Ruth Pelz. Illustrated by Leandro Della Piana. (Open Hand Publishing, 1990) 55 pages. ISBN: 0-940880-26-1. Level: Ages 7-9 and older.

Short biographical essays highlight the lives of African American explorers, pioneers, entrepreneurs, and cowboys who helped shape the West. Six men and three women are featured in a highly accessible volume that pulls together much hard-to-find information.

BLOOMERS!

Rhoda Blumberg. Illustrated by Mary Morgan. (Bradbury, 1993) 32 pages. ISBN: 0-02-711684-0. Level: Ages 7-10 and older.

Hooray for Libby Miller! In 1851, Libby arrived in Seneca Falls, New York, for a visit with her cousin, Elizabeth Cady Stanton, dressed not in the tight-fitting corset and skirt of convention, but in free-flowing trousers that ballooned from her waist to her knees. One look and Elizabeth was convinced that this liberating outfit was for her as well. The rest, as they say, is history—women's history! An engaging text introduces young readers to women's rights pioneers Stanton, Amelia Bloomer, and Susan B. Anthony, presenting the basic tenets of the fight for equal rights in direct, accessible language as the history of bloomers, a fashion that was much more than a fad, is told.

A BOY BECOMES A MAN AT WOUNDED KNEE

Ted Wood and Wanbli Numpa Afraid of Hawk. (Walker, 1992) 42 pages. ISBN: 0-8027-8175-6. Level: Ages 8-13 and older.

A photo-essay with color photographs traces the dramatic journey made in December 1990 by the descendants of survivors of the Wounded Knee Massacre. The account is told from the point of view of eight-year-old Wanbli Numpa, the youngest Lakota to make the trip. Throughout their treacherous six-day journey on horseback in subzero temperatures, they are continually reminded of the suffering of their ancestors along this same trail one hundred years ago and of the seriousness of their mission: to mend the sacred hoop of the world that was broken at Wounded Knee in 1890.

THE BOYS' WAR: CONFEDERATE AND UNION SOLDIERS TALK ABOUT THE CIVIL WAR

Jim Murphy. (Clarion, 1990) 110 pages. ISBN: 0-89919-893-7. Level: Age 9 and older.

Using excerpts from letters and diaries written by boys between the ages of twelve and eighteen who served in the Confederate and Union armies, the author provides an intriguing history of the Civil War that focuses on the experiences of the war's youngest soldiers. Some of the boys were "tall 14 year olds who lied about their ages," and others were drummer boys who took up arms on the battlefield. The fifty accompanying documentary photographs were carefully chosen; in most of them, the youthfulness of the soldiers pictured is obvious, sometimes shockingly so.

CHEROKEE SUMMER

Diane Hoyt-Goldsmith. Photographs by Lawrence Migdale. (Holiday House, 1993) 32 pages. ISBN: 0-8234-0995-3. Level: Ages 7-11.

Bridget is a ten-year-old Cherokee girl who lives in a mobile home near Tahlequah, Oklahoma, with her parents, brother, and sister. An upbeat first-person text describes Bridget's typical summer activities: drawing pictures, hunting for crawdads, spending time with her grandparents, studying the Cherokee language on a computer at the library, and attending a summer stomp dance. Information about Cherokee history, culture, and contemporary issues is woven throughout Bridget's discussion, accompanied by color photographs of this energetic girl.

CHILDREN OF PROMISE: AFRICAN-AMERICAN LITERATURE AND ART FOR YOUNG PEOPLE

Charles Sullivan, editor. (Harry N. Abrams, 1991) 126 pages. ISBN: 0-8109-3170-2. Level: Age 5 and older.

A curious mix of African American and other voices from U.S. history shows "the evidence of a country striving toward the reconciliation between the real and the ideal." The written and visual statements of a surprising range of public servants, philosophers, writers, and artists bear witness both to a proud and painful past. At the back of this anthology is a poetry, title, and author index, as well as an alphabetical listing of the 111 contributors represented by more than one hundred texts and eighty color or black-and-white illustrations. Examples of the wide range of the people included within Children of Promise are James Baldwin, Imamu Amiri Baraka, Romare Bearden, Gwendolyn Brooks, Lucille Clifton, Countee Cullen, W.E.B. Du Bois, Paul Laurence Dunbar, Bob Dylan, Amos Fortune, Stephen Foster, and Meta Vaux Warwick Fuller.

CHRISTMAS COUNTING

Lynn Reiser. (Greenwillow, 1992) 32 pages. ISBN: 0-688-10677-3. Level: Ages 2-5.

Each December for ten years, an evergreen tree is carried with its surrounding dirt inside the house. Each year, a new person or pet joins the family, additional decorations (three paper chains, five colored balls, etc.) are added to the tree, and the cumulative story grows a bit longer. Every year "after Christmas / the father planted / the . . . tree / back in the clearing in the forest / under the moon shining down." Reiser's counting book offers a patterned text, a conservation theme, and much to notice and count in wonderfully developed watercolor-and-pen illustrations.

THE CHRISTMAS TREE SHIP

Jeanette Winter. (Philomel, 1994) 32 pages. ISBN: 0-399-22693-1. Level: Ages 5-9.

For twenty-five years, beginning in 1887, Captain Herman Schuenemann cut evergreens to load in a ship he then sailed south on Lake Michigan from Manistique, Michigan, to Chicago. In 1912, a bottle washed up on the Wisconsin shore containing Captain Herman's message to his wife Hannah and their girls about a storm's severity, confirming his death and the loss of the ship. For twenty-two more years, Hannah Schuenemann and her three daughters continued to sail to Chicago bringing trees in time for Christmas. Based on a true event and real people, a relatively small (9¼ x 8¾ in.) full-color picture book briefly relays this amazing piece of Great Lakes history.

THE DAYS BEFORE NOW: AN AUTOBIOGRAPHICAL NOTE BY MARGARET WISE BROWN

Joan W. Blos, adapter. Illustrated by Thomas B. Allen. (Simon & Schuster, 1994) 32 pages. ISBN: 0-671-79628-3. Level: Ages 3-9.

When asked in 1951 to write an autobiographical essay for H. W. Wilson's Junior Book of Authors, Margaret Wise Brown submitted a characteristically lyrical, sensuous, and direct piece of prose. More than forty years later, Blos recognized the essay as "vintage Margaret Wise Brown," in other words, a perfectly paced, child-centered picture-book text that required only a little shaping and editing by Blos and Allen's pleasingly soft-edged illustrations to bring it to life. Their combined efforts have given us Brown's own autobiography, written in the style and form she single-handedly invented, nurtured, and passed on to future generations.

DICK KING-SMITH'S ANIMAL FRIENDS: THIRTY-ONE TRUE LIFE STORIES

Dick King-Smith. Illustrated by Anita Jeram. (U.S. edition: Candlewick, 1996) 95 pages. ISBN: 1-56402-960-3. Level: Ages 4-12.

What at first glance seems to be a collection of animal stories is actually an autobiographical portrait of the author, told through his recollections of animals he has known. Beginning with one of his earliest memories (riding an elephant at the zoo) and ending with an animal he encountered while writing this book (a crow that perches outside his study window), the chronological arrangement serves to show us King-Smith's growth from boyhood through young adulthood and middle age to his present status as an elderly gent. Throughout, he has maintained his lifelong interest in animals of all species (though long-haired dachshunds figure prominently, and deservedly so). Anita Jeram's lively watercolor illustrations perfectly complement King-Smith's light, humorous tone and make this volume a perfect selection as a family read-aloud.

DISCOVERING CHRISTOPHER COLUMBUS: HOW HISTORY IS INVENTED

Kathy Pelta. (Lerner, 1991) 112 pages. ISBN: 0-8225-4899-2. Level: Ages 7-11 and older.

The author pieces together the facts known about Christopher Columbus during his lifetime and in succeeding centuries. She demonstrates how historians persevere in finding out more about the past as well as how human knowledge continues to grow accordingly. Using an engaging, narrative style, Pelta shows how historical material is documented and, likewise, how a legend about someone who once lived can grow and take on its own life. Archival materials, maps, art reproductions, and contemporary photographs provide an abundance of visual information on the pages of this absorbing book. Pelta's excellent bibliographic narrative describes her sources; she points out the resources young readers will most likely want to use. This outstanding book about both Columbus and historiography will no doubt still be compelling reading after the year 2000.

DON'T YOU KNOW THERE'S A WAR ON?

James Stevenson. (Greenwillow, 1992) ISBN: 0-688-11384-2. Level: Ages 6-11.

In the style of his earlier autobiographical picture books—WHEN I WAS NINE (Greenwillow, 1986); HIGHER ON THE DOOR (Greenwillow, 1987); and JULY (Greenwillow, 1990)—Stevenson reminisces about growing up in the United States during World War II. The artist's memories of his father's enlistment provide a poignant counterpoint to the wry, childlike self-importance he exhibits in describing his own contribution to the war effort: collecting tin foil, buying war stamps, eating spam, and watching newsreels. Stevenson manages to suggest a lot of emotion and detail with just a few brush strokes in his expressive watercolor illustrations.

THE FEATHER-BED JOURNEY

Paula Kurzband Feder. Illustrated by Stacey Schuett. (Albert Whitman, 1995) ISBN: 0-8075-2330-5. Level: Ages 5-8 and older.

Grandma tells Rachel and Lewis how the feather pillow she treasures was once a huge feather bed made by their great-grandmother in Poland. Grandma slept on the bed as a little girl and shared it with five other children after the sad times came and the Germans forced Jewish people into the ghetto: "They didn't want Jews in Poland. They didn't want Jews anywhere." An introduction to the Holocaust is skillfully presented for younger readers in this picture book that also tells of the kindness of a Polish farmer who helped save Grandma's life, and later sent the remnants of the feather bed to her in America. Full-page illustrations balance images of fearful times with those of a warm, secure, loving family.

FIRE IN THE FOREST: A CYCLE OF GROWTH AND RENEWAL

Laurence Pringle. Illustrated by Bob Marstall. (Atheneum, 1995) 32 pages. ISBN: 0-689-80394-X. Level: Ages 7-11.

"Fires bring change, diversity and new life," Pringle tells us in his opening paragraphs. Using the Yellowstone fires of 1988 as an example, the author writes about how forest fires fit into the natural cycle of forest ecology. His compelling text alternates with wordless double-page illustrations that show the same expanse of forest before, during, and after a fire.

FLIGHT: THE JOURNEY OF CHARLES LINDBERGH

Robert Burleigh. Illustrated by Mike Wimmer. (Philomel Books, 1991) 32 pages. ISBN: 0-399-22272-3. Level: Ages 5-10.

Burleigh uses short sentences to recount the historic first airplane flight across the Atlantic that transformed a twenty-five year-old pilot into a hero in 1927. The terse, present-tense narrative conveys elements of the risk Lindbergh took and the courage he exhibited only twenty-four years after the Wright Brothers successfully flew the first airplane. Wimmer's full-color artwork provides a suitably heroic perspective on this exciting achievement.

FUN—NO FUN

James Stevenson. (Greenwillow, 1994) 32 pages. ISBN: 0-688-11674-4. Level: Ages 4-8.

Stevenson catalogs a collection of his own childhood memories, categorizing each recollection as "Fun" or "No Fun." From joyous ("Fun was when we raked up all the leaves, when my friends and I could jump in the pile") to sad ("No fun was when my parents went on a trip without me"), each reminiscence is enhanced with simple watercolor illustrations that are visual extensions of the mood. Children will recognize the truth in these memories and the feelings they evoke as if they were their own.

FUN WITH 9UMBERS

Massin. Illustrated by Les Chats Peles: Lionel Le Neouanic, Benoit Morel, and Christian Oliver. (Creative Editions/Harcourt Brace, 1995) 32 pages. ISBN: 0-15-200962-0. Level: Ages 7-11.

Phil the dog and Pippo, his human companion, travel through time to discover intriguing facts about systems of counting and numerical representation developed by many cultures. An informative and imaginative $13\frac{1}{4}$ x $9\frac{1}{4}$ in. towering text is accompanied by delightfully zany illustrations in which personified numbers dance, roll, and fly across pages. Other full-page art shows Phil and Pippo among the Aztecs, Ancient Egyptians, Sumerians, and others whose numerical achievements continue to be counted today.

GRANDADDY AND JANETTA

Helen V. Griffith. Illustrated by James Stevenson. (Greenwillow, 1993) 32 pages. ISBN: 0-688-11227-7. Level: Ages 4-8.

Young listeners and readers will again encounter the spunky protagonist and amiable grandparent enjoyed earlier in GEORGIA MUSIC (Greenwillow, 1986) and GRANDADDY'S PLACE (Greenwillow, 1987). This third five-chapter story begins as Janetta travels alone by train from Baltimore to Georgia. She wonders what has changed during the year that has elapsed since her last visit to Momma's rural childhood home. Does Grandaddy remember what she looks like? Will she remember him? At once Janetta notices that Grandaddy's beard is gone, while he wastes no time living up to his reputation in the humor department: "I thought to myself, if that child has grown a beard, how will I ever know her?" Yes, there are changes at Grandaddy's, small ones contributing to a family's memory of itself. Grandaddy is good at telling stories, sometimes ones from Momma's childhood. Janetta is good at listening and also at enjoying the mule she once named Star, the egg-laying chickens, and the cat. Griffith's ability to create distinctive, plausible, likable characters through dialogue, and Stevenson's skill in creating full-color art done in black line with watercolors, combine once again with success to delineate a heart-warming bond between two generations.

GRANDMOTHER BRYANT'S POCKET

Jacqueline Briggs Martin. Illustrated by Petra Mathers. (Houghton Mifflin, 1996) 48 pages. ISBN: 0-395-68984-8. Level: Ages 5-7.

Sarah Bryant has nightmares after her little dog Patches is killed in a barn fire. Grandmother Bryant knows roots and herbs that might make bad dreams go away. But just as important to Sarah's healing are the stories, songs, and patience that make a little girl feel safe and loved. A one-eyed cat, a gaggle of geese, a selfish old neighbor, and the small, special things in Grandmother Bryant's pocket also play a role in Sarah's recovery. Set in 1787, this comforting story with its down-to-earth characters is charmingly told. Mathers's watercolor illustrations are detailed and lively; perfect for this intimate 6 x 7 in. book.

A GREAT MIRACLE HAPPENED THERE: A CHANUKAH STORY

Karla Kuskin. Illustrated by Robert Andrew Parker. (Willa Perlman Books/HarperCollins, 1993) 32 pages. ISBN: 0-06-023618-3. Level: Ages 5-10.

Kuskin's artfully written first person narrative features the voice of a boy who invites a non-Jewish friend, Henry, to join his family's celebration of the first night of Hanukkah on the twenty-fifth of Kislev. Members of three generations express distinctive understandings of the evening's events. Grandma remembers that people didn't give Hanukkah presents at all when she was a girl and indicates that "the older she gets, the more things she can think of that cannot be explained in scientific ways." The family members' comments about the nature of miracles constitute a memorable portion of Kuskin's amazingly natural dialogue that integrates elements of history and human nature. Whether Parker paints a flaming sunset, dinner candlelight, torches from the past, or the fire of anger, his masterful watercolor and ink images illuminate every page with one or another source of light. Kuskin's matchless text achieves the same in this handsome 9 by 10¼ in. book.

HARD TO BE SIX

Arnold Adoff. Illustrated by Cheryl Hanna. (Lothrop, Lee & Shepard, 1991) 32 pages. ISBN: 0-688-09013-3. Level: Ages 4-6.

"Hard to be six / when your sister is ten. / There are things she can do that / must wait until then: when I am / seven or eight, nine or ten. / Hard to be six until then." Adoff's poems about the ups and downs of a typical six-year-old who can't wait to grow up are marvelously illustrated with full-color paintings that show the six-year-old and his sister as biracial children with a white father and an African American mother.

THE HEROINE OF THE TITANIC: A TALE BOTH TRUE AND OTHERWISE OF THE LIFE OF MOLLY BROWN

Joan W. Blos. Illustrated by Tennessee Dixon. (William Morrow, 1991) 40 pages. ISBN: 0-688-07546-0. Level: Ages 7-10.

A sequence of visually boxed rhymes is interspersed between eight easy-to-read dramatic episodes from the life of the woman known to some as "the unsinkable Molly Brown." Molly became infamous after she moved from Hannibal, Missouri, to Leadville and Denver, Colorado. As the spouse of J. J. Brown, she became wealthy. As a survivor of the Titanic, Molly Brown also became somewhat famous. Just before her death in 1932, she became a benefactor to the children of the then-depressed mining town of Leadville. In a brief note at the end, Blos documents the factual sources she consulted to create this breezy, engaging historical fiction. Dixon's theatrically presented illustrations for the 11½ x 9½ in. picture book were created with watercolors and ink.

THE HIRED HAND

Robert D. San Souci. Illustrated by Jerry Pinkney. (Dial, 1997) 40 pages. ISBN: 0-8037-1296-0. Level: Ages 8-11.

To find out the secret of how the New Hand hired by his good-hearted father was able to cure the misery of someone with a bad back, New Sam, the lazy, careless son of this black sawmill owner, spies on the New Hand to learn the secrets of his healing powers. New Sam doesn't know the full requirements involved in healing, however, and when he tries to heal someone himself, his patient doesn't survive. New Sam is charged with murder. A ghostly tale full of tension is set in what might have been Waterford, Virginia, during the early 1800s, when antislavery Quakers who settled there welcomed blacks. Pinkney's trademark skill with historic details such as clothing and machinery is evident in his complex pencil and watercolor artwork. Helpful source notes are provided by San Souci and Pinkney.

HOME PLACE

Crescent Dragonwagon. Illustrated by Jerry Pinkney. (Macmillan, 1990) 32 pages. ISBN: 0-02-733190-3. Level: Ages 7-10.

"Every year, / These daffodils come up. / There is no house near them … But once, someone lived here. How can you tell? Look. A chimney, made of stone … Look. Push aside these weeds—here's a stone foundation, laid on earth …" Three white people—a man, woman, and school-aged girl—discover more: "A round blue glass marble, a nail, a horseshoe and a piece of plate. A small yellow bottle. A china doll's arm." Contemporary hikers and readers alike imagine the family that once lived here. The illustrations show an African American family; fragments of their conversations are imagined. Beautifully rendered full-color paintings depict flowers and people of today along with the imaginative flowering of life and living in another time.

HOMEPLACE

Anne Shelby. Illustrated by Wendy Anderson Halperin. (A Richard Jackson Book/Orchard, 1995) 32 pages. ISBN: 0-531-06882-X. Level: Ages 4-8 and older.

"Your great-great-great-great grandpa built this house," a grandmother tells her granddaughter one day. Together the two imagine all the changes that have occurred in the house through six generations. Halperin's cozy pencil and watercolor illustrations are filled with details of everyday life in the past, cast against a backdrop of constancy (the house) and continuity (the family).

HUSH! A THAI LULLABY

Minfong Ho. Illustrated by Holly Meade. (Orchard, 1996) 32 pages. ISBN: 0-531-09500-2. Level: Ages 2-5.

A worried Thai mother tries to quiet all the animals and insects that might wake her napping baby in rhythmic verse graced with gentle humor. Observant readers and listeners will find delight in the supposedly sleeping baby's active endeavors while his mother appeals to each animal in turn to "Hush!," and all will enjoy the soothing pattern of the text. Cut-paper collage illustrations in warm earth tones fill each double-page spread with varied visual perspectives.

I THOUGHT MY SOUL WOULD RISE AND FLY: THE DIARY OF PATSY, A FREED GIRL

Joyce Hansen. (Dear America). (Scholastic, 1997) 202 pages. ISBN: 0-590-84913-1. Level: Ages 10-13 and older.

The Civil War is over, but Patsy doesn't feel free. Little has changed on the plantation for this girl who has been a house slave all of her life. Even as some of the older black men and women start brave journeys into difficult but hopeful new lives, Patsy is still tending to the needs of Master, Mistress, and the house. She has no one with whom to start her own life of freedom. Instead, Patsy continues the work she has always done, waiting for the promised plantation school that she and others look upon as a beacon of hope. Patsy, who learned how to write by surreptitiously listening when the children of the house had their lessons, finds solace in her diary, where she describes these new and confusing times. These daily entries in Patsy's authentic, believable voice constitute a captivating narrative in Hansen's novel, articulating the emotional weight and historical significance of these times of slow yet sweeping change.

INDIGO AND MOONLIGHT GOLD

Jan Spivey Gilchrist. (Black Butterfly/Writers and Readers, 1993) 32 pages. ISBN: 0-86316-210-X. Level: Ages 5-8.

Standing on her front porch gazing at the nighttime sky, Autrie wishes she could freeze time. Not only could she keep the stars forever, but Mama would always be watching over her from the window, bathed in night's colors of indigo and moonlight gold. Yet Autrie knows that night turns to day, warm breezes grow cold, and "Mama's don't sit and watch forever." The prospect of change doesn't frighten her, however, because mama's love has helped her grow strong. Gilchrist's luminous oil paintings lend a quality of mystery to this African American mother's and daughter's special bond.

THE INNER CITY MOTHER GOOSE

Eve Merriam. Illustrated by David Diaz. Introduction by Nikki Giovanni. (Simon & Schuster, 1996. Introduction from the 1982 edition by Eve Merriam. Text: 1969, 1982, 1996) 70 pages. ISBN: 0-689-80677-9. Level: Age 14 and older.

Poet Nikki Giovanni writes, "Eve Merriam took the spirit of Mother Goose to the inner city to give voice to those who were being silenced. . . She had the moral indignation of a just cause." Many of Merriam's seventy-one poems will startle some readers today, just as they did when they were first published in 1969. Since 1969, an introduction has been added, but the content remains virtually the same, and is as relevant and eye opening today as it was thirty years ago. Merriam's poems continue to "carry some healing," offering truth, insight, and perspective at a time when these are very much needed. From Diaz's eleven full-color illustrations rendered in acrylic to accompany this slim 9 x 5 in. volume, one can gain a strong sense of human need within urban immediacy.

JOHN HENRY

Julius Lester. Illustrated by Jerry Pinkney. (Dial, 1994) 40 pages. ISBN: 0-8037-1607-9. Level: Ages 4-12.

The mythic railroad worker from the African American oral tradition comes to life in this outstanding retelling that recounts John Henry's extraordinary accomplishments. Lester's uses of anthropomorphism and anachronism mark the story with his own distinctive flair. Pinkney's vibrant colored pencil and watercolor paintings depict John Henry as an ordinary mortal, just a little taller than everybody else. This is in keeping with Lester's historical note concerning the academic research into whether or not the legendary John Henry was based on a real man. The story retold for this picture book account is based on three specific versions of the African American folk ballad about the famous contest between John Henry and a steam drill in the building of Big Bend Tunnel in the Allegheny Mountains. Visual images of rainbows and meteors add cosmic scope throughout. The final page combines John Henry with another icon of power: the White House.

THE JOURNEY: JAPANESE AMERICANS, RACISM AND RENEWAL

Sheila Hamanaka. (Richard Jackson/Orchard Books, 1990) 40 pages. ISBN: 0-531-08449-3. Level: Age 9 and older.

Children's book illustrator and art director Sheila Hamanaka is also a mural artist. Her five-panel, 25' x 8' mural depicting the World War II internment of her Japanese American elders forms the basis for this distinctive, distinguished, and important book. As a child in the generation born after the war, Hamanaka and most other Americans were unaware that 120,000 male and female American citizens and residents of all ages with up to one-sixteenth Japanese ancestry were abruptly rounded up and imprisoned in ten concentration camps early in 1942. Readers are witnesses to Hamanaka's journey through justifi-

able anger as she provides thirty close-up glimpses of mural sections accompanied by a terse, uncompromising account of the conditions of this imprisonment. One portion of the mural uses the Japanese Bunraki puppet tradition to show U.S. military personnel acting in the "theatre of war," while a Noh drama pose is incorporated into the section about the U.S. Supreme Court challenge to the internment camps. The full mural is reproduced on a double-page spread at the end of the book. The $9^{3}/_{4}$ x $11^{3}/_{4}$ in. book begins and ends with the visual and intellectual connection of tradition (the tale of Momotaro, or Peach Boy), U.S. labor history (peach picker), and hope (a contemporary preschool-aged child offering a peach to the viewer of the artistic commentary). Readers, too, receive a new perspective of history, tradition, and hope.

JUNE 29, 1999

David Wiesner. (Clarion, 1992) 32 pages. ISBN: 0-395-59762-5. Level: Ages 4-9.

In Ho-Ho-Kus, New Jersey, child scientist Holly Evans uses helium balloons to launch vegetable seedlings into the sky so that she can study the effects of extraterrestrial conditions on their development. Six weeks later, giant turnips descend on Montana. In fact, each region of the United States is soon dealing with giant vegetables of some form or another. Wiesner's hilarious paintings of citizens throughout the nation creatively coping with an increase in produce (peas, for example, must be floated like barges down the Mississippi) are accompanied by cleverly understated captions that make this spoof on American resourcefulness even funnier. And what does scientist Evans conclude from her experiment? Even though she knows the giant vegetables aren't the results of her experiment (she never launched arugula!), only readers are let in on the truth behind this strange series of events.

KENNEDY ASSASSINATED! THE WORLD MOURNS: A REPORTER'S STORY

Wilborn Hampton. (Candlewick, 1997) 96 pages. ISBN: 1-56402-811-9. Level: Ages 9-14 and older.

The author was a young reporter trying to stay out of the way in the Dallas office of United Press International on November 22, 1963, when he found himself in the midst of what became one of the biggest stories of U.S. history. Hampton's sense of how to be helpful in what immediately became a highly competitive situation helped to give UPI an edge as the news broke. The gripping narrative reads like breaking news and is abundantly illustrated with both familiar and unfamiliar press photos reproduced in black and white. Subsequent changes in technology and other aspects of public life can be easily identified as a second level of information.

THE LEAVING MORNING

Angela Johnson. Illustrated by David Soman. (Orchard, 1992) 32 pages. ISBN: 0-531-08592-9. Level: Ages 3-6.

"The leaving happened on a soupy, misty morning," begins this account by a young African American boy of the day the van came to help his family move from a city apartment to a new home. Although his narration focuses on the neighborhood he's leaving and the difficulty of leaving friends and family ("We said good-bye to the cousins all day long."), Johnson's text carries a subtle undercurrent of excitement and anticipation. The boy's changing moods are aptly depicted in Soman's watercolor illustrations, which also realistically show his older sister looking wistful and tentative while his parents seem to glow with happiness and confidence.

MA DEAR'S APRONS

Patricia C. McKissack. Illustrated by Floyd Cooper. (Anne Schwartz/Atheneum, 1997) 32 pages. ISBN: 0-689-81051-2. Level: Ages 4-7.

History comes to life in a story inspired by an apron that once belonged to McKissack's great-grandmother, an African American domestic worker who lived in rural Alabama a hundred years ago. Young David Earl can always tell the day of the week by the apron his mother is wearing when he wakes up in the morning. Each Monday, for example, is wash day, and Ma Dear wears the apron with the big pockets across the front that hold clothespins. On Tuesday she wears a bright yellow apron to remind herself of sunshine on a long day of ironing. Not only does McKissack's story pay tribute to women who worked hard to support their families, it also demonstrates some of the ingenious ways parents helped their children cope with drudgery: "Inch along, inch along, like an inch worm," Ma Dear sings to her son as he helps her scrub floors. Later, he sticks to the arduous task of pulling weeds by pretending to be an inchworm. Cooper's compelling brown-tone paintings give the story a strong sense of its historical setting, even as they provide a timeless quality in depicting the love between a mother and her child.

MAILING MAY

Michael O. Tunnell. Illustrated by Ted Rand. (Tambourine/ Greenwillow, 1997) 32 pages. ISBN: 0-688-12878-5. Level: Ages 5-9.

In 1914 the train was the only way to travel the seventy-five mountainous miles between May's home and Grandma Mary's in Idaho. May's parents can't afford a $1.55 train ticket for May. Ingenuity and lots of luck make it possible for May to be mailed from Grangeville to Lewiston as a package weighing less than fifty pounds. She is mailed to Grandma Mary's legally for fifty-three cents, like a parcel post shipment of baby chicks might be sent. Tunnell uses postal history information and May's family sources to develop a story based on the real Charlotte May Pierstorff's trip in the mail car. Rand's watercolor paintings reflect the time, and the author's note provides facts about travel and communication in the early 1900s.

MARVEN OF THE GREAT NORTH WOODS

Kathryn Lasky. Illustrated by Kevin Hawkes. (Harcourt Brace, 1997) 44 pages. ISBN: 0-15-200104-2. Level: Ages 6-9 and older.

When the 1918 influenza epidemic hits Duluth, Minnesota, Marven Lasky's family decides to isolate him from the disease. They choose the unlikely scenario of sending their ten-year-old Jewish son to a French-Canadian logging camp far from the train station in Bemidji. Fortunately Marven has a head for numbers and figures out how he can become useful at the camp. Marven weathers the winter, and he also finds ways to adhere to some of the dietary rules observed by his birth family. The author's father actually was sent by his family to such a logging camp to escape influenza. Hawkes's paintings were rendered in acrylic and provide a strong sense of frigid landscapes, large lumberjacks, and a small, strong-willed lad.

ME, DAD AND NUMBER 6

Dana Andrew Jennings. Illustrated by Goro Sasaki. (Gulliver Books/Harcourt Brace, 1997) 32 pages. ISBN: 0-15-200085-2. Level: Ages 6-8.

Six-year-old Andy catches his father's contagious enthusiasm one Saturday morning when Dad and his pals bring home an old junker, a 1937 Pontiac coupe he bought for $20.00. For two solid months they spend their free time working on the car, bringing it back to life so Dad can race it in the stock car races every summer weekend. He rarely places in any race, but for Andy and his parents, the thrill is measured in possibilities. Jennings's homey, first-person narrative and Sasaki's violet-tinted watercolor paintings bring to life a fond childhood memory from an earlier era.

MY DADDY WAS A SOLDIER: A WORLD WAR II STORY

Deborah Kogan Ray. (Holiday House, 1990) 40 pages. ISBN: 0-8234-0795-0. Level: Ages 7-10.

Accurately reflecting specifics of girlhood in the United States during the Second World War, Ray's fictional portrait features Jeannie, whose father was drafted in 1943 to serve in the Pacific before returning home after V-J Day. The frankly sentimental account of domestic life on the home front is illustrated with more than twenty black-and-white drawings showing Jeannie tending a Victory Garden, collecting scrap metal with her wagon, food shopping using a ration book, trying to sleep during a blackout, writing and waiting for letters from her father, and finding things to do while her mother works her defense plant shift. The text is set in a large typeface.

ON BOARD THE TITANIC

Shelley Tanaka. Illustrated by Ken Marschall. (I Was There) (U.S. edition: Madison Press/Hyperion, 1996) 48 pages. ISBN: 0-7868-0283-9. Level: Ages 8-14.

Harold Bride worked in the wireless room of the *Titanic*, while Jack Thayer and his parents had access to the luxury oceanliner's first class accommodations. Bride later became an important witness during subsequent U.S. and British investigations. Thayer insisted for years he had seen the *Titanic* break in two on the night it sank, and in 1985 he was proved right. Based largely on these two survivor's experiences, this easy fictionalized narrative is filled with dialogue. A wide range of compelling photographs, cross-section illustrations, drawings and paintings in full color, charts, and other visual material is handsomely placed on all pages of this gripping account. Daisy Spedden's POLAR, THE TITANIC BEAR (Little, Brown, 1994) is an excellent companion to this book.

OUR HOUSE: THE STORIES OF LEVITTOWN

Pam Conrad. Illustrated by Brian Selznick. (Scholastic, 1995) 65 pages. ISBN: 0-590-46523-6. Level: Ages 9-12 and older.

Levittown, Pennsylvania, was once a potato field, but in the aftermath of World War II, houses grew there and a community was born. The houses looked almost identi-cal on the outside, but inside lived families as singular as the stories they have to tell. Conrad explores our history and our sense of belonging with six funny, moving stories told in the voices of children living in Levittown in the six decades from 1940 to the present. Each one masterfully captures a sense of the times in which the children live, marking the changes from decade to decade in the social climate of our nation. But they are unified by a palpable sense of place, which, like the times in which they live, leaves a visible imprint on each child's life.

OUR OLD HOUSE

Susan Vizurraga. Illustrated by Leslie Baker. (Henry Holt, 1997) 32 pages. ISBN: 0-8050-3911-2. Level: Ages 5-8.

"There's a wisteria vine that curls around a post on our front porch . . . It's an old vine and it's an old house. It's our house now . . . It used to belong to someone else." This picture story gives examples of ways to find out about the earlier inhabitants of a house, including finding a marble, a name written on the back of the mantle, and earlier layers of wallpaper, and noticing a distinctive color to the roses growing in the neighborhood. Illustrations were rendered in watercolors that show the girl narrator, the people she imagines once living there, and an old woman who visits the family and shares her first-hand memories.

OUR PEOPLE

Angela Shelf Medearis. Illustrated by Michael Bryant. (Atheneum, 1994) 32 pages. ISBN: 0-689-31826-X. Level: Ages 4-8.

An African American girl proudly compares the realities of her everyday life to the accomplishments of people of African descent throughout history. The stories her daddy has told her of builders, explorers, inventors, adventurers, and heroes influence her present-day play and inspire her dreams for the future. The connections between past and present are imaginatively drawn with watercolor and colored pencil illustrations for this cheerful picture book.

POPCORN AT THE PALACE

Emily Arnold McCully. (Browndeer/Harcourt Brace, 1997) 40 pages. ISBN: 0-15-277699-0. Level: Ages 6-9.

Based on real events originating in McCully's hometown of Galesburg, Illinois, this picture story takes place during the mid-1800s and involves Galesburg newcomers Maisie Ferris and her open-minded parents. The Ferris family reads the Bible, but they also read the latest books and magazines. Most of all, Maisie enjoys reading about the English royal family and playing with her homemade Queen Victoria doll. The neighbors raise corn and hogs, but Mr. Ferris plants canary seed and mustard. There's no American market for either one, but he thinks there might be a British market for a recent American phenomenon: popcorn. Mr. Olmstead travels to England, taking Maisie along in case they get to visit royalty. Prince Albert finds out about their public demonstrations of a peculiar kind of corn and invites them to the Palace. McCully's watercolors have rarely been more effective than the one in which Maisie and her father practice curtsies on the wordless double page spread picturing their carriage trip to Windsor. Queen Victoria gave the real Olmstead daughter a French wax doll with real hair and a velvet-and-lace gown; the girl McCully names Maisie in this heartwarming historical story receives one, too. However, popcorn did not gain a market outside of America as a result of the Ferris business trip.

THE RED COMB

Fernando Pico. Illustrated by Maria Antonia Ordonez. (BridgeWater, 1994) 48 pages. ISBN: 0-8167-3539-5. Level: Ages 7-11.

Because Pedro Calderion has received rewards for capturing runaway slaves, considered "lawbreakers," he is envied by other young men in his Puerto Rican village. However, "black folks should help black folks, not hurt them," counsels Old Rosa Bultron. Ultimately, Rosa tricks Pedro and saves a runaway girl. Pico is a history professor in Puerto Rico. The Cuban-born artist, whose illustrations appear in full color in this $8\frac{1}{2}$ x $9\frac{1}{4}$ in. book, has lived in Puerto Rico since 1961.

RUN AWAY HOME

Patricia C. McKissack. (Scholastic, 1997) 160 pages. ISBN: 0-590-46751-4. Level: Ages 10-12.

In 1888, Apache Indians who had been held as prisoners of war in Florida were transported to Alabama. McKissack's own great-great-great grandfather was a Native American whose tribal ancestry remains undetermined, and in *Run Away Home*, she has written a story based on "what might have been" as she imagines the meeting between a fictional Apache boy and a rural African American family in Alabama at that time. The novel is told from the point of view of eleven-year-old Sarah

Crossman, an African American child who lives with her mother and father on a small farm. When an Apache boy escapes from the train transport and hides in the Crossman family barn, Sarah discovers him and he is sheltered and cared for by her parents. At first Sarah is jealous of Sky and the attention he receives from both her parents, but he soon becomes like an older brother to her. Sky's values and way of life blend with those of Sarah's family, and he stands with them when white supremacists are angered and threatened by the very idea of a black man voting. A strong African American family and community, whose understanding of freedom embraces the desire for self-determination of an American Indian child and his people, form the strong foundation of this novel.

A SEPARATE BATTLE: WOMEN AND THE CIVIL WAR

Ina Chang. (Lodestar Books, 1991) 103 pages. ISBN: 0-525-67365-2. Level: Age 9 and older.

Women played an important part in the U.S. Civil War, serving such varied roles as volunteers, nurses, soldiers, and spies in both the North and the South. Drawing on nineteenth century women's letters, diaries, speeches, and essays, Chang eloquently tells the story of these women, placing them within the historical context of the abolitionist movement and the struggle for women's rights. The handsome volume, generously illustrated with photographs and prints from the era, is exemplary nonfiction for young readers.

SERENA KATZ

Charlotte Pomerantz. Illustrated by R. W. Alley. (Macmillan, 1992) 32 pages. ISBN: 0-02-8774901-0. Level: Ages 4-7.

Serena Katz, a New York City hardware store employee, is one of Mr. Duncan's best paint sale customers. The two establish such a good business relationship that Serena invites the entire Duncan family for a weekend visit from their Pennsylvania home. As they plan for their trip, the Duncans find, to their surprise, that everyone knows of Serena Katz: the postmistress says she's a famous pool player, the school librarian saw her perform daredevil motorcycle stunts, and the garbage collector describes her legendary wedding cakes. Just who is the real Serena Katz? A charming story of a woman who has (and continues) to do it all!

SEVEN BRAVE WOMEN

Betsy Hearne. Illustrated by Bethanne Andersen. (Greenwillow, 1997) 24 pages. ISBN: 0-688-14502-7. Level: Ages 5-11 and older.

Family history meets fine art in this singular tribute to women, written from the perspective of a young girl who recounts the family stories she has heard about her female forebears, going back to her great-great-great grandmother. Each of the women is placed in the context of her time as the child cites the name of the war era she lived through but pointedly states each time that "she did not fight in it." This brilliant device aptly serves more than one purpose: it playfully gives young readers a clear historical text-book time line; it contrasts the lives of men and women; it underscores the book's premise that women have contributed to history by leading everyday lives requiring strength and courage; and, most importantly perhaps, it gives the story continuity through a lyrical use of repetition that reminds us this history is alive due to an oral tradition. The colorful figures in the young girl's past—an artist, a missionary, an architect, a secretary—seem at once ordinary and extraordinary. The naïve style of Andersen's rich oil paintings perfectly capture the story's sense of history, as well as its serious, yet celebratory, tone. Just as Hearne uses the repeated phrase about women not fighting in wars to tie the story together, Andersen uses a rose-colored ribbon, seen streaming horizontally across the background of each page and held at the book's beginning and end in the beak of a dove. Both devices are subtle, artfully adding depth and meaning to an inspiring picture book for older readers.

SHORTCUT

David Macaulay. (Houghton Mifflin, 1995) 64 pages. ISBN: 0-395-52436-9. Level: Ages 4-10.

On his way to the market, Albert opts for a short cut, instead of the "long, long way," and his simple acts of hanging his jacket on a post, hitching his horse June to a railroad switch, and cutting a rope that blocks his path set off a chain reaction of events that spell disaster for others. A delightful cause-and-effect story is told in just fifty-two short sentences spread out over nine chapters and an epilogue. Most of the plot, however, unfolds in the pictures, which require a careful reading in order to make sense of how and why things happen as they do.

SILENT NIGHT: THE SONG FROM HEAVEN

Linda Granfield. Illustrated by Nelly and Ernst Hofer. (Tundra Books, 1997) 24 pages. ISBN: 0-88776-395-2. Level: Age 7 and older.

On December 24, 1818, young Hans and Maria hurry through the winter streets of Oberndorf, Austria, to join other villagers in assembling the Christmas *crèche* in the Church of St. Nicola. On this night Father Josef Mohr was to ask organist Frans Gruber to compose music for verses he wrote earlier that day. On this night—according to tradition—the carol "Stille Nacht" was first sung because the organ was broken. An unusual book about the familiar hymn provides several levels of information about the history of "Silent Night." The gold and black visual elements on every page are reproductions of the Hofer's *scherenschnitte*, or scissors-cut silhouette pictures of the assemblage of the *crèche scherenschnitte* explained later as an art developed centuries earlier in China. The last page contains two verses of "Silent Night" in English and in German.

SOME OF THE PIECES

Melissa Madenski. Illustrated by Deborah Kogan Ray. (Little, Brown, 1991) 32 pages. ISBN: 0-316-54324-1. Level: Ages 4-8.

A boy remembers his father's made-up stories, wrestling with him on the rug, listening together to cello music, and enjoying early breakfasts together before the others woke up. He also recalls his father's sudden fatal heart attack and the great sadness of the past year. Somehow, the scattering of his father's ashes in all the places he loved confirms that loss and assists the boy in grieving. A gentle picture story provides an example of suffering and healing with an emotional tone appropriate to the developmental need of its intended audience. The full-color illustrations reinforce all dimensions of this subdued book.

STORIES IN STONE: ROCK ART PICTURES BY EARLY AMERICANS

Caroline Arnold. Photographs by Richard Hewett. (Clarion, 1996) 48 pages. ISBN: 0-395-72092-3. Level: Ages 9-12 and older.

Line drawings on rock walls and boulders across the Americas provide evidence of human habitation between several hundred to six thousand (or more) years ago. Ancient artists engraved or painted human figures, abstract designs, and animals that are often identifiable today. Arnold's thorough explanations and Hewitt's distinctive color photographs of the astonishing petroglyphs within the Coso Range of contemporary California provide an excellent general overview of petroglyphs in the western hemisphere. Readers will find a helpful glossary, index, and listing of thirteen of the North American locations where these old, permanent art forms can be seen.

SWEET WORDS SO BRAVE: THE STORY OF AFRICAN AMERICAN LITERATURE

Barbara K. Curry and James Michael Brodie. Illustrated by Jerry Butler. (Zino Press, 1996) 64 pages. ISBN: 1-55933-179-8. Level: Ages 9-16 and older.

A fictional grandfather relates the history of African Americans in North America to his granddaughter by telling her about early storytellers and writers as well as recent literary activists. He points out that centuries ago a black person who picked up a book and learned to read was both defiant and brave. The narrative pays homage to enslaved and oppressed people who kept their heritage alive through deed and word and to those who continue in this tradition. Thirty published writers are featured in the visually exciting, multidimensional presentation linking text, photographs, varied uses of type size, page designs, and paintings in bold colors. The writers include Maya Angelou, James Baldwin, Amiri Baraka, Gwendolyn Brooks, Countee Cullen, Frederick Douglass, W.E.B. Du Bois, Paul Laurence Dunbar, Ralph Ellison, Olaudah Equiano, Nikki Giovanni, Lorraine Hansberry, Langston Hughes (from whose poem the title originated), Zora Neale Hurston, James Weldon Johnson, Martin Luther King Jr., Malcolm X, Paule Marshall, Toni Morrison, Sonia Sanchez, Alice Walker, and Richard Wright. A glossary and list of selected readings accompany a volume tall in more ways than one.

TELL THEM WE REMEMBER: THE STORY OF THE HOLOCAUST

Susan D. Baachrach. Photographs from the United States Holocaust Memorial Museum. (Little, Brown, 1994) 112 pages. ISBN: 0-316-69264-6. Level: Age 9 and older.

A sampling of materials from the U.S. Holocaust Memorial Museum includes the excerpted texts from taped oral and video histories and photos of people, artifacts, and maps. The specific stories of twenty young people link the artifacts through the effective device of museum-created "identity cards." The featured youth were born between 1911 and 1934 in Austria, Denmark, Germany, Greece, Hungary, Poland, and Romania; they suffered or died during the Holocaust in Europe between 1933 and 1945. The book is divided into sections: Nazi Germany; The "Final Solution"; and Rescue, Resistance, and Liberation. A lengthy chronology, suggestions for further reading, and a glossary place the highly emotional material within its historical context.

THIS LAND IS MY LAND

George Littlechild. (Children's Book Press, 1993) 32 pages. ISBN: 0-89239-119-7. Level: Ages 9-14 and older.

Seventeen dazzling, thought-provoking paintings by artist George Littlechild, a member of the Plains Cree nation, are the focus of this stunning book. In the open, engaging narrative that accompanies the vivid reproductions, most of which are full page, the artist explains the meaning and symbolism found in his paintings, making both the art and the artistic process wholly accessible to children. Describing the painting "Red Horse in a Sea of White Horses," he writes, "An Indian Warrior sits atop a red horse. Not at home in his own territory, the red horse sits among the white horses, who find him different and don't understand him … The red horse represents me." The artist paints a moving portrait in words of his own life and of Native experience in this singular book that celebrates the relationship between individual, art, and culture.

TILL YEAR'S GOOD END: A CALENDAR OF MEDIEVAL LABORS

W. Nikola-Lisa. Illustrated by Christopher Manson. (Atheneum, 1997) 32 pages. ISBN: 0-689-80020-7. Level: Ages 7-11.

"July—Thick rows of peas I hoe and weed. Vile brine I boil for salt I need." This and similar verses open each double-page spread on which a full color pen-and-ink and watercolor illustration shows typical tenant farmer life. A short explanation of the hard labor of rural men and women during each particular season accompanies each picture spread. Inspired by the Books of Hours so popular during the Middle Ages, the author and illustrator have labored to create the feeling of a similarly illustrated calendar.

TOMMY TRAVELER IN THE WORLD OF BLACK HISTORY

Tom Feelings. (Black Butterfly/Writers & Readers, 1991) 42 pages. ISBN: 0-86316-202-9. Level: Ages 7-11 and older.

Significant historical events in the lives of Phoebe Fraunces, Emmet Till, Aesop, Frederick Douglass,

Crispus Attucks, and Joe Louis are dramatized in a comic-strip format. Each event is introduced by Tommy Traveler, an African American child fascinated with the private library collection of his neighbor, Dr. Gray, who has had a life-long interest in collecting books, magazines, and newspaper clippings related to black history. As Tommy reads, he is transported back in time and becomes a first-hand observer and participant in the events he describes. Originally published as a weekly comic strip in 1958-59, this presentation of black history is as fresh and original today as it was thirty years ago and will appeal to a new generation of children.

TOMORROW'S ALPHABET

George Shannon. Illustrated by Donald Crews. (Greenwillow, 1996) 56 pages. ISBN: 0-688-13505-6. Level: Ages 4-9.

Just when you think you've read every possible idea for an alphabet book, a new one comes along. In this book, the letters stand for the promise of what things will be in the future, e.g., B is for eggs, tomorrow's birds" and "T is for bread, tomorrow's toast." Part puzzle, part poetry, and all concept, Shannon's original approach will provide creative inspiration to countless young visionaries who probably think they're too old for alphabet books.

TREEMONISHA

Angela Shelf Medearis. Illustrated by Michael Bryant. (Henry Holt, 1995) 37 pages. ISBN: 0-8050-1748-8. Level: Ages 9-12 and older.

Scott Joplin created a musical autobiography in his ragtime opera *Treemonisha*, first performed in Harlem in 1915. Although the opera received a Pulitzer Prize in 1976, *Treemonisha* was first produced without costumes or scenery. Joplin choreographed that production and played the orchestral score on the piano himself. Even though he realized his work was ahead of its time, Joplin viewed this effort as a failure. He died two years later. The theme of *Treemonisha* honors African American heritage, while the story involves the daughter of freed slaves who works on behalf of her people in the post-Civil War South. Medearis's fictionalized version of the plot includes excerpts from the libretto. Rendered in watercolor and colored pencil, Bryant's many illustrations costume lively characters and stage vivid scenes in an important book that should be read as if it were a short novel.

THE WALL

Eve Bunting. Illustrated by Ronald Himler. (Clarion, 1990) 30 pages. ISBN: 0-395-51588-2. Level: Ages 4-9 and older.

"This is the wall, my grandfather's wall. On it are the names of those killed in a war, long ago." So begins the first visit of a young boy and his father to the Vietnam Veterans Memorial in Washington, D.C. The child experiences other "firsts," too: weeping adults and a wheelchair-mobile veteran. The father is quiet and moved; the boy has questions. The illustrations suggest that this family is Hispanic or American Indian. Four sentences on the final page explain the Memorial. Restraint marks this strong evocation of the emotion people generally feel at the memorial.

WAR GAME

Michael Foreman. (Arcade, 1994) 72 pages. ISBN: 1-55970-242-7. Level: Ages 8-12 and older.

Following a summer of soccer practice, four British youths enlist in the British Army, expecting to be home for the Christmas of 1914. After becoming immersed in war's realities, the young soldiers lose their innocence and—some of them—their lives. The heart of this story is based on the documented instance of a Christmas cease fire during which British and German soldiers took time to bury their respective dead in a joint service, share food and gifts mailed from families, give haircuts, and play soccer—all in a self-declared No-Man's-Land. That emotional oasis contrasts powerfully with final pages showing a bleak snowy terrain dotted with bloodstains transformed by Foreman's paintbrush into images of the poppies that later symbolized the casualties of that war. The $7\frac{7}{8}$ x $10\frac{1}{2}$ in. book's fictionalized text contains several deftly conceived light moments, an abundance of full-color original artwork, and occasional black-and-white reproductions of posters, letters, and photos. Foreman also created WAR BOY (U.S. edition: Arcade, 1990.), also about World War I.

THE ZEBRA-RIDING COWBOY: A FOLK SONG FROM THE OLD WEST

Angela Medearis. Illustrated by Maria Cristina Brusca. (Henry Holt, 1992) 32 pages. ISBN: 0-8050-1712-7. Level: Ages 5-9.

Created by an unknown songwriter between 1870 and 1890, this song features an "educated fellow with jaw-breaking words" who might have been an African American man (as he is pictured here) or a Mexican vaquero or one of any number of cowboys from the documented frontier history to which Medearis refers in her two-page afterword. The song lyrics, which read like a tall tale in verse, form the basis for this humorous picture book about a city-slicker cowboy who accepts the challenge of riding Zebra Dun. An easy arrangement for the song is printed on the endpapers.

Children's Trade Books with Time, Continuity, and Change as a Second Thematic Strand

The title index on pp. 173-180 lists the number of the page on which each book is annotated.

TITLE	AUTHOR	DATE	AGE LEVEL
Abuelita's Paradise	Carmen Santiago Nodar	1992	Ages 4-7
Afro-Bets First Book about Africa	Veronica Freeman Ellis	1990	Ages 6-12
Ahyoka and the Talking Leaves	Peter and Connie Roop	1992	Ages 7-10 and older
All the Lights in the Night	Arthur A. Levine	1991	Ages 5-9
The *Amistad* Slave Revolt and American Abolition	Karen Zeinert	1997	Age 11and older
Anastasia's Album	Hugh Brewster	1996	Ages 10-13 and older
Arctic Hunter	Diane Hoyt-Goldsmith	1992	Ages 9-13
Arctic Memories	Normee Ekoomiak	1990	Age 5 and older
Artist in Overalls: The Life of Grant Wood	John Duggleby	1996	Ages 9-14 and older
Aunt Harriet's Underground Railroad in the Sky	Faith Ringgold	1992	Ages 6-11
Big Meeting	Dee Parmer Woodtor	1996	Ages 3-8
Billy and Belle	Sarah Garland	1992	Ages 3-6
Bras Button	Crescent Dragonwagon	1997	Ages 6-8 and older
The Children of Topaz: The Story of a Japanese-American Internment Camp, Based on a Classroom Diary	Michael O. Tunnell and George W. Chilcoat	1996	Ages 8-14 and older
Christmas in the Big House, Christmas in the Quarters	Patricia C. and Fredrick L. McKissack	1994	Ages 8-13 and older
Christmas Tree Memories	Aliki	1991	Ages 3-6
Coming Home: From the Life of Langston Hughes	Floyd Cooper	1994	Ages 4-12
Compost Critters	Bianca Lavies	1993	Ages 7-11
Dear Benjamin Banneker	Andrea Davis Pinkney	1994	Ages 5-9
Dear Rebecca, Winter Is Here	Jean Craighead George	1993	Ages 3-7
Dia's Story Cloth: The Hmong People's Journey to Freedom	Dia Cha	1996	Ages 8-11 and older
Dream Catcher: The Legend and the Lady	Karen Hartman	1992	Ages 6-13
Eleanor	Barbara Cooney	1996	Ages 7-10
End of Winter	Sharon Chmielarz	1992	Ages 6-9

Everglades: Buffalo Tiger and the River of Grass	Peter Lourie	1994	Ages 9-11 and older
Faith Ringgold and Frida Kahlo	Robyn Montana Turner	1993	Ages 7-12
Fire at the Triangle Factory	Holly Littlefield	1996	Ages 8-11 and older
Four Seasons of Corn: A Winnebago Tradition	Sally M. Hunter	1996	Ages 7-11
Frozen Man	David Getz	1994	Ages 8-16 and older
Georgia O'Keefe	Linda Lowery	1996	Ages 6-8
Going Back Home	Michelle Wood with Toymi Igus	1996	Ages 9-12
The Green Frogs: A Korean Folktale	Yumi Heo, reteller and illustrator	1996	Ages 3-8
Growing Up in Coal Country	Susan Campbell Bartoletti	1996	Ages 9-16
Hanna's Cold Winter	Trish Marx	1993	Ages 6-9 and older
Happy Birthday, Martin Luther King	Jean Marzollo	1993	Ages 3-8
Harlem: A Poem	Christopher Myers	1997	Age 12 and older
Harvest Year	Cris Peterson	1996	Ages 6-8
Hiawatha: Messenger of Peace	Dennis Brindell Fradin	1992	Ages 7-11 and older
I'll See You in My Dreams	Mavis Jukes	1993	Ages 4-8
I've Got an Idea: The Story of Frederick McKinley Jones	Gloria M. Swanson and Margaret V. Ott	1994	Ages 9-11 and older
Kisses from Rosa	Petra Mathers	1995	Ages 4-8
Laura Ingalls Wilder Country	William Anderson	1990	Age 7 and older
Life around the Lake: Embroideries by the Women of Lake Patzcuaro	Maricel E. Presssilla and Gloria Soto	1996	Ages 9-12 and older
The Lily Cupboard	Shulamith Levey Oppenheim	1992	Ages 5-8
Many Thousand Gone: African Americans from Slavery to Freedom	Virginia Hamilton	1993	All ages
Marvin's Best Christmas Present Ever	Katherine Paterson	1997	Ages 4-7
The Milkman's Boy	Donald Hall	1997	Ages 5-9
Minty: The Story of Young Harriet Tubman	Alan Schroeder	1996	Ages 7-10

Mirette on the High Wire	Emily Arnold McCully	1992	Ages 6-9
Monarch Butterflies: Mysterious Travelers	Bianca Lavies	1992	Ages 9-12 and older
My Place	Nadia Wheatley and Donna Rawlins	1990	Ages 6-12 and older
Native American Rock Art: Messages from the Past	Yvette La Pierre	1994	Ages 8-12 and older
Oh, Freedom! Kids Talk about the Civil Rights Movement with the People Who Made It Happen	Casey King and Linda Barrett Osborn	1997	Ages 8-14 and older
The Old Dog	Charlotte Zolotow	1995	Ages 3-8
On the Wings of Peace: Writers and Illustrators Speak Out for Peace in Memory of Hiroshima and Nagasaki	Sheila Hamanaka, coordinator	1995	Age 8 and older
Orphan Train Rider: One Boy's True Story	Andrea Warren	1996	Ages 9-16 and older
Peacebound Trains	Haeme Balgassi	1996	Ages 8-12 and older
Polar, The Titanic Bear	Daisy Corning Stone Spedden	1994	Ages 7-9 and older
Radio Boy	Sharon Phillips Denslow	1995	Ages 7-10 and older
Red Scarf Girl: A Memoir of the Cultural Revolution	Ji-Li Jiang	1997	Age 12 and older
The Return of the Buffaloes: A Plains Indian Story about Famine and Renewal of the Earth	Paul Goble, reteller and illustrator	1996	Ages 8-12
Rocket! How a Toy Launched the Space Age	Richard Maurer	1995	Ages 8-12
Rosa Bonheur	Robyn Montana Turner	1991	Ages 7-12
Ruth Law Thrills a Nation	Don Brown	1993	Ages 4-8 and older
Sadako	Eleanor Coerr	1993	Ages 8-11
Sky Pioneer: A Photobiography of Amelia Earhart	Corinne Szabo	1997	Ages 7-11 and older
Snowed In	Barbara M. Lucas	1993	Ages 4-7
Surtsey: The Newest Place on Earth	Kathryn Lasky	1992	Ages 9-14 and older
Teammates	Peter Golenbock	1990	Ages 5-10
Thirteen Moons on Turtles: A Native American Year of Moons	Joseph Bruchac and Jonathan London	1992	Ages 4-9 and older
Uncertain Roads: Searching for the Gypsies	Yale Strom	1993	Ages 9-14 and older
The Uninvited Guest and Other Jewish Holiday Tales	Nina Jaffe	1993	Ages 5-10 and older

Visions: Stories about Women Artists	Leslie Sills	1993	Ages 9-14 and older
Waiting for Christmas	Monica Greenfield	1996	Ages 3-6
Weaving a California Tradition: A Native American Basketmaker	Linda Yamane	1996	Ages 7-11
What's in Aunt Mary's Room?	Elizabeth Fitzgerald Howard	1996	Ages 4-7
When Birds Could Talk and Bats Could Sing: The Adventures of Bruh Sparrow, Sis Wren, and Their Friends	Virginia Hamilton, reteller	1996	Ages 7-12 and older
When I Left My Village	Maxine Rose Schur	1996	Ages 8-10 and older
When Jo Louis Won the Title	Belinda Rochelle	1994	Ages 5-8
The Widow's Broom	Chris Van Allsburg	1992	Ages 6-11
Wilma Mankiller	Linda Lowery	1996	Ages 6-8 and older
Wilma Unlimited: How Wilma Rudolph Became the World's Fastest Woman	Kathleen Krull	1996	Ages 5-10 and older
Window	Jeannie Baker	1991	Age 9 and older
With Love from Koko	Faith McNulty	1990	Ages 8-10
With Needle and Thread	Raymond Bial	1996	Ages 9-16 and older

Children's Trade Books with Time, Continuity, and Change as a Third Thematic Strand

The title index on pp. 173-180 lists the number of the page on which each book is annotated.

Back Home	Gloria Jean Pinkney	1992	Ages 4-8
The Ballot Box Battle	Emily Arnold McCully	1996	Ages 5-8
Baseball Saved Us	Ken Mochizuki	1993	Ages 7-11 and older
The Bobbin Girl	Emily Arnold McCully	1996	Ages 8-11 and older
Buffalo Days	Diane Hoyt-Goldsmith	1997	Ages 7-11
The Day Gogo Went to Vote: South Africa, April 1994	Elinor Batezat Sisulu	1996	Ages 7-10 and older
Earth, Fire, Water, Air	Mary Hoffman	1995	Ages 8-14
Eleanor Roosevelt: A Life of Discovery	Russell Freedman	1993	Ages 9-14 and older
Everglades	Jean Craighead George	1995	Ages 7-10 and older
Follow That Trash! All about Recycling	Francine Jacobs	1996	Ages 5-7
Fort Chipewyan Homecoming: A Journey to Native Canada	Morningstar Mercredi	1997	Ages 8-11

Georgia O'Keefe	Robyn Montana Turner	1991	Ages 7-12
Gonna Sing My Head Off!: American Folk Songs for Children	Kathleen Krull	1992	All ages, especially ages 8-12
Good-Bye, Curtis	Kevin Henkes	1995	Ages 3-6
The Great Migration: An American Story	Jacob Lawrence	1993	Age 9 and older
Her Stories: African American Folktales, Fairy Tales, and True Tales	Virginia Hamilton	1995	Ages 7-14 and older
A House by the River	William Miller	1997	Ages 5-8
I Have a Dream	Martin Luther King, Jr.	1997	Age 5 and older
I Was a Teenage Professional Wrestler	Ted Lewin	1993	Ages 8-14
In the Heart of the Village: The World of the Indian Banyan Tree	Barbara Bash	1996	Ages 8-11
In the Street of the Temple Cloth Printers	Dorothy Field	1996	Ages 9-14
Jacques-Henri Lartigue: Boy with a Camera	John Cech	1994	Ages 8-11
Kids at Work: Lewis Hine and the Crusade Against Child Labor	Russell Freedman	1994	Ages 8-14 and older
Little White Cabin	Ferguson Plain	1992	Ages 5-8
Lives of the Musicians	Kathleen Krull	1993	Ages 7-14 and older
Lukas Quilt	Georgia Guback	1994	Ages 4-8
Mary Cassatt	Robyn Montana Turner	1992	Ages 7-12
Mimi's Tutu	Tynia Thomassie	1996	Ages 3-5
My Fellow Americans: A Family Album	Alice Provensen	1995	Ages 5-14 and older
A Picture Book of Jesse Owens	David A. Adler	1992	Ages 5-9
Quilted Landscape: Conversations with Young Immigrants	Yale Strom	1996	Ages 11-14 and older
Remember That	Leslea Newman	1996	Ages 4-8
Rome Antics	David Macaulay	1997	Ages 9-12
Sami and the Time of the Troubles	Florence Parry Heide and Judith Heide Gilliland	1992	Ages 8-11
The Seasons Sewn: A Year in Patchwork	Ann Whitford Paul	1996	Ages 9-12
The Snow Walker	Margaret K. Wetterer and Charles M. Wetterer	1996	Ages 7-10
Star of Fear, Star of Hope	Jo Hoestlandt	1995	Ages 7-10 and older

The Tie Man's Miracle	Steven Schnur	1995	Ages 5-8
Toussaint L'Ouverture: The Fight for Haiti's Freedom	Walter Dean Myers	1996	Ages 9-12
The Ugly Menorah	Marissa Moss	1996	Ages 5-8
Up North at the Cabin	Marsha Wilson Chall	1992	Ages 4-9
The Wright Brothers: How They Invented the Airplane	Russell Freedman	1991	Ages 9-14 and older

CHILDREN'S TRADE BOOKS WITH PEOPLE, PLACES, AND ENVIRONMENTS AS THE MAJOR THEMATIC STRAND

ABUELA

Arthur Dorros. Illustrated by Elisa Kleven. (Dutton Children's Books, 1991) 40 pages. ISBN: 0-525-44750-4. Level: Ages 4-7.

Rosalma and her Spanish-speaking abuela (grandmother) spend the day together in a city park where the two of them share an imaginary flight over the city. All of Abuela's comments and observations are made in Spanish, while either the context or Rosalma's translations into English make her statements clear for non-Spanish speakers. Kleven's vibrant, mixed-media collages add colorful whimsy to this visual and verbal delight.

ABUELITA'S PARADISE

Carmen Santiago Nodar. Illustrated by Diane Paterson. (Albert Whitman, 1992) 32 pages. ISBN: 0-8075-0129-8. Level: Ages 4-7.

After her abuelita (grandmother) dies, Marita cuddles up in the rocking chair and faded blanket that Abuelita has left to her. As she rocks, she remembers stories her grandmother told her about her childhood in Puerto Rico, a time and place that seemed like a paradise to her. Brightly colored watercolor illustrations skillfully blend the present, recent past, and a distant past into a visual continuum of family traditions.

AFRO-BETS FIRST BOOK ABOUT AFRICA

Veronica Freeman Ellis. Illustrated by George Ford. (Just Us Books, 1990) 32 pages. ISBN: 0-940975-12-2. Level: Ages 6-12.

A Ghanaian visitor to a classroom answers questions about his continent posed by a group of curious African American children. Mr. Amegashi's natural-sounding conversation with the children provides a wealth of information about Africa's history, geography, and cultures, stressing the diversity of this rich continent. Outstanding page designs use full-color illustrations and a combination of color and black-and-white photographs, all clearly reproduced and perfectly placed.

AKIAK: A TALE FROM THE IDITAROD

Robert J. Blake. (Philomel, 1997) 32 pages. ISBN: 0-399-22798-9. Level: Ages 7-11.

Akiak has been at the head of her team for seven Iditarod races. She knows the 1,151 miles of Alaskan terrain between Anchorage and Nome better than any other dog, perhaps even better than Mick, the woman whose sled she pulls. In all those tries, they've never won; the closest they've come is second. In this eighth attempt, the ten-year-old Akiak has her final chance to win. But Mick must pull Akiak out of the race on day four because of an injured paw, and the team heads on without her. On day five, Akiak breaks free from the volunteers who are supposed to fly her home and sets off down the Iditarod trail alone, in pursuit of her team, in pursuit of her victory. Blake's dramatic story is powerfully illustrated with sweeping oil paintings that span each two page spread, capturing a fierce and stunning frozen landscape and the spirit of those who cross it.

ANTARCTICA: THE LAST UNSPOILED CONTINENT

Laurence Pringle. (Simon & Schuster, 1992) 56 pages. ISBN: 0-671-73850-X. Level: Ages 8-12 and older.

Once called terra incognita—the unknown land—Antarctica has only recently become accessible to scientists from many countries as they study the continent's unique biosystem. The author describes the discovery and exploration of Antarctica, the treaties that control it, and current scientific, tourist, and private use of the area, as well as its physical features and plant and animal life.

APPALACHIA: THE VOICES OF SLEEPING BIRDS

Cynthia Rylant. Illustrated by Barry Moser. (Harcourt Brace Jovanovich, 1991) 32 pages. ISBN: 0-15-201605-8. Level: Ages 7-11.

A short essay eloquently characterizes the people of Appalachia as inexorably tied to the landscape and each other. Moser's softly colored watercolor illustrations realistically capture ordinary movements in ordinary lives. The text and pictures combine to present a loving and respectful, slightly romanticized, portrait of a people and place frequently misunderstood and stereotyped by outsiders.

ARCTIC HUNTER

Diane Hoyt-Goldsmith. Photographs by Lawrence Migdale. (Holiday House, 1992) 30 pages. ISBN: 0-8234-0972-4. Level: Ages 9-13.

For most of the year, ten-year-old Reggie lives with his family in a modern three-bedroom house in Kotzebue, Alaska, but every summer, he and his family spend several weeks in a traditional Inupiaq camp where they fish and hunt to store up food for the long winter months ahead. Through color photographs and first-person narration, Reggie introduces the basic values and traditions of his people, the Inupiat, which represent perhaps the most ingenious human adaptations to an ungiving natural environment.

ARCTIC SON

Jean Craighead George. Illustrated by Wendell Minor. (Hyperion, 1997) 32 pages. ISBN: 0-7868-2255-4. Level: Ages 5-9.

On the day Luke is born in the Arctic, his parents are visited by an Inupiat friend, Aalak, who offers the baby an Inupiat name. "His name may be 'Kupaaq,' for my papa," Aalak tells them, "an Eskimo name to go with his English name." George's restrained, lyrical text cycles through the seasons of a harsh and beautiful landscape, and through the years of a young boy's life. Kupaaq grows from infant to toddler to school-age child, learning the ways of the Arctic, and the ways of the Eskimo, from Aalak and others in the village. He witnesses the northern lights in the cold of winter, and welcomes back the sun. He sees millions of birds returning in the spring, and helps on a whale hunt as the weather begins to warm. This fictional work that looks at contemporary life in an Arctic village is based on the experience of the author's grandson, who lives with his parents in the Arctic and was given an Inupiat name when he was born. The text is graced by Minor's richly colored illustrations that emphasize the many moods of dark and light in the far northern part of the world.

BASEBALL IN THE BARRIOS

Henry Horenstein. (Gulliver/Harcourt, Brace, 1997) 36 pages. ISBN: 0-15-200499-8. Level: Ages 8-11.

Hubaldo Antonie Romero Páez falls asleep each night dreaming of cheering fans. In his imagination, he is the hero, hitting the home run that means the national victory for his baseball team. Hubaldo's dream is one shared by many U.S. children, but this nine-year-old boy lives in Venezuela, where *béisbol* is more than a national pastime—it's a national passion. In Hubaldo's own *barrio* (neighborhood), children of all ages play many types of baseball, and when they're not playing the game or practicing, they are often trading cards and talking about their favorite players and teams in the country's two professional leagues. Active color photographs of Hubaldo and his friends and reproductions of Venezuelan team logos and baseball cards add to the visual interest of a book in which young Hubaldo describes the love of baseball in this South American country. (Hubaldo notes that the fact that baseball is played in both North and South America makes it a truly *all*-American sport.) Baseball fans will especially enjoy learning about different types of baseball played by Venezuelan children and the Spanish language words for many baseball terms, which are provided in a glossary at the back.

BEACH FEET

Lynn Reiser. (Greenwillow, 1996) 32 pages. ISBN: 0-688-14401-2. Level: Ages 3-8.

There's more to this book than first meets the eye— or foot! On one level, it's a simple rhyming story about feet on the beach ("Scrunch feet, squash feet/squish feet, splash feet . . ."). But on every page we also find several "foot notes" that provide information about marine biology, and each of these is cleverly related to the human feet described in the rhyming story. The footnote accompanying "squash feet," for example, tells us that the air bladder on sargassum seaweed pops when stepped on. Reiser's expert design holds it all together and makes it easy to read in several different ways. All in all, a remarkable feat!

A BELLBIRD IN A FLAME TREE

Kilmeny Niland. (Tambourine Books, 1991) 32 pages. ISBN: 0-688-10798-2. Level: All ages.

A rollicking, full-color send-up of "The Twelve Days of Christmas" features koalas, lizards, dingoes, numbats, quokkas, mice, penguins, crocodiles, pelicans, lorikeets, and wallabies. The creatures sing carols, open gifts, parade with candy canes, hang up stockings, bake cookies, and engage in other secular activities requisite to the season. An easy notation for the music and a tree pyramid visually summarizing the final chorus are at the end of this Australian slant on the traditional English cumulative song.

BIRDIE'S LIGHTHOUSE

Deborah Hopkinson. Illustrated by Kimberly Bulcken Root. (Anne Schwarz/Atheneum, 1997) 32 pages. ISBN: 0-689-81052-0. Level: Ages 7-10.

Diary entries from January 1855 to January 1856 document a year in the life of a fictional girl based on a composite of the many true-life female lighthouse keepers. Her family's move to a new lighthouse island, the departure of her older brother, Nate, and increasing responsibilities for ten-year-old Birdie are the highlights of her year. Exquisite pen-and-ink and watercolor illustrations enliven an already adventurous tale, bound in a $6\frac{1}{4}$ x $11\frac{1}{2}$ in. volume that resembles, appropriately, a lighthouse.

BITTER BANANAS

Isaac Olaleye. Illustrated by Ed Young (Boyds Mills Press, 1994) 32 pages. ISBN: 1-56397-039-2. Level: Ages 4-8.

Set in the heart of the African rain forest, this original story by a Nigerian writer has many folkloric qualities. Young Yusef gathers palm sap to sell at the market but notices with dismay that someone has been raiding his stores. When he discovers that the thieves are a family of baboons, he devises a scheme to discourage them from stealing from him. Frequent repetition of the phrases "Oh no! Oh no!" and "Oh yes! Oh yes!" to signal a bad or good turn of events, along with a generous use of onomatopoeia, makes this a great read-aloud. Young's stunning artwork features his pastel and watercolor paintings, used with a cut-paper technique that layers images to give a three-dimensional sense of the dense rain forest.

THE BLOCK

Langston Hughes. Collage by Romare Bearden. (The Metropolitan Museum of Art, 1995) 32 pages. ISBN: 0-670-86501-X. Level: Age 11 and older.

Full-color reproductions from Bearden's 1971 mural "The Block" are accompanied by twelve poems by Hughes. In his introduction to the elegant, almost cinematic volume measuring $12\frac{1}{4}$ x $9\frac{1}{4}$ in., Bill Cosby relates how the mural reflects the people and events of a busy, exciting Harlem neighborhood. He comments that "it is also a universal place, a recognizable and familiar environment for many people from around the world," pointing out that while "Bearden shows us the sights, Hughes gives us the sounds." A full-page biography of each man with his photograph completes this singular book.

BUFFALO DAYS

Diane Goldsmith-Hoyt. Photographs by Lawrence Migdale. (Holiday House, 1997) 32 pages. ISBN: 0-8234-1327-6. Level: Ages 7-11.

Clarence Three Irons, Jr., a member of the Crow tribe, loves riding horseback and helping out on his family's forty-acre ranch. Ten-year-old Clarence, his father, and older brothers also participate in the Crow's annual buffalo roundup, a crucial part of the nation's efforts to restore the buffalo to reservation lands. And each summer, Clarence and his entire family take part in Buffalo Days, a Crow fair and rodeo that celebrates American Indian traditions. A brief history of the Crow, including the critical role that wild buffalo once played in their survival and the devastation that the slaughtering of the buffalo by settlers brought to their way of life in the nineteenth century, is summarized as part of the text of this lively, hopeful profile of an American Indian boy who is taking part in his nation's efforts to build hope for the present and future by restoring and honoring the ways of the past.

BUILDING AN IGLOO

Ulli Steltzer. (Henry Holt, 1995) 32 pages. ISBN: 0-8050-3753-5. Level: Ages 7-11.

In the frozen arctic landscape on Ellsmere Island in northern Canada, Inuit Tookillkee Kiguktak builds an igloo with his son, Jopee, for shelter during a winter hunting expedition. It is a skill he learned as a child, and one he has taught his own children. Full-page black-and-white photographs as sharp as the winter's cold show Tookillkee and Jopee at work. A brief text describes their progress as the igloo takes shape.

BUTTERFLY BOY

Virginia Kroll. Illustrated by Gerado Suzán. (Boyds Mills, 1997) 32 pages. ISBN: 1-56397-371-5. Level: Ages 5-8.

Even though his grandfather can no longer speak or smile, Emilio can sense Abuelo's pleasure at the sight of the red admiral butterflies that fly into their yard. Every summer afternoon Emilio wheels Abuelo outside so they can watch them together. When the weather cools and the butterflies disappear, Emilio brings home a library book so he can tell Abuelo more about red admirals: how they hibernate in the winter but return in the spring, and how they are attracted to brighter white surfaces, like the family's garage. Kroll's warm, charming story depicts a rich relationship between a young boy and his grandfather in the context of a loving Latino family, all magnificently illustrated by Suzán. The vibrant, stylized paintings aptly suggest magical realism and show the bond between Emilio and Abuelo with a joyous sense of celebration. At the same time they reveal that behind Abuelo's silence is a lively, active mind that soars with imagination and love.

C IS FOR CITY

Nikki Grimes. Illustrated by Pat Cummings. (Lothrop, Lee & Shepard, 1995) 40 pages. ISBN: 0-688-11809-7. Level: Ages 3-6.

Rhyming verses for each letter of the alphabet celebrate the sights and sounds of a lively Manhattan neighborhood. Cummings's shimmering color illustrations extend the text even further by adding several objects for children to identify in each picture. At the end of the book, she has provided an alphabetical key that lists the illustrated objects corresponding to each letter, right down to the names of typefaces she has used (Airkraft, Benguiat, Cooper Black, etc.), which also go in corresponding alphabetical order.

CAMPING IN THE TEMPLE OF THE SUN

Deborah Gould. Illustrated by Diane Paterson. (Bradbury, 1992) 32 pages. ISBN: 0-02-736355-4. Level: Ages 3-7.

The orange and yellow dome tent named by Dad "Temple of the Sun" seems right for a family of two children and two adults taking their first camping trip. But Jeannie and her parents discover that camping involves more than selecting a tent. Baby Billy needs to be comforted when everyone else is sleepy, the tent has to be kept dry inside during a downpour, and walking to the bathroom building at night is an excursion in itself. But hiking, swimming, picnicking, and finding constellations in the clear night sky made up for any inconveniences, making the sometimes damp, sometimes dark Temple of the Sun begin to feel homey.

CHIBI: A TRUE STORY FROM JAPAN

Barbara Brenner and Julia Takaya. Illustrated by June Otani. (Clarion, 1996) 63 pages. ISBN: 0-395-69623-2. Level: Ages 7-10.

An inviting design and engaging story distinguish this chapter book in which a mother duck hatches and raises her ducklings in the midst of a Tokyo business park. The book is based on a true story, and the author was one of the thousands of Tokyo residents who waited and watched each day for the moment the mother duck would lead her ducklings across a busy, congested roadway to the pond on the other side. Mr. Sato, a news photographer sent to cover the story, names the smallest duckling Chibi, which means "tiny" in Japanese. The ducks make a safe journey, but when a typhoon strikes, Mr. Sato and others go for days not knowing the fate of Chibi or his family. Full-color illustrations in water color and ink on each double-page spread are a charming accompaniment to a warm, dramatic, satisfying story for young readers.

CHILDREN OF CLAY: A FAMILY OF PUEBLO POTTERS

Rina Swentzell. Photographs by Bill Steen. (Lerner, 1992) 40 pages. ISBN: 0-8225-2654-9. Level: Ages 7-13.

Eliza, Zachary, and Devonna are Tewa children living in Santa Clara Pueblo, New Mexico, who are learning the traditions of making clay pottery from their grandmother, Gia Rose. Together the family members dig for clay, clean it, and mix it with sand to make it ready for sculpting. Later they will sand, polish, and fire the pottery they have made. Even the youngest children in this large, extended family have a job to do, and everyone is delighted to see the final results of all their hard work.

CHRISTMAS AT LONG POND

William T. George. Illustrated by Lindsay Barrett George. (Greenwillow, 1992) 32 pages. ISBN: 0-688-09214-4. Level: Ages 4-8.

A father and son pull a toboggan carrying the spruce tree they just selected and cut. Trying not to disturb the winter creatures of frozen Long Pond, they also fell an old poplar to create something for deer to eat and start the growth of new shoots by spring. While coming and going, they hear a woodpecker, see deer, notice fox prints, and listen to activity within a beaver lodge. Gouache paints were used for the full-color art detailing the winter landscape and its inhabitants and visitors in this lovely picture book, the Georges' fourth about Long Pond. Lindsay Barrett George's superior draftsmanship and personal understanding of her subjects bring to life the wildlife and vegetation on each page, while William T. George writes with an equally sensitive pen.

CINNAMON, MINT, & MOTHBALLS: A VISIT TO GRANDMOTHER'S HOUSE

Ruth Tiller. Illustrated by Aki Sogabe. (Browndeer Press/Harcourt Brace Jovanovich, 1993) 32 pages. ISBN: 0-15-276617-0. Level: Ages 4-8.

A city child's description of her grandmother's rural home includes ordinary details that she herself finds extraordinary: the pantry, the bathtub with feet, the dirt-floor in the cellar and, of course, the cistern out back. Coziness and quiet comfort are the hallmarks of her overnight visit with her grandma and great aunt. Stunning illustrations were created from black paper cut freehand and placed over sheets of painted ricepaper, giving an ethereal quality to everyday places and occurrences. Outstanding reproduction and distinguished book design enhance the mood of sharing a special place with a beloved family member. Grandmother is depicted in the illustrations as Asian American, while her grandchildren are biracial (Asian/white).

CLIMBING KANSAS MOUNTAINS

George Shannon. Illustrated by Thomas B. Allen. (Bradbury, 1993) 32 pages. ISBN: 0-02-782181-1. Level: Ages 4-8.

When they made a flour-dough map of their home state, Kansas, there was hardly a bump on it, so what in the world was his dad talking about when he invited Sam to go mountain-climbing one Sunday afternoon? Out of curiosity and boredom, Sam agreed to go but he couldn't see any mountains, not even when his dad stopped the car next to the grain elevators where he worked. "The thing that makes a mountain is a high, quiet view," his dad tells him, after he grins his "got you" grin. Viewing Kansas from their "mountaintop" Sam sees that it looks the same—and different. And driving home across the flat landscape, the father and son together are the same—and different. An exquisitely eloquent story uses humor and metaphorical language to bring two characters to life as they share an un-

forgettable yet private experience. With very few words, the author has managed to reveal truths and complexities of human relationships that many novelists fail to elicit— perhaps that's what happens when you set out to climb a Kansas mountain.

COMPOST CRITTERS

Bianca Lavies. (Dutton, 1993) 32 pages. ISBN: 0-525-44763-6. Level: Ages 7-11.

The mysteries of nature are once again revealed by Lavies, who this time focuses her camera on the dozens of living creatures, many too small for the unassisted eye to see, which turn our daily bread (and many other things) into rich, fertile soil through the compost process. Incredible photographs reveal a minute world of hardworking "critters," from sow bugs to earthworms, bacteria to fungi, all of which are part of our world, too, helping to keep it clean. The informative text is written in straightforward language that children will find anything but dull (because tomatoes really are mushy, and the hyphae of mold really is white and hairy looking).

COUNTRY FAIR

Elisha Cooper. (Greenwillow, 1997) 40 pages. ISBN: 0-688-15531-6. Level: Ages 3-8.

Early one summer morning, trucks, tractors, and trailers rumble into an empty field and workers begin to set up tents for the country fair that will take place that day. Some farmers groom their prize animals to get them ready for the competition, while others wrestle "uncooperative pumpkins" in preparation for the vegetable weigh-in. A judge samples banana bread. A bald man shears sheep. A yellow jacket hovers around a man eating an enormous lunch. In every little corner a small drama takes place. Collectively, they add up to a lively country fair, gracefully captured in Cooper's understated watercolor paintings and matter-of-fact, yet witty, prose.

DARKNESS

Mildred Pits Walter. Illustrated by Marcia Jameson. (Simon & Schuster, 1995) 24 pages. ISBN: 0-689-80305-2. Level: Ages 3-7.

Many small children who are afraid of the dark will find reassurance in this evocative story that reminds us of all the good things darkness brings us: our shadows and cool shade, soothing rain from dark clouds, dreamtime, and the bright stars that can only be seen at night. The comforting, poetic text is nicely interpreted by Jameson's abstract acrylic paintings that contrast deep shades of blue and purple with occasional touches of orange and gold to express the beauty of darkness.

A DAY AT DAMP CAMP

George Ella Lyon. Illustrated by Peter Catalanotto. (Orchard, 1996) 28 pages. ISBN: 0-531-09504-5. Level: Ages 6-9.

Three pairs of rhyming one-syllable words on each double-page spread highlight the ups and downs of life at summer camp (e.g., "Damp camp/Green screen/Hot cot"). Catalanotto illustrates each pair with separate paintings, layered one on top of another like a stack of postcards or like windows on a web site. This technique gives viewers a sense of zeroing in on the small details suggested by the rhymes. Together the text and illustrations create an effective picture of a typical fast-paced, regimented day in a young camper's life.

THE DAY OF AHMED'S SECRET

Florence Parry Heide and Judith Heide Gilliland. Illustrated by Ted Lewin. (Lothrop, Lee & Shepard, 1990) 32 pages. ISBN: 0-688-08895-3. Level: Ages 5-9.

As Ahmed drives a donkey cart through busy streets and delivers heavy canisters filled with butane gas, he thinks of his father's advice: "Hurry to grow strong . . . But do not hurry to grow old." Contemporary Cairo is the setting for a young "butagaz boy" to tell the story of the day on which he learns to write his own name. Well-patterned sentences shaped into a wonderfully paced narrative are extended with full-color watercolor illustrations detailing cultural information.

DEAR REBECCA, WINTER IS HERE

Jean Craighead George. Illustrated by Loretta Krupinski. (HarperCollins, 1993) 32 pages. ISBN: 0-02-021140-7. Level: Ages 3-7.

In a letter dated December 21st, a grandmother living in the Northern Hemisphere writes to her grandchild about seasonal changes marking winter, even though "you can't touch it or … make it do anything. But it makes us do all sorts of things. I turn on my lights. You put on your mittens. The birds fly to the sunny underside of the Earth." She writes about streams turning to ice and creatures hibernating, observing how, on December 22nd, "little hands of light begin to push back the edges of darkness minute by minute" to begin the natural cycle leading to

summer. Details from the brief letter are shown in full-color illustrations created with gouache opaque watercolor and colored pencil for the 9 by 10¼ in. book.

DRYLONGSO

Virginia Hamilton. Illustrated by Jerry Pinkney. (Harcourt Brace Jovanovich, 1992) 54 pages. ISBN: 0-15-224241-4. Level: Ages 7-11.

Growing up on a farm in the drought-stricken Midwest of the 1970s, Lindy can barely remember a time when mud and cloudbursts were ordinary features of her landscape. She is sustained by the memories of her gentle, loving parents who patiently answer Lindy's questions about life in easier times past. But even her parents' stories haven't prepared her for the day of the windstorm when a strange young man named Drylongso literally blows into their lives. Full-page, full-color pastel and watercolor paintings appear on nearly every double-page spread of this powerful story about hope, hard work, and gifted people who can make something out of nothing.

EAGLE

Judy Allen. Illustrated by Tudor Humphries. (Candlewick Press, 1994) 24 pages. ISBN: 1-56402-143-2. Level: Ages 4-8.

Despite his teacher's assurances, young Miguel worries that he'll be attacked by an eagle when he and his class make a field trip to the Philippine rain forest near their school. His obsessive fear nearly ruins the trip for Miguel and just about everyone else, until a chance encounter with a real eagle absolves the boy of his worries. Softly colored realistic paintings skillfully capture the drama of Miguel's story, as well as the majesty of the rain forest.

EMEKA'S GIFT: AN AFRICAN COUNTING STORY

Ifeoma Onyefulu. (Cobblehill & Dutton, 1995) 20 pages. ISBN: 0-525-65205-1. Level: Ages 4-7.

Photographic images of village life among the Igala people in Nigeria shine from the pages of this unique counting book that follows the short journey of one small boy to his grandmother's house. Along the way, Emeka passes people and objects numbered from two to ten (four brooms, six beaded necklaces, seven musical instruments, etc.). Brief sidebars provide information on the items and activities shown in the lively color photographs in this wonderful companion to the author's earlier work A IS FOR AFRICA (Cobblehill & Dutton, 1993).

EVERGLADES

Jean Craighead George. Illustrated by Wendell Minor. (HarperColllins, 1995) 32 pages. ISBN: 0-06-021228-4. Level: Ages 7-10 and older.

Five children in a dugout canoe listen to the words of the storyteller as he poles the canoe through the waters of the vanishing Everglades. He tells them the history of this "living kaleidoscope of color and beauty," from the earliest days in the Age of Seashells up to our present time, which threatens to destroy it. George's poetic words combine with Minor's lush watercolor paintings to inspire reverence for this fragile ecosystem.

EVERGLADES: BUFFALO TIGER AND THE RIVER OF GRASS

Peter Lourie. (Boyds Mills Press, 1994) 47 pages. ISBN: 1-878093-91-6. Level: Ages 9-11 and older.

Writer-photographer Peter Lourie's desire to learn about the Everglades takes him on a journey into the "River of Grass." His guide is Buffalo Tiger, chief of the Miccosukee Indians, who grew up in the Everglades more than sixty years ago, when the area was not yet polluted and the tribe could still live off the land. Lourie's appreciation for this unique and fragile environment, and for Buffalo Tiger's willingness to share his personal experience and expertise, unfolds through full-color photos and a text that skillfully weaves a brief, fascinating history of the Miccosukee into a compelling portrait of nature in the "grassy water," an environment which is in danger of dying.

●●●

THE FIDDLER OF THE NORTHERN LIGHTS

Natalie Kinsey-Warnock. Illustrated by Leslie W. Bowman. (Cobblehill/Dutton, 1996) 32 pages. ISBN: 0-525-65215-9. Level: Ages 7-10.

Eight-year-old Henry had heard just about all of Grandpa Pepin's wild stories, and he didn't believe them, either. How was he to know that when he and Grandpa went skating up the frozen river one winter night they would actually see the Northern Lights dance? Could he have imagined that later they would be visited by the legendary fiddler? When the wind is howling, this fanciful winter story might come to mind. If so, listen for the sound of a fiddle. Striking artwork in full color suggests a winter landscape in an earlier time.

●

FLOOD

Mary Calhoun. Illustrated by Erick Ingraham. (Morrow, 1997) 40 pages. ISBN: 0-688-13919-1. Level: Ages 5-8.

If she stands on her tiptoes, Sarajean can just reach the high water mark on the wall of the fire station in her small Iowa town. Sarajean's grandmother remembers the Big Flood that left it there when Sarajean's father was just a baby. Now everyone in her town is preparing for another big flood. Calhoun's somber picture story is filled with everyday details of an ordinary Midwestern family that is hoping for the best but preparing for the worst. Her tone is perfectly matched by Ingraham's realistic pastel pencil and watercolor illustrations that show Sarajean's family as strong, distinctive individuals, busying themselves with the small things that need to be done, all action taking place against the ominous backdrop of a bruised sky.

FORT CHIPEWYAN HOMECOMING: A JOURNEY TO NATIVE CANADA

Morningstar Mercredi. Photographs by Darren McNally (We Are Still Here). (Lerner, 1997) 48 pages. ISBN: 0-8225-2659-X. Level: Ages 8-11.

Twelve-year-old Matthew Dunn accompanies his mother, author Morningstar Mercredi, to her hometown of Fort Chipewyan, Alberta, to visit family and friends. For Matthew, whose parents are divorced and who lives every other year with his father, who is white, the trip also provides the opportunity for his mother to share more about their Native heritage, a mixture of Cree, Denedeh (Chipewyan), and Métis. In a visit with a Métis elder who does traditional beadwork, Matthew learns more about Native arts. A Cree family cousin takes Matthew and his mom for a boat ride and talks about Native respect for animals and the environment. When Matthew goes fishing with a Chipewyan friend of his mother's, he sees firsthand the way Native people once lived off the land. Matthew's visit culminates with Treaty Days, an annual Fort Chipewyan event that honors the treaty signing that gave Native peoples in large parts of Canada reservations lands and hunting and fishing rights. At Treaty Days, Matthew participates in games, dances to the drums, and shares in the celebration of Native traditions. This informative photo-documentary provides another welcome profile of a contemporary Native child.

GABRIELLA'S SONG

Candace Fleming. Illustrated by Giselle Potter. (Anne Schwartz & Atheneum, 1997) 32 pages. ISBN: 0-689-80973-5. Level: Ages 4-7.
As she walks through Venice, young Gabriella hears music in the hustle and bustle of city life. The tune she hums has been inspired by the calls of street vendors, church bells, and the sound of boats gently bumping against the canal walls. Her infectious song is picked up and passed along from one person to another, until it reaches the ears of the brilliant composer Giuseppe Del Pietro who turns it into a full symphony. Porter's distinctive watercolor paintings use curved lines and leaning figures to give a sense of music wafting through the streets of Venice.

THE GARDENER

Sarah Stewart. Illustrated by David Small. (Farrar, Straus, Giroux, 1997) 36 pages. ISBN: 0-374-32517-0. Level: Ages 5-9.
At the height of the U.S. Depression, Lydia Grace Finch must leave home to spend a year living with her stodgy uncle in the city to help out in his bakery. The story of how she transforms his tenement apartment (and eventually her uncle) with her gardening skills is told through a series of letters she writes from August 27, 1935, to July 11, 1936, and through Small's detailed pen-and-ink illustrations, as well. Small's linework, in particular, shows the determination of the plucky young heroine, contrasted with the gruff character of her hard-working uncle.

GIVING THANKS: A NATIVE AMERICAN GOOD MORNING MESSAGE

Chief Jake Swamp. Illustrated by Erwin Printup. (Lee & Low, 1995) 24 pages. ISBN: 1-880000-15-6. Level: Ages 5-10.
Based on what is known as the Iroquois Nation's Thanksgiving Address, the text of this picture book caries the "ancient message of peace and appreciation of Mother Earth and all her inhabitants" to her family. The words are still used at contemporary governmental and ceremonial gatherings of the Six Nations: Mohawk, Oneida, Cayuga, Onondaga, Seneca, and Tuscarora. Children of these Native peoples are taught the concept of greeting the world each morning by saying thank you to all living things, which is what this picture book expresses. Swamp has delivered the Thanksgiving Address at the United Nations and throughout the world. The illustrations rendered in acrylic on canvas show images of Native people with Earth's creatures. Printup is a Cayuga/Tuscarora painter.

GOING HOME

Eve Bunting. Illustrated by David Diaz. (HarperCollins, 1996) 32 pages. ISBN: 0-06-026296-6. Level: Ages 5-9.
After sleeping under the stars for three nights, Carlos and his family finally arrive by car in time to celebrate Christmas in La Perla, Mexico. Even though there is no work for Mama and Papa in their village, La Perla is still home for them. Mama even blows kisses "at the sun-filled winter sky" as soon as the family car crosses the border from the United States into Mexico. Warm welcomes and celebrations of Christmas await the family in La Perla, along with expressions of pride in the English language Carlos and his sisters have acquired since their last visit. The walls of Grandfather's La Perla house "bulge with talk and rememberings." Distant La Perla has never felt like home to five-year-old Nora, ten-year-old Delores, and young Carlos. Home for them is the house where they live all year while working in the fields with their parents. During this visit, Carlos begins to understand about the "opportunities" his parents and grandparents hold in such high regard. Exuberant paintings superimposed over full-color photographs of folk art assemblages detail the specific people and locales of a joyous reunion. The composition of several paintings suggests the traditional Christmas story. A font designed especially for the dialogue-filled text is set on sun-colored pages. This rich story for all seasons has multidimensional characters and a plot that does not minimize hard labor at the expense of hope.

GRANDFATHER'S JOURNEY

Allen Say. (Houghton-Mifflin, 1993) 32 pages. ISBN: 0-395-57035-2. Level: Ages 8-12.
Wearing European clothes for the first time, a young Japanese man travels alone across the Pacific and then throughout the United States during the early twentieth century. He marvels at the expanses of ocean and land. "The endless farm fields reminded him of the ocean he had crossed." Finally returning to Japan years later with his wife and daughter, he establishes a life in his birth nation and culture but never quite settles there emotionally. This young man was the grandfather of the narrator/artist who, like his elder, now understands longing for the home left behind and yet living where one has also experienced wonder. The juxtaposition of deep feeling with emotional distance underscores the theme. Say's full-page watercolor paintings present an 11 ¼ by 9 ¼ in. album-like sequence of landscapes and people with effective uses of light in this unique perspective on immigration.

GRANDPAPPY

Nancy White Carlstrom. Illustrated by Laurel Molk. (Little, Brown, 1990) 32 pages. ISBN: 0-316-12855-4. Level: Ages 5-8.

During Nate's visit, he and his grandfather share quiet beach walks, trips to town for supplies, and a midnight look at the stars. No matter whether the affectionate story takes place now or decades earlier, the central idea is timeless: live "as a light in a dark place." Grandpappy does.

THE GREAT MIGRATION: AN AMERICAN STORY

Jacob Lawrence. (HarperCollins, 1993) 48 pages. ISBN: 0-06-023038-X. Level: Ages 9 and older.

According to Lawrence, his sequence of paintings, begun in 1940 when he was twenty-two years old, involves the "exodus of African-Americans who left their home and farms in the South around the time of World War I and traveled to northern industrial cities in search of better lives." This book that reproduces the entire series in full color was published on the occasion of the 1993 exhibition "Jacob Lawrence: The Migration Series." Images of dignity and hope are mingled with those of hard work and harsh experience into panels depicting an epic sweep of a people on the move. Lawrence's introduction and brief narrative accompanying the paintings offer insights into this aspect of U.S. history and his immediate family's migration experience. The closing page of this significant book contains a poem by Walter Dean Myers in which tribute is paid to the theme of the paintings and to the people they represent.

GREAT-GRANDMA TELLS OF THRESHING DAY

Verda Cross. Illustrated by Gail Owens. (Albert Whitman, 1992) 40 pages. ISBN: 0-8075-3042-5. Level: Ages 5-8, or older for oral history purposes.

During the early twentieth century, the annual harvest in many parts of the United States typically required the labor of the entire farm family, and represented a cooperative, intergenerational, rural neighborhood effort to bring in a crop. Some Great Plains landowners of today display the machines that became the dinosaurs of threshing, and certain historical museums interpret the social and economic dimensions of threshing as well. Cross's autobiographical account of winter wheat threshing in one part of Missouri provides impressions of an earlier time, telling about the hard work in which relatives and neighbors usually had gender-determined roles and also about that work's unexpected pleasures. Illustrated with nostalgic full-color paintings, the picture story can stimu-

late some readers to ask long-lived community members to recount personal threshing anecdotes or to compare those experiences with ones in this book.

HARVEST YEAR

Cris Peterson. Photographs by Alvis Upitis. (Boyds Mills, 1996) 32 pages. ISBN: 1-56397-571-8. Level: Ages 6-8.

Wisconsin author Cris Peterson teams with photographer Alvis Upitis to look at harvest time across the nation throughout the calendar year in a simple, effective photodocumentary. Each two-page spread focuses on one month's harvest with color photographs, crisp, enticing prose, and a map that highlights the mentioned states. The purpose is not to show every food crop in every state, but rather to give readers a sense of the many kinds of food that are grown or harvested throughout the country, as well as the endless cycle of the harvest year.

HAYSTACK

Bonnie Geisert and Arthur Geisert. (Houghton Mifflin, 1995) 32 pages. ISBN: 0-395-69722-0. Level: Ages 4-9.

Bonnie Geisert's carefully crafted words paired with Arthur Geisert's finely detailed color etchings paint a delicate and satisfying portrait of life on a Midwest farm "in a time not so long ago" when "haystacks stood high, long, and wide on the prairie." Following the cycle of the seasons, Haystack begins in the spring, when everyone on the farm pitches in to harvest and stack the hay. Through summer's heat and the cold bite of fall and winter, the haystack provides food and shelter for the animals. In the greening of a new spring, the last remnants of hay are eaten, and rich manure from the field where the haystack once stood is spread so that new hay will grow. An unusual and engaging entry into the past is presented in this haystack-shaped 7½ x 12 in. volume.

A HOUSE BY THE RIVER

William Miller. Illustrated by Cornelius Van Wright and Ying-Hwa Hu. (Lee & Low, 1997) 32 pages. ISBN: 1-880000-48-2. Level: Ages 5-8.

Belinda dislikes the old house down by the river where she lives with her mother. She wishes she could live up on higher ground as her school friends do, so that she and her mother wouldn't have to worry about their house getting flooded when the rains come. During a big summer storm, as they prepare to wait out the flood by heading for the attic, Belinda's mother explains to her why the house is important to her family, how her daddy worked so hard to buy it, just as her great-grandfather Elias had worked during slavery times, and that, like Belinda's family, the house is stronger than the storm. Realistic watercolor illustrations show Belinda and her mother preparing to ride out the storm as her mother comforts her with a story that can be understood either literally or metaphorically in the context of African American history.

A HOUSE BY THE SEA

Joanne Ryder. Illustrated by Melissa Sweet. (Morrow, 1994) 32 pages. ISBN: 0-688-12676-6. Level: Ages 3-5.

"If I could live in a little house / I'd live in a house by the sea …" Ryder's gentle, rhyming text voices the dreams of a small boy and his sister who long for the everyday adventure and excitement a seaside home would provide. Charming watercolor paintings of the two brown-skinned siblings deftly depict their wildly imaginative and playful vision of a perfect life.

HOUSES OF ADOBE: THE SOUTHWEST

Bonnie Shemie. (Tundra, 1995) 24 pages. ISBN: 0-88776-353-7. Level: Ages 9-11.

The "great houses" of Chaco Canyon, the cliff dwellings of Mesa Verde, and Hopi pueblos are examples of the enduring architectural structures built over hundreds of years by the indigenous people of what is now the southwest United States. These buildings and what is known about the peoples who constructed them are the subject of an appreciative paperback text emphasizing the unique function and form of the ingenious designs. Like those in her other excellent books in this valuable series, Shemie's black-and-white drawings illustrate art and architectural elements, and two-page color spreads show how people lived in the buildings.

HOUSES OF BARK: TIPI, WIGWAM AND LONGHOUSE

Bonnie Shemie. (Tundra Books, 1990) 24 pages. ISBN: 0-88776-246-8. Level: Ages 6-9.

Line drawings accompany a brief text which describes the three basic traditional types of shelters built by Woodland Indians. Pictures show both an exterior and interior view of each dwelling while the text explains how the structures were built and why they were particularly well suited to the environment.

HUNTING THE WHITE COW

Tres Seymour. Illustrated by Wendy Anderson. (Orchard, 1993) 32 pages. ISBN: 0-531-05496-9. Level: Ages 3-8.

When a white cow gets loose from a Kentucky family's pasture, first Daddy and Mr. Matthew try to catch it and can't; then Daddy, Mr. Matthew, Uncle Bill, and Uncle Bob go after it and miss; and finally Daddy, Mr. Matthew, Uncle Bill, Uncle Bob, and Papaw try to find it and fail. "That cow is one tough dude," comments Mr. Matthew after every unsuccessful attempt. A white Southern cadence adds character and humor to the delightful story, traits that are further enhanced with distinctive details in the softly shaded watercolor and pencil illustrations. Multiple layers of plot are skillfully depicted in the illustrations, which are themselves layered to show simultaneous actions. For example, a single spread shows the hunting party setting out while the cow grazes peacefully in a field beyond them and a child sits impatiently on the front porch behind them.

IN FOR WINTER, OUT FOR SPRING

Arnold Adolf. Illustrated by Jerry Pinkney. (Harcourt Brace Jovanovich, 1991) 48 pages. ISBN: 0-15-238637-8. Level: Ages 5-8.

The youngest child in a rural African American family expresses her delight with the Earth's vivid show in the ever-changing cycle of seasons. Twenty-six poems written in a young girl's voice celebrate the beauty of nature and the security of family. Pinkney's detailed pencil, watercolor, and pastel paintings perfectly complement the child's exuberant moods within the cozy circle of her family.

IN THE HEART OF THE VILLAGE: THE WORLD OF THE INDIAN BANYAN TREE

Barbara Bash. (Sierra Club, 1996) 32 pages. ISBN: 0-87156-575-7. Level: Ages 8-11.

Beneath a banyan tree's broad, expansive covering, the people of a small village in India find a center for community life. School children gather for a class, traders exchange goods, and villagers seek shelter from the mid-day sun. Later in the day, children will play in and around the tree and elders will gather to talk. All the while, high up in its branches, egrets and owls nest, langur monkeys play, and rose finches, fairy bluebirds, and other birdlife feast on ripe red figs. The human and wildlife activity in and around this tree that is sacred to the people of India is followed from dawn to dusk to dawn in a singular, informative text with full-color illustrations that stretch across each two-page spread.

IN THE WOODS: WHO'S BEEN HERE?

Lindsay Barrett George. (Greenwillow, 1995) 40 pages. ISBN: 0-688-12319-8. Level: Ages 3-6.

While walking through the woods on an early autumn afternoon, Cammy and her older brother see many signs of animals who have preceded them, including a red squirrel, a blue jay, and a family of foxes. Double-page spreads show the clues and ask the question "Who's been here?" while alternating pages give a visual and verbal reply. The same device is used with Cammy and William's winter walk in George's IN THE SNOW: WHO'S BEEN HERE? also published in 1995.

INTO THE DEEP FOREST WITH HENRY DAVID THOREAU

Jim Murphy. Illustrated by Kate Kiesler. (Clarion, 1995) 39 pages. ISBN: 0-395-60522-9. Level: Ages 10-16 and older.

Carefully excerpted entries from Thoreau's journals concerning his third and earlier trips into the wilderness of Maine provide valuable insights from this reverent observer of nature. Murphy's note about the text indicates that he tried to use a light hand when creating transitions and other necessary alterations within Thoreau's original writing. The brief passages written in third person are effectively illustrated with Kiesler's oil paintings and pencil drawings.

JACKAL WOMAN: EXPLORING THE WORLD OF JACKALS

Laurence Pringle. Photographs by Patricia D. Moehlman. (Scribners, 1993) 42 pages. ISBN: 0-684-19435-X. Level: Ages 7-13.

Behavioral ecologist Patricia Moehlman's two decades of field observations of two jackal species on the Serengeti Plain of Tanzania in East Africa are summarized in language easily understood by anyone unfamiliar with this community of creatures and with the findings of this world authority on jackals. Moehlman's color photographs of her subjects offer superb support to Pringle's absorbing report of Moehlman's work and studies showing that jackal behavior differs from what is commonly attributed to them in folklore and fiction. Pringle explains Moehlman's reluctance to use the radio collars and dart guns often used to track and study many wildlife species, and he tells of her conservation work with others in Tanzania.

JULY

James Stevenson. (Greenwillow, 1990) 32 pages. ISBN: 0-688-08822-8. Level: Ages 5-9.

"When I was young, each month was like a glacier slowly melting . . ." begins a largely visual autobiographical narrative about the summers fifty years ago when this popular *New Yorker* cartoonist and children's book humorist spent a month with this grandparents at their beach house. New rules, old summer friends, varying oceanside weather, sticky toasted marshmallows, and almost-scary stories are remembered in a spare, witty narrative punctuated with small watercolor paintings reproduced in full color. WHEN I WAS NINE (Greenwillow, 1986) and HIGHER ON THE DOOR (Greenwillow, 1987) are companion picture book volumes.

KOFI AND HIS MAGIC

Maya Angelou. Photographs by Margaret Courtney-Clarke. Designed by Alexander Isley Design. (Clarkson Potter, 1996) 36 pages. ISBN: 0-517-704530-6. Level: Ages 6-8.

A dazzling photoessay combines an energizing, poetic text with crisp, colorful photographs and an engaging, playful design. Seven-year-old Kofi lives in Bonwire, the Ghanian village known for its beautiful Kente cloth. Kofi likes to weave, and he likes to travel. "I sit down, Close my eyes, Open my mind," Kofi explains, and he is transported to other places in Africa that he has always wanted to see. Kofi's magic is his vivid imagination, but his journey comes alive for readers through words and images depicting both his own life and each place he visits with a joyous sense of appreciation and discovery.

LAST LEAF FIRST SNOWFLAKE TO FALL

Leo Yerxa. (Orchard, 1994) 32 pages. ISBN: 0-531-06824-2. Level: Age 10 and older.

A Woodland Indian child travels by canoe and on foot with a parent to an island campsite. During a day and a night, autumn becomes winter. Details of the familiar transition seem new within a wondrous, sophisticated account distinctive in design and voice. First, a lengthy poetic commentary on creation: "before seeing, before being / before valentines and wild flowers … snow was born," and then—a unique naturalistic first person narrative. Neither uses conventional punctuation. "The blanket of leaves that yesterday / covered the earth / was now covered with a blanket / of snow / to keep her warm during her long winter sleep of yesterday / I arose from the earth / and walked into the light / of a new season." Stunning full-color collage assemblages sometimes fill double-page spreads and at other times decorate one corner of a full page of text. Illuminated letters and images of falling leaves assist in expressing the delicate instant when the season changes.

LAURA INGALLS WILDER COUNTRY

William Anderson. Photographs by Leslie A. Kelly. (Harper Perennial/HarperCollins, 1990) 119 pages. ISBN: 0-06-097346-3. Level: Age 7 and older.

Numerous color photographs and black-and-white documentary photographs depict the people and places of Laura Ingalls Wilder's well-known series based on her early life in Wisconsin, Minnesota, Kansas, Iowa, and South Dakota. Brief explanatory text and reproductions of Little House illustrations by Helen Sewell, Mildred Boyle, and Garth Williams serve to link Wilder's fiction with the real people and places that inspired her work.

THE LIVING EARTH

Eleonore Schmid. (North-South, 1994) 28 pages. ISBN: 1-55858-298-3. Level: Ages 4-8.

"There are more living organisms in a single handful of soil than there are people on the entire earth." An appealing, highly visual science book introduces young readers to the busy, intriguing world that lives just beneath their feet and describes how this world is affected by human activity on the surface just above it.

LOST

Paul Brett Johnson and Celeste Lewis. Illustrated by Paul Brett Johnson. (Orchard, 1996) 32 pages. ISBN: 0-531-09501-0. Level: Ages 4-7.

While camping in the desert, a little girl and her dad lose their beagle, Flag, and for weeks they do everything they can to try to find him. Finally, after a month, they are reunited. Written in the first-person voice of the girl, line drawings on the right-hand side on the page show their search efforts while full-color paintings on the left-hand side of the page show what Flag is actually doing in the desert to survive while they are searching for him.

A MILLION FISH ... MORE OR LESS

Patricia C. McKissaack. Illustrated by Dena Schutzer. (Alfred A. Knopf, 1992) 32 pages. ISBN: 0-679-80692-X. Level: Ages 4-7.

Inspired by the tall tales of Papa-Daddy and Elder Abbajon, young Hugh Thomas recounts a whopper of a fish tale of his own after a day of fishing on the Bayou Clapateaux. On his way home after having caught a million fish, he loses half of them to a wily alligator, half of the remaining lot to a band of pirate raccoons, and several thousand more to a flock of attacking crows before running into his neighbor's greedy cat. A well-paced, wildly funny story set in the Louisiana bayou and whimsically illustrated with boldly colored oil paintings.

MONARCH BUTTERFLIES: MYSTERIOUS TRAVELERS

Bianca Lavies. (Dutton, 1992) 32 pages. ISBN: 0-525-44905-1. Level: Ages 9-12 and older.

After introducing the egg-to-butterfly cycle of a Monarch butterfly, the author describes the work of Dr. Fred Urquhart and Norah Urquhart, scientists who have spent their lives researching the migratory behavior of these insects. When Ken and Cathy Burgger first located a central Mexican wintering site of the Monarch, the Urquharts and the author-photographer arrived soon after to study and document this long-awaited discovery. Full-page photographs aptly convey the overwhelming number of butterflies found at the mountain site.

THE MOON WAS THE BEST

Charlotte Zolotow. Photographs by Tana Hoban. (Greenwillow, 1993) 32 pages. ISBN: 0-688-09941-6. Level: Ages 3-5.

When a little girl's parents leave for a trip to Paris, she tells them, "Remember the special things to tell me ... the things I'd like if I were there ... So the mother remembered." This beautifully composed book pairs Zolotow's quiet, gentle narrative with full-page photographs by Hoban in which each of the mother's treasured memories is visually realized. An enlarged detail of the photo appearing opposite enhances each page of text. The perfect resolution of this warm, loving book will leave those who experience it sighing with pleasure and satisfaction.

MORNING MILKING

Linda Lowe Morris. Illustrated by David Deran. (Picture Book Studio, 1991) 32 pages. ISBN: 0-88708-173-8. Level: Ages 7-11.

Although she doesn't have to get up when she is awakened by her parents' alarm clock before dawn, a young girl living on a dairy farm in northern Maryland forces herself out of bed. A lyrical first-person narrative describes the small details of the morning milking routine that make it a special time shared by a father and daughter. Softly colored, realistic watercolor paintings aptly reflect the quiet yearning of a child's wish to hold onto the perfect moments at the start of every day.

MY PLACE

Nadia Wheatley and Donna Rawlins. (Kane-Miller, 1990) 48 pages. ISBN: 0-7328-0010-2. Level: Ages 6-12 and older.

A powerful cultural history of a fictional Australian neighborhood begins in 1988. This and subsequent double-page spreads are written, designed, and illustrated according to a pattern: "My name's Laura, and this is my place … Our house is the one with the flag on the window … This is a map of my place. We've got a McDonalds right on the corner. In the … yard, there's this big tree … There's a canal … Mum said it must have been a creek once. It's too dirty to swim in …" The visual chronology moves backward ten years at a time through twenty-one decades of Australian immigrations (Asian, German, Irish, English prisoners); world events (Vietnam War, World Wars, U.S. gold rush); and economic changes (land ownerships and uses, Labor movement) affecting ordinary families. Differences and effects of cultures and classes are suggested. The tree and the water represent steady points of reference and subtle change in each decade. The people indigenous to Australia claim the dramatic final double-page spread showing a rural sunset before contact with the British. This stunning intellectual and political reiteration of the Aboriginal flag mentioned and seen at the beginning of this outstanding, award-winning $10^{1}/_4$ x $9^{3}/_4$ in. book invites already-intrigued readers into repeated experiences with the narrations and detailed images.

MY PRAIRIE CHRISTMAS

Brett Harvey. Illustrated by Deborah Kogan Ray. (Holiday House, 1990) 32 pages. ISBN: 0-8234-0827-2. Level: Ages 4-8.

"I loved our new home on the prairie, sitting in the middle of its ocean of grass. But how would we celebrate Christmas?" Mama knows. Cornhusks are twisted into decorations. Popcorn strings become a substitute for the cranberries strung for past Christmas trees in Maine. Mama and the three children trudge through deep snow to get a cottonwood even though they are frantic because Papa didn't return home before a blizzard began. Full-color illustrations evoke the open prairie, late-nineteenth century homesteading life and the loving family of young Eleanore's first prairie December. The companion book, MY PRAIRIE YEAR (Holiday, 1986), is also based on a diary written by Eleanore Plaisted.

MY STEPS

Sally Derby. Illustrated by Adjoa J. Burrowes. (Lee & Low, 32 pages. ISBN: 1-880000-40-7. Level: Ages 3-6.

An African American girl describes all the fun she has year round (but especially in summer) playing on the front steps of her house in a busy urban neighborhood with her friends Essie and Nicholas. Two elements work particularly well to bring the book to life: the realistic voice of the child narrator and the bright cut-paper collages used to illustrate the story. The collages give both texture and dimension to the illustrations, making every scene look like a real front stoop.

NATIVE AMERICAN ROCK ART: MESSAGES FROM THE PAST

Yvette La Pierre. Illustrated by Lois Sloan. (Thomasson-Grant, 1994) 48 pages. ISBN: 1-56566-064-1. Level: Ages 8-12 and older.

Petroglyphs and pictographs—carvings and paintings on rocks—done by the earliest human inhabitants of North America, can be found from Nova Scotia to the deserts of the Southwest. La Pierre explores what is known and how it was determined, as well as what is not known, about these ancient forms of art and communication and the people who created them. Though the illustrations and the fictionalized scenarios that open each chapter seem to assume that rock artists were always male, the unique information presented here makes this a valuable text, which includes photographs of rock art throughout North America.

NIGHT ON NEIGHBORHOOD STREET

Eloise Greenfield. Illustrated by Jan Spivey Gilchrist. (Dial Books for Young Readers, 1991) 32 pages. ISBN: 0-8037-0778-9. Level: Ages 3-9.

Each of the seventeen poems in this collection offers glimpses into the lives of African American children on a single night in an urban neighborhood. Nerissa is telling her parents bedtime jokes; Tonya is hosting a sleepover. Darnell is afraid of nighttime noises; independent Lawanda is determined not to let her daddy carry her from the car to the front door even though she's very sleepy; Juma is talking his daddy into letting him stay up just a little longer; and Buddy is already asleep and dreaming of impressing the world with his wonderful, amazing self. Gilchrist's full-color gouache paintings evoke a perfect nighttime mood in Greenfield's celebratory tribute to African American families and communities.

NIGHT OWLS

Sharon Phillips Denslow. Illustrated by Jill Kastner. (Bradbury, 1990) 32 pages. ISBN: 0-02-728681-9. Level: Ages 4-7.

Aunt Charlene "has always been afraid she will miss something wonderful if she goes to bed too early." She and her nephew William enjoy being night owls together during his summer visits. They roast corn over a bonfire, count the night songs of crickets and frogs, climb a tree, and decorate the night with soap bubbles. A colorful loving account of a colorful loving relationship.

NIGHT TREE

Eve Bunting. Illustrated by Ted Rand (Harcourt Brace Jovanovich, 1991) 32 pages. ISBN: 0-15-257425-5. Level: Ages 3-7.

On the cold night before Christmas, a mother, father, and two children drive their pickup truck out from the city to a forested area to find a perfect Christmas tree. Instead of cutting it down, however, they decorate it with apples, tangerines, balls of sunflower seeds and pressed millet, and a popcorn chain. They enjoy a picnic by moonlight before leaving the tree as a gift to the forest animals. The deep solitude of the forest on a winter night is aptly depicted with dark blues and greens in double-page watercolor illustrations, highlighted with bright red and pink clothing worn by the family members. This understated story provides a satisfying blend of traditional values and original expressions of generosity and celebration.

ON THE PAMPAS

Maria Cristina Brusca. (Henry Holt, 1991) 32 pages. ISBN: 0-8050-1548-5. Level: Ages 4-8.

A young girl from Buenos Aires, Argentina, spends the summer on her grandfather's ranch on the pampas, enjoying a thrilling camaraderie with her cousin and age-mate, Susanita, who knows "everything about horses, cows, and all the other animals that live on the pampas." Together the two girls ride horses, go swimming, search for nandu eggs, and listen to the gauchos tell ghost stories. There are plenty of activities to fill the days of these tireless and adventuresome cousins, both of whom aspire to be gauchos some day themselves. This autobiographical reminiscence by Argentinean Maria Cristina Brusca is filled with visual and textual details about life on a South American ranch.

ONLY A PIGEON

Jane Kurtz and Christopher Kurtz. Illustrated by E. B. Lewis. (Simon & Schuster, 1997) 40 pages. ISBN: 0-689-80077-0. Level: Ages 4-8.

Ondu-ahlem goes to school every morning and spends his afternoons shining shoes in the market area to earn some spending money. Busy as he is, his thoughts are never far from the homing pigeons he is raising. He spends most of his free time caring for them—checking on the eggs that are just about ready to hatch and protecting them from the pesky mongoose who visits frequently at night. Inspired by the experiences of a real boy Jane and Christopher Kurtz met in Addis Ababa, Ethiopia, the story captures the child's deep devotion to his pigeons. Lewis's rich watercolor illustrations shimmer with small details of Ondu-ahlem's everyday life.

PLACES OF REFUGE: OUR NATIONAL WILDLIFE REFUGE SYSTEM

Dorothy Hinshaw Patent. Photographs by William Munoz. (Clarion, 1992) 80 pages. ISBN: 0-899-19-846-5. Level: Ages 9-12 and older.

The United States Wildlife Refuge System is described from its inception in 1903 by President Theodore Roosevelt to its current state. Various types of refuges, including national parks, national forests, national resource lands, and wilderness areas, are defined and their differences outlined. An emphasis on human uses of refuge land is present throughout the text, as the author discusses the impact of logging, farming, mining, hunting, and recreational activities on these protected areas and their animal inhabitants. Numerous color photographs are clearly captioned.

RAPTOR RESCUE! AN EAGLE FLIES FREE

Sylvia A. Johnson. Photographs by Ron Winch. (Dutton, 1995) 32 pages. ISBN: 0-525-45301-6. Level: Ages 7-11.

When a bald eagle wounded by shotgun pellets is found in a roadside ditch by a conservation officer, he is taken to the Gabbert Raptor Center at the University of Minnesota. This compelling photoessay follows the steps taken by the Raptor Center staff to heal patient S-137's wounds and eventually return him to the wild.

ROME ANTICS

David Macaulay. (Houghton Mifflin, 1997) 79 pages. ISBN: 0-395-82279-3. Level: Ages 9-12 and older.

Macaulay's bird's-eye view of modern-day Rome follows the journey of a homing pigeon released by a woman in the hills outside the city. The pigeon decides to take the scenic route on her way to deliver her message. As the pigeon travels, she flies over a city where ancient ruins, historic sites, and thoroughly modern life coexist. Macaulay reveals all three in his distinctive black-and-white drawings that fill the oversized pages. The pigeon's path through the city is marked by a bold red line that loops and curves, zips and arcs across the otherwise colorless pages. A droll narrative gives insight into what the pigeon is thinking ("She firmly resolves to stay on course, at least until she reaches this piazza") in addition to documenting her adventures and mishaps. This wholly original book includes information about the sites the pigeon sees: each building or ruin is labeled at the bottom of the full-page illustrations, and a brief description of each one is provided at the book's end. And as for the pigeon message? She delivers it at last, to an anxious man in Rome. It is one word: "Yes."

SCORPION MAN: EXPLORING THE WORLD OF SCORPIONS

Pringle, Laurence. Photographs by Gary A. Polis. (Charles Scribner's Sons, 1994) 42 pages. ISBN: 0-684-19560-7. Level: Ages 8-12.

Continuing his line of books about the life and works of contemporary natural scientists (Bat Man, Bear Man, Jackal Woman), Pringle turns our attention to desert biologist Gary Polis. This scientist's studies of scorpions living in their natural habitat, along with Pringle's cogent description of the scorpion's life cycle, do much to belie the creature's universally bad reputation. Accompanied by full-color pictures of Gary Polis at work, as well as some dazzling close-up shots of scorpions in the wild, it's sure to be a hit with young readers interested in "scary" animals.

THE SEASHORE BOOK

Charlotte Zolotow. Illustrated by Wendell Minor (HarperCollins, 1992) 32 pages. ISBN: 0-06-020213-0. Level: Ages 3-8.

To answer his question about the seashore, a little boy's mother invites him to pretend to "pick up a stone washed smooth by the sea" and notice tiny oyster shells "crusty gray outside and smooth, pearly pink inside." By suggesting sensory ways to experience a specific place, Zolotow's affectionate text bids children to use imagination to recapture experience and/or companionship. Minor's full-page illustrations for this lovely $11\frac{1}{4}$ x $9\frac{1}{4}$ in. book for all seasons were painted with gouache and watercolors on cold-press watercolor board.

THE SEASONS SEWN: A YEAR IN PATCHWORK

Ann Whitford Paul. Illustrated by Michael McCurdy. (Browndeer/Harcourt Brace, 1996) 40 pages. ISBN: 0-15-276918-8. Level: Ages 9-12.

In three opening pages, the author invites readers to imagine the life and work of a rural family in the northern United States throughout one year more than a hundred years ago. She then suggests that patchwork patterns and their names give clues about life in earlier centuries. The central portion of this book is organized according to the four seasons. Each seasonal section is introduced by colored scratchboard artwork on a double page spread. Paul discusses six quilt patterns for each season. In her one-paragraph accompaniment for each pattern, she speculates about its possible historical origin. That historic activity or event is pictured in McCurdy's scratchboard art on the top half of each page. This nicely designed $10\frac{1}{4}$ in. square book includes a selective bibliography.

SNOW ON SNOW ON SNOW

Cheryl Chapman. Illustrated by Synthia Saint James. (Dial, 1994) 32 pages. ISBN: 0-8037-1457-2. Level: Ages 3-6.

Inspired by Christina Rossetti's poem "In the Bleak Midwinter," this picture story begins "Once upon a winter's day / I woke up / under blankets under blankets under blankets." Using repeating prepositional phrases, Chapman's young narrator tells of going out with a dog and sled to play. Although the dog disappears for a moment, all live "happily ever after ever after ever after." Saint James' artwork picturing a brown-skinned child and mother with abstract features was rendered in oil and acrylic on canvas. Her landscapes are filled with bright skies and a rainbow of playmates and snowsuits.

THE SNOW WALKER

Margaret K. Wetterer and Charles M. Wetterer. Illustrated by Mary O'Keefe Young. (On My Own) (Carolrhoda, 1996) 48 pages. ISBN: 0-87614-891-7. Level: Ages 7-10.

During the record-breaking blizzard of 1888 in the Northeast, a twelve-year-old named Milton Daub and his father make snow shoes because Milton wants to go out and get milk needed at home. He ends up doing errands for snowbound neighbors in the Bronx at great risk of becoming a blizzard victim. This easy-to-read story about a real boy in Old New York who found a way to earn money despite severe weather is illustrated in full color on every page spread.

THE SNOW WHALE

Caroline Pitcher. Illustrated by Jackie Morris (Sierra Club, 1996) 24 pages. ISBN: 0-87156-915-9. Level: Ages 3-6.

After a snowstorm, Laurie and her little brother, Leo, build a great white whale in the snow. "Where does the snow come from?" Leo asks, and Laurie, in an exasperated, big-sisterly tone, tells him how "the water rises up from the ocean and goes into the clouds" to fall down again as rain or snow. The children's snow whale is a gentle and magnificent beast that spurs their imaginations until the weather warms and a heartbroken Laurie asks "Where has the whale gone?" to which Leo gently replies, "Snow whale's gone home." A captivating story is matched by outstanding design and lovely full-color illustrations.

SNOWED IN

Barbara M. Lucas. Illustrated by Catherine Stock. (Bradbury, 1993) 32 pages. ISBN: 0-02-761465-4. Level: Ages 4-7.

As winter begins in Wyoming in 1915, young Grace and Luke said good-bye to their teacher for the season and go by horse and wagon with their father to town to stock up on pencils and paper at the store and borrow a box of books from the library. These preparations for winter's inevitable isolation provide the children with certain resources for studying, with their parents as teachers, and enjoying the reading that takes them beyond Wyoming winter confinement. The watercolor illustrations and the spare text for the 8¼ by 10¼ in. book were influenced by LETTERS OF A WOMAN HOMESTEADER, by Elinore Pruitt Stewart (University of Nebraska Press, 1961).

SPILL! THE STORY OF THE EXXON VALDEZ

Terry Carr. (Frankllin Watts, 1991) 64 pages. ISBN: 0-531-15217-0. Level: Ages 9-14 and older.

An editorial writer for the *Anchorage Daily News* documents events before and after the historic collision. He describes the impact of the resulting oil spill on the ecosystem. Vivid color photographs on every page amplify the details. Volunteer efforts to rescue and recover affected wildlife are also emphasized.

STARRY NIGHT

David Spohn. (Lothrop, Lee & Shepard, 1992) 32 pages. ISBN: 0-688-11171-8. Level: Ages 3-7.

When Nate, Matt, and Dad go camping near their house in August, everyone helps with preparations. Nate assembles snacks, Matt packs his stuffed animal, and Dad takes a harmonica. They establish their campsite, build a fire, and settle in for singing, stories, and locating the Big Dipper, the Great Bear, and Cassiopeia. Observant readers will notice practical details about camping unobtrusively woven within the brief, quiet 8 x 6¼ in. book about two boys and their father. The same biracial (African American / white) family pictured in the full-color illustrations appears in NATE'S TREASURE AND WINTER WOOD (Lothrop, 1991).

STREET MUSIC: CITY POEMS

Arnold Adoff. Illustrated by Karen Barbour. (HarperCollins, 1995) 32 pages. ISBN: 0-06-021522-4. Level: Ages 7-11.

Feel the cold shiver of water from a hydrant spray relief on a steaming summer day. Listen as the clang and bang of a garbage truck sounds the alarm for morning. See the woman and her young daughters sharing fruit in the doorway of the cash machine, where they spend each day in search of survival. A child offers images and observations of life in the big city in this collection of fifteen original poems that vibrate with edginess and excitement. Barbour's illustrations echo the energy of the poems and pulse with the intensity and abandon of city life.

SUNFLAKES: POEMS FOR CHILDREN

Lilian Moore. Illustrated by Jan Ormerod. (Clarion, 1992) 96 pages. ISBN: 0-395-58833-2. Level: Ages 2-7.

The poet-anthologist states that poems can assist children to "connect with feelings of others, to hear the music of language and to see the details in the world around them more vividly, more truthfully." Moore writes her own poems and collects the poems of others with grace. Her accurate scenes of very young children are reflected in her names for sections of this collection: I Am Very Fond Of Bugs, I Like To Look In Puddles, Me And Potato Chips, The Night Is Long But Fur Is Deep, and Breathing On The Window Pane In Winter. Ormerod's full-color illustrations enliven each page with images that do not limit a poem's possibility. Poets represented in the seventy-five poems include Arnold Adoff, Frank Asch, Margaret Wise Brown, John Ciardi, Eloise Greenfield, Mary Ann Hoberman, Edward Lear, Dennis Lee, Eve Merriam, Kazue Mizumura, Jack Prelutsky, Nancy Willard, Jane Yolen, and Charlotte Zolotow.

SURTSEY: THE NEWEST PLACE ON EARTH

Kathryn Lasky. Photographs by Christopher G. Knight. (Hyperion, 1992) 64 pages. ISBN: 1-56282-300-0. Level: Ages 9-14 and older.

When the crew of an Icelandic fishing vessel smells sulfur early on the morning of November 14, 1963, they radio the coast guard to see if any ships in the area are reporting a fire. The crew soon discovers that the fire they are smelling is originating from a nearby submarine volcano that has reached the water's surface after days of burning beneath the waves. Stunning photographs and a fascinating text describe the events of the next several years as the newest island on earth forms and evolves into a habitat capable of supporting plant and animal life.

TAR BEACH

Faith Ringgold. (Crown Publishers, 1991) 32 pages. ISBN: 0-517-58030-6. Level: Ages 5-11.

In one of the most visually exciting books to appear in a long time, artist Faith Ringgold has created a picture book based on her story quilt "Tar Beach." Eight-year-old Cassie Lightfoot and her baby brother Be Be lie stretched out on a mattress on the rooftop of their Harlem apartment while her parents play cards with their next-door neighbors. During that magical time that comes between wakefulness and sleep, the adult conversation blends into Cassie's daydream as she envisions herself flying high above the city, claiming that she owns it all and can change anything to make life come out the way she wants it to be. Ringgold's boldly imaginative acrylic paintings brilliantly capture the power of a child's soaring imagination on the twilight edge of dreams. Set in 1939, Tar Beach succeeds as an appealing story for children illustrated with fine art, an astute societal commentary, and a new variation on a traditional African American liberation motif.

THIRTEEN MOONS ON TURTLE'S BACK: A NATIVE AMERICAN YEAR OF MOONS

Joseph Bruchac and Jonathan London. Illustrated by Thomas Locker. (Philomel, 1992) 32 pages. ISBN: 0-399-22141-7. Level: Ages 4-9 and older.

In many Native cultures, seasonal changes in the natural world are noted by naming a month with a descriptive phrase. The Micmac, for example, call the ninth month "the moose-calling moon" while the Cherokee call the tenth "the moon of falling leaves." Each of the thirteen months included in this book is illustrated with an oil painting accompanied by a three-verse poem about the distinctive features that led to its name. Potawatomi, Anishnabe (Ojibway), Menominee, and Winnebago are four of the thirteen tribes represented.

TOMORROW ON ROCKY POND

Lynn Reiser. (Greenwillow, 1993) 32 pages. ISBN: 0-688-10673-0. Level: Ages 3-6.

Tucked in bed at night, a young girl is filled with excitement about the fishing trip her family has planned for the next day. She runs through a mental list of the special fishing clothes they'll wear and the equipment they'll carry, the animals they'll hear and plants they'll see on their walk through the woods to reach their canoe, and then all the bird and fish they'll encounter once they reach the lake. All the exuberance of a child's anticipation of good times ahead is deftly expressed in text and pictures that make this family fishing trip appropriately idealized.

TONIGHT IS CARNAVAL

Arthur Dorros. Illustrated with arpilleras sewn by the Club de Madres Virgen del Carmen de Lima, Peru. (Dutton Children's Books, 1991) 24 pages. ISBN: 0-525-44641-9. Level: Ages 4-8.

A Peruvian child describes family and community preparations during a three-day period prior to the first night of Carnaval. His story is illustrated with brightly colored folk-art wall hangings (arpilleras), which were sewn by women in Lima, Peru. A final double-page spread titled "How Arpilleras Are Made" includes captioned color photographs of the artists at work, adding another dimension of cultural detail to the book. A Spanish language edition of this book was also published in 1991.

TWO LANDS, ONE HEART: AN AMERICAN BOY'S JOURNEY TO HIS MOTHER'S VIETNAM

Jeremy Schmidt and Ted Wood. Photographs by Ted Wood. (Walker, 1995) 44 pages. ISBN: 0-8027-8357-0. Level: Ages 7-10.

Seven-year-old T. J. Sharp is accompanying his mother on a journey to Vietnam—the homeland she fled as a child in the midst of the war. T. J. is eager to meet his Vietnamese grandparents, aunts, uncles, and cousins and see the country about which he has been hearing for so long. Color photographs and text document T. J.'s experience as he travels to a far-away land that holds the familiar embrace of family even though the language and customs differ from his own.

UP NORTH AT THE CABIN

Marsha Wilson Chall. Illustrated by Steve Johnson. (Lothrop, Lee & Shepard, 1992) 32 pages. ISBN: 0-688-09733-2. Level: Ages 4-9.

Chall and Johnson successfully pinpoint the experiences of many who regularly vacation "up north." "I know the way by heart:/past the big walleye statue on Lake Mille Lacs,/a few more miles to the Live Deer Park,/till all the trees are birch and pine/and houses are made from logs that look like shiny pretzels. . .", a girl says as she anticipates another summer at a family cottage. She thinks of herself as a smart angler (fishing), a great gray dolphin (diving), a fearless voyager (portaging with a canoe), and a daredevil (waterskiing). This non-Indian child realizes that the Ojibway people were once the only inhabitants of this woods-and-lakes region enjoyed today by others. The details in Johnson's fourteen full-color paintings add immediacy, clarifying Chall's skillfully employed figurative language; his art is also noteworthy in its interpretations of various types of summer light.

WAKE UP, CITY!

Alvin Tresselt. Illustrated by Carolyn Ewing. (Lothrop, Lee & Shepard, 1990) 32 pages. ISBN: 0-688-08652-7. Level: Ages 3-7.

People stir and wake up on an early morning in a city. "In a harbor a great freighter from across the world comes in on the morning tide . . ." Food is unloaded at noisy markets. Buses run. A pajama-clad child notices birds at the window feeder. The cat goes inside. Nothing and everything happens. All children, workers, police officers, and others represent the ordinary busyness and racial diversity common to a city. New, full-color illustrations update a picture book text more than thirty years old.

WATER BUFFALO DAYS: GROWING UP IN VIETNAM

Quang Nhuong Huynh. Illustrated by Jean and Mou-Sien Tseng. (HarperCollins, 1997) 116 pages. ISBN: 0-06-024957-9. Level: Ages 9-11.

Huynh Quang Nhuong's memories of his childhood in Vietnam are fresh, appealing stories perfectly suited to child readers. The narratives focus on Nhuong's relationship as a child with the water buffalo bulls owned by his family. Tank, whom Nhuong's father acquired as a calf after the bull Water Jug's death, grows to be Nhuong's friend and protector as well as his companion in adventure. Nhuong's charming recollections give a sense of the peaceful, quiet agrarian life that his own and many other families were living in Vietnam during the years just prior to the war that would tear the country in two. The war does finally intrude in Nhuong's life in the book's final chapter, and with it's arrival he loses a very good friend. Children will understand why Nhuong felt his life would never be the same again after the death of his beloved Tank. That it was not the same again for many other reasons, and that Nhuong would face many other losses in his life, is only hinted at in a narrative that movingly concludes "How could future losses surprise me now that I knew a single misplaced bullet could destroy. . . such a benevolent being, such a good friend?"

Ⅲ Ⅳ Ⅸ

WHEELS

Shirley Hughes. (Lothrop, Lee & Shepard Books, 1991) 24 pages. ISBN: 0-688-09880-0. Level: Ages 3-8.

Trotter Street is full of Spring motion and locomotion. Sanjit Lal has roller skates; Barney, a skateboard; and Mae's baby sister, a stroller. Carlos deals gamely with the disappointment of receiving perfectly fine birthday presents but no bike like Billy's. Mum had warned Carlos in advance about this, but he was completely unprepared for his brother Marco's handmade surprise. This gift and a subsequent neighborhood non-bicycle race exhibit the small moments of high drama at which Hughes excels. Hughes's full-color artwork harmonizes wonderfully with the down-to-earth fictional Trotter Street community she has populated with appealing folks living their daily lives next to each other. An outstanding addition to a great series.

Ⅲ Ⅳ Ⅴ

WHEN I GO CAMPING WITH GRANDMA

Marion Dane Bauer. Illustrated by Allen Garns. (Bridge Water, 1995) 32 pages. ISBN: 0-8167-3448-8. Level: Ages 3-6.

A young girl lyrically describes the quiet moments she and her grandmother share when they camp together: sleeping in a tent, fishing from a canoe, roasting hot dogs and marshmallows over an open campfire. Throughout the busy day, there is still plenty of time and space for them to observe the wonders of nature. Garns's soft, hazy illustrations provide just the right mood for this evocative story.

Ⅲ Ⅳ

WHERE DOES THE TRAIL LEAD?

Burton Albert. Illustrated by Brian Pinkney. (Simon & Schuster, 1991) 32 pages. ISBN: 0-671-73409-1. Level: Ages 4-7.

A short, lyrical text traces the steps of an African American boy on Summer Island as he follows a rustic trail along the beach until he reaches his family at a seaside picnic. Pinkney's scratchboard illustrations are colored with aqua, green, brown, and purple oil pastels, providing the perfect ambiance for the quiet story of a solitary journey.

WHERE ONCE THERE WAS A WOOD

Denise Fleming. (Henry Holt, 1996) 28 pages. ISBN: 0-8050-3761-6. Level: Ages 5-10.

When a wood, meadow, and creek vanish due to modern development of the land, the flora and fauna are also directly affected. Children will notice more animals, birds, reptiles, and plants than the few named in the brief, lyrical text of a provocative picture book. The final four pages contain detailed directions for creating a family backyard wildlife habitat. Fleming's trademark illustrations were created with cotton rag fiber. The bold shapes and distinctive full-color images can be easily seen in a large group setting.

Ⅲ

WINDOW

Jeannie Baker. (Greenwillow Books, 1991) 32 pages. ISBN: 0-688-08917-8. Level: Age 9 and older.

Complex, full-color collage constructions in a thirteen-part sequence show the view from one person's window. At the beginning, an adult holding an infant is inside. Several years elapse between each turn of the page, and the child grows up as the book's images unfold. Over the years, each neighborhood change is seen as exacting a cumulative toll on the landscape. What was once a green residential area becomes a commercial district throughout two or three decades. A final double-page spread displays the former child, now a parent himself, looking out the window of his new home located beyond the suburbs. Distant green hills appear to be newly scarred by construction. This disturbing, provocative wordless essay invites reflection and discussion as well as real-life observation and action.

WINTER POEMS

Barbara Rogasky, selector. Illustrated by Trina Schart
Hyman. (Scholastic, 1994) 40 pages. ISBN: 0-590-42872-1.
Level: Ages 5-14.

Twenty-five poems evoke possibilities of the season—its
weather, bird-watching, skiing, moon, deer, geese, even
its germs, as well as its indoor warmth. It's the warmth
that readers of this incomparable anthology can experience, the warmth resulting from reading or hearing superb classic poetry in many voices and forms; from seeing pictures of a home, its people, its work, and its pleasure; from noticing landscapes and families in new ways.
Hyman's paintings reproduced in full color on every page
were rendered in acrylics on illustration board, contributing
significantly to the excellence of the appealing volume.

WINTER RESCUE

W. D. Valgardson. Illustrated by Ange Zhang. (Mnargaret K.
McElderry, 1995) 40 pages. ISBN: 0-689-80094-0. Level: Ages 6-9.

This picture story adventure takes place on Lake
Winnipeg during a frigid day when Grandfather decides
Thor is old enough to help him set nets. The boy will
miss his Saturday TV cartoons—a serious matter. Zhang's
illustrations done with colored pencil detail how the two
transport an icehouse fitted with skis so far out on the
large frozen lake that they will need a compass to get
back. Explosive sounds made by cracking ice and
Grandfather's explanations of pressure ridges remind
Thor to watch for cracks and not fall in. Readers see an
experienced ice fisherman at work, and they witness fast-
driving snowmobiles getting into trouble on thin ice.
They discover that a child can muster more courage than
a Saturday morning cartoon hero.
Ⅲ Ⅳ Ⓧ

THE YEAR OF NO MORE CORN

Helen Ketteman. Illustrated by Robert Andrew. (Orchard, 1993)
32 pages. ISBN: 0-531-05950-2. Level: Ages 4-8.

Because Beanie is too young to help with the corn planting
and Old Grampa's too old, the two of them share a story on
the front porch instead. Old Gramps tells Beanie about a planting season long ago when the farmers were besieged with
first a flood, then a tornado, next a hot spell, and finally crows,
so that every last kernel of corn had been carried away by
one natural disaster or another. Ever resourceful, Old Grampa
had whittled corn to plant that year. Parker's expressive watercolor paintings accompany a text that is half tall tale, half
family story, and completely entertaining.
Ⅲ Ⅴ

Children's Trade Books with People, Places, and Environments as a Second Thematic Strand

The title index on pp. 173-180 lists the number of the page on which each book is annotated.

TITLE	AUTHOR	DATE	AGE LEVEL
Amelia's Road	Linda Jacobs Altman	1993	Ages 7-9
Back Home	Gloria Jean Pinkney	1992	Ages 4-8
Bat in the Dining Room	Crescent Dragonwagon	1997	Ages 4-8
Batman: Exploring the World of Bats	Laurence Pringle	1991	Ages 9-11
A Bear for All Seasons	Diane Marcial Fuchs	1995	Ages 3-7
A Blue Butterfly: A Story about Claude Monet	Bijou Le Tord	1995	Ages 5-8
Bread Is for Eating	David Gershator	1995	Ages 4-8
Calling the Doves/El Canto de las Palomas	Juan Felipe Herrera	1995	Ages 4-8
The Circle of Thanks: Native American Poems and Songs of Thanksgiving	Joseph Bruchac	1996	Ages 7-11 and older
Cocoa Ice	Diana Applebaum	1997	Ages 5-9
Cuckoo: A Mexican Folktale/Cucú	Lois Ehlert	1997	Ages 3-9
The Dancing Fox: Arctic Folktales	John Bierhorst	1997	Ages 9-14 and older
The Days before Now: An Autobiographical Note by Margaret Wise Brown	Joan W. Blos, Adapter	1994	Ages 3-9
Dick King-Smith's Animal Friends: Thirty-One True Life Stories	Dick King-Smith	1996	Ages 4-12
Diego	Jonah Winter	1991	Ages 5-9
Diez Deditos/Ten Little Fingers and Other Play Rhymes and Action Songs from Latin America	Jose-Luis Orozco	1997	Babies-age 8, adults
Dolphin Man: Exploring the World of Dolphins	Laurence Pringle	1995	Ages 7-11
Dreamcatcher	Audrey Osofsky	1992	Ages 4-9
Earth, Fire, Water, Air	Mary Hoffman	1995	Ages 8-14
Extra Cheese, Please! Mozzarella's Journey from Cow to Pizza	Cris Peterson	1994	Ages 5-8
Farmer's Market	Paul Brett Johnson	1997	Ages 4-7
Fire in the Forest: A Cycle of Growth and Renewal	Laurence Pringle	1995	Ages 7-11
Gathering the Sun: An Alphabet in Spanish and English	Alma Flor Ada	1997	Ages 5-10
Global Warming	Laurence Pringle	1990	Ages 7-10

The Golden Lion Tamarin Comes Home	George Ancona	1994	Ages 7-11
Harlem: A Poem	Walter Dean Myers	1997	Age 12 and older
Hattie and the Wild Waves: A Story from Brooklyn	Barbara Cooney	1990	Ages 6-9
The Heart of the Wood	Marguerite W. Davol	1992	Ages 3-8
Here Comes the Mail	Gloria Skurzynski	1992	Ages 4-8
Home Place	Crescent Dragonwagon	1990	Ages 7-10
Hopscotch around the World	Mary D. Lankford	1992	Ages 6-9
Kodomo: Children of Japan	Susan Kuklin	1995	Ages 5-11
Laura Loves Horses	Joan Hewett	1990	Ages 4-9
Luka's Quilt	Georgia Guback	1994	Ages 4-8
Mac & Marie & the Train Toss Surprise	Elizabeth Fitzgerald Howard	1993	Ages 5-8
Marven of the Great North Woods	Kathryn Lasky	1997	Ages 6-9 and older
Meet Danitra Brown	Nikki Grimes	1994	Ages 7-10
Moon Festival	Ching Yeung Russell	1997	Ages 6-9
The Most Beautiful Roof in the World: Exploring the Rainforest Canopy	Kathryn Lasky	1997	Ages 7-11 and older
My Mexico/Mexico Mio	Tony Johnston	1996	Ages 5-8
Nana's Birthday Party	Amy Hest	1993	Ages 4-8
Night Driving	John Coy	1996	Ages 4-8
Our House: The Stories of Levittown	Pam Conrad	1995	Ages 9-12 and older
Our Journey from Tibet: Based on a True Story	Laurie Dolphin	1997	Ages 9-12 and older
Pueblo Storyteller	Diane Hoyt-Goldsmith	1991	Ages 6-10
Quilted Landscape: Conversations with Young Immigrants	Yale Strom	1996	Ages 11-14 and older
The Sacred Harvest: Ojibway Wild Rice Gathering	Gordon Regguinti	1992	Ages 7-13
Sami and the Time of the Troubles	Florence Parry Heide and Judith Heide Gilliland	1992	Ages 8-11
Señor Cat's Romance and Other Favorite Stories from Latin America	Lucia M. Gonzalez	1997	Ages 4-11

Sitti's Secrets	Naomi Shihab Nye	1994	Ages 6-10
Taxi! Taxi!	Cari Best	1994	Ages 4-8
The Third Planet: Exploring the Earth from Space	Sally Ride and Tam O'Shaughnessy	1994	Ages 7-11
Tree of Cranes	Allen Say	1991	Ages 5-7
Tunnels, Tracks, and Trains: Building a Subway	Joan Hewett	1995	Ages 7-10
Turtle Bay	Saviour Pirotta	1997	Ages 5-8
V for Vanishing; An Alphabet of Endangered Animals	Patricia Mullins	1994	Ages 5-10
The Whispering Cloth	Pegi Deitz Shea	1995	Ages 7-11

Children's Trade Books with People, Places, and Environments as a Third Thematic Strand

The title index on pp. 173-180 lists the number of the page on which each book is annotated.

Abuela's Weave	Omar S. Castaneda	1993	Ages 6-9
Alphabet City	Stephen T. Johnson	1995	Ages 3-6
At the Beach	Huy Voun Lee	1994	Ages 6-10
Be Patient, Abdul	Dolores Sandoval	1996	Ages 5-7
Bravo, Tanya	Patricia Lee Gauch	1992	Ages 4-7
Chicken Soup Boots	Maria Kalman	1993	Ages 4-8
Christmas in the Big House, Christmas in the Quarters	Patricia C. and Fredrick L. McKissack	1994	Ages 8-13 and older
Clambake: A Wampanoag Tradition	Russell M. Peters	1992	Ages 7-13
Down the Road	Alice Schertle	1995	Ages 4-7
End of Winter	Sharon Chmielarz	1992	Ages 6-9
Faith Ringgold and Frida Kahlo	Robyn Montana Turner	1993	Ages 7-12
Father's Rubber Shoes	Yumi Heo	1995	Ages 4-8
Four Seasons of Corn: A Winnebago Tradition	Sally M. Hunter	1996	Ages 7-11
The Gift of Changing Woman	Tryntje Van Ness Seymour	1993	Ages 9-14 and older
Grandaddy's Stars	Helen V. Griffith	1995	Ages 6-8
Grandmother Bryant's Pocket	Jacqueline Brigs Martin	1996	Ages 5-7

Homeplace	Anne Shelby	1995	Ages 4-8 and older
Life around the Lake: Embroideries by the Women of Lake Patzcuaro	Maricel E. Presilla and Gloria Soto	1996	Ages 9-12 and older
My Mama Had a Dancing Heart	Libba Moore Gray	1995	Ages 7-10
Mayeros: A Yucatec Maya Family	George Ancona	1997	Ages 7-11
Patrick Desjarlait: Conversations with a Native American Artist	Neva Williams	1995	Ages 8-14 and older
Serena Katz	Charlotte Pomerantz	1992	Ages 4-7
Songs from the Loom: A Navajo Girl Learns to Weave	Monty Roessel	1995	Ages 7-11
Sugaring Season: Making Maple Syrup	Diane L. Burns	1990	Ages 6-10
Visions: Stories about Women Artists	Leslie Sills	1993	Ages 9-14 and older
Wearing a California Tradition: A Native American Basketmaker	Linda Yamane	1996	Ages 7-11
What a Wonderful World	Ashley Bryan, illustrator	1995	Ages 2-8
Working Cotton	Sherley Anne Williams	1992	Ages 6-9

Children's Trade Books with Individual Development and Identity as the Major Thematic Strand

ALL THE LIGHTS IN THE NIGHT

Arthur A. Levine. Illustrated by James E. Ransome. (Tambourine, 1991) 32 pages. ISBN: 0-688-10107-0. Level: Ages 5-9.

After the tsar spreads word that the Jews are responsible for the country's poverty, an ugly mood overwhelms a Russian village just before Hanukkah begins. Just in time, a family receives a letter containing what it thinks will be adequate money for Moses and Benjamin to join their older brother in Palestine. As they travel, the lonely boys use their grandmother's brass lamp to gain needed comfort, to sustain their faith, and, finally, to secure passage for the final leg of their perilous journey. Oil paintings reproduced in full color illustrate a story based on the experiences in 1914 of the author's grandfather and great-uncle.

ⒾⓋ ⒾⒾ Ⓥ

AMELIA'S ROAD

Linda Jacobs Altman. Illustrated by Enrique O. Sanchez. (Lee & Low, 1993) 32 pages. ISBN: 1-880000-04-0. Level: Ages 7-9.

A young child living in a Mexican migrant family hates "the road," which to her symbolizes another round of backbreaking work, degradation, and insecurity. More than anything else she would like to feel a sense of belonging in one place, but it is unlikely that will ever happen. Then she discovers the "accidental road," an overgrown path that leads to a place no one else frequents, and she claims it for her own. This poignant yet realistic story of a plucky young girl who comes up with her own solution to a problem is stunningly illustrated with full-color acrylic paintings.

ⒾⓋ ⒾⒾⒾ Ⓥ ⒾⒾ

ANGELA WEAVES A DREAM: THE STORY OF A YOUNG MAYA ARTIST

Michelle Solá. Photographs by Jeffrey Jay Foxx. (Hyperion, 1997) 47 pages. ISBN: 0-7868-2060-8. Level: Ages 8-11.

From the time she was a small child, Angela has been learning the skills of a weaver. Now this young Mayan girl has prepared her first sampler and is about to enter it in a weaving competition. But it is far more than technical expertise on which Angela will be judged. Angela's work must show she understands the seven sacred designs of San Andreas

weavers—symbols that incorporate elements of Mayan spiritual beliefs and traditions into weaving. Angela's sampler must also reflect her ability to weave these symbols—and their meanings—into an original, unified pattern, a pattern inspired by a dream. Only when Angela has mastered the technique and dreamed her first weaver's dream is she ready to make her first sampler. Accompanying a text that describes the years of Angela's education as a weaver are well-captioned photographs showing Angela and other weavers at work, and lovely up-close looks at Mayan weavings. A welcome, well-written glossary of terms relating to weaving and other facets of Angela's life is also provided.

ⒾⓋ Ⓘ

ARTIST IN OVERALLS: THE LIFE OF GRANT WOOD

John Duggleby. (Chronicle, 1996) 56 pages. ISBN: 0-8118-1242-1. Level: Ages 9-14 and older.

Although Grant Wood's "American Gothic" is known throughout the world, little or nothing about the artist who painted it has been written for children prior to now. This biography is worthy of attention. It includes more than a dozen reproductions of his works in full color and several black-and-white photographs of other works and of Wood himself. The conversational tone of the narrative will engage readers in finding out about the Iowa artist who elevated the places and people around him in his paintings during a time when the style of art called Regionalism had not reached a respected status. Source documentation and an index should have been included in this wonderfully designed book, which is, otherwise, exemplary.

 ⒾⓋ ⒾⒾ Ⓘ

AUNT FLOSSIE'S HATS (AND CRAB CAKES LATER)

Elizabeth Fitzgerald Howard. Illustrated by James E. Ransome. (Clarion Books, 1991) 32 pages. ISBN: 0-395-54682-6. Level: Ages 4-9.

Susan and her sister Sarah love to visit their Great Aunt Flossie's house each Sunday afternoon because Aunt Flossie lives in "a house crowded full of stuff and things." The sisters are particularly intrigued with Aunt Flossie's collection of hats—she has saved every hat she has ever owned and each one reminds her of a story from her past. Ransome's elegant oil paintings move easily from the present to the past as he illustrates Aunt Flossie's stories, as well as the context in which she is telling them. A skillful use of dialogue aptly portrays a strong intergenerational relationship in an African American family.

BACK HOME

Gloria Jean Pinkney. Illustrated by Jerry Pinkney. (Dial, 1992) 40 pages. ISBN: 0-8037-1168-9. Level: Ages 4-8.

Eight-year-old Ernestine travels south by train for a mid-twentieth century summer visit with relatives in rural North Carolina. Except for Cousin Jack's teasing, she immediately feels at home in her mother's childhood environs. Ernestine tries to overlook Jack's condescending attitude while exploring the farm, learning about its animals, visiting a family cemetery, and seeing the house where she was born. Period details support the text and can also be found in household objects, clothing, and vehicles so faithfully pictured in Pinkney's luminous illustrations created with pencil, colored pencils, and watercolor. Heritage, memory, renewal, and family ties are linked in a strong vignette about an African American family's warm welcome to their city relative.

BAT IN THE DINING ROOM

Crescent Dragonwagon. Illustrated by S. D. Schindler. (Marshall Cavendish, 1997) 32 pages. ISBN: 0-7614-5007-6. Level: Ages 4-8.

Pandemonium breaks out when a bat swoops into a hotel restaurant. While the staff tries to keep the customers calm, young Melissa imagines what the situation must feel like to the bat. Her empathy and quick thinking help her to figure out just what to do to help the bat find its way back outside. Schindler's colored pencil and watercolor illustrations humorously show the contrast between the panic-stricken diners and quiet, observant Melissa.

BATMAN: EXPLORING THE WORLD OF BATS

Laurence Pringle. Photographs by Merlin Tuttle. (Charles Scribner's Sons, 1991) 42 pages. ISBN: 0-684-19232-2. Level: Ages 9-11.

Bats, constituting nearly one-quarter of all mammals on earth, are often maligned and feared as revolting pests. Beginning in high school, Merlin Tuttle, an internationally recognized bat expert, devoted his life to the study of bats, and later to increasing human understanding of bat characteristics, behaviors, and their contributions to the ecosystem. Tuttle trains bats to come when called and to respond to simple hand signals, demonstrating their amazing intelligence. Human threats to bat populations are discussed and the formation and continuing efforts of Bat Conservation International's protection program is outlined. Striking clear color photographs of several species of bats help to promote Tuttle's goal of seeing bats as the unique, appealing creatures they are.

A BEAR FOR ALL SEASONS

Diane Marcial Fuchs. Illustrated by Kathryn Brown. (Henry Holt, 1995) 32 pages. ISBN: 0-8050-2139-6. Level: Ages 3-7.

Drowsy Bear is ready to snuggle beneath a thick quilt for the winter when Fox appears at the door, full of energy and ready to discuss the merits of the seasons. Agreeable Bear remembers why he enjoys each one in a fluid text with pleasant repetitions. "Are you sure?" Fox always asks, because he can only recall the problems a season presents: mud, mosquitoes, and chilly winds. Bear decides that "The company of a good friend is what I love best—no matter what the season." Hilarious images of big Bear's hairy front sticking out of his vest and bathrobe are just one aspect of the comical pictures that show how Bear enjoys himself and Fox doesn't. Brown uses watercolors and color pencil to create the cheerful pictures of two congenial woodland gents at ease.

BEIN' WITH YOU THIS WAY

W. Nikola-Lisa. Illustrated by Michael Bryant. (Lee & Low, 1994) 32 pages. ISBN: 1-880000-05-9. Level: Ages 3-6.

A rhyming, patterned text celebrates human diversity with an otherwise straightforward series of observations about physical differences. Energetic watercolor and colored pencil illustrations show children of various colors and sizes at play in a busy city park.

BILLY THE GREAT

Rosa Guy. Illustrated by Caroline Binch. (Delacorte, 1992) 32 pages. ISBN: 0-385-30666-0. Level: Ages 4-8.

From the time he was a baby, Billy's parents have had big plans for his future. When Billy was six, ten-year old Rod moved in next door. Billy's parents think Rod plays too roughly and they are wary of Rod's dad because he's a truck driver with broad shoulders and tattoos on his arms. But Billy thinks Rod is wonderful! After all, Rod always treats him like a big kid and teaches him how to do a handstand after just three tries. This appealing picture story deals with the issue of class prejudice in an urban British neighborhood. Binch's marvelous watercolor paintings of Billy (who is black) from babyhood through young childhood capture the childlike energy and openness that make him truly great.

THE BLUSHFUL HIPPOPOTAMUS

Chris Raschka. (Orchard, 1996) 32 pages. ISBN: 0-531-09532-0. Level: Ages 2-5.

When Roosevelt, a baby hippopotamus, gets things wrong (as he often does), his older sister is always standing by to point out his mistakes. "Are you blushing again, baby brother?" she asks him, looming large, and he usually is. He turns pink with embarrassment whenever she teases him. Lombard, Roosevelt's feathered friend, restores his ego by assuring him he's not blushful; he's "hopeful, mindful, thoughtful, skillful and wonderful." With every positive adjective, Roosevelt's sister gets a little smaller and the background color gets a little less pink. Raschka excels at reinforcing meaning with subtle changes in shape and color.

BRAVO, TANYA

Patricia Lee Gauch. Illustrated by Satomi Ichikawa. (Philomel, 1992) 32 pages. ISBN: 0-399-22145-X. Level: Ages 4-7.

The star of DANCE, TANYA (Philomel, 1989) still loves to dance and now she's old enough to attend ballet classes as a bonafide member. But she finds that dancing is hard work and, though she manages to keep up with her classmates, she still prefers dancing outdoors to the music in her head. Ichikawa's softly colored illustrations capture the exuberance and enthusiasm of an energetic child who loves to dance.

BROWN HONEY IN BROOMWHEAT TEA

Joyce Carol Thomas. Illustrated by Floyd Cooper. (HarperCollins, 1993) 32 pages. ISBN: 0-06-021088-5. Level: Ages 5-10.

African American experience is depicted in twelve original poems that exquisitely express feelings of pride, joy, love, wonder, sorrow, and hope, and delicately extract and magnify moments imbedded in everyday life. "I spring up from mother earth / She clothed me in her own colors / I was nourished by father sun / He glazed the pottery of my skin," begins the affirming opening poem, "Cherish Me." The simplest gestures take on the significance of ritual in "Mama": "She bows to the plant for permission / Prunes a small twig / Carries it like a healing flower / Over and over the rising road." "Family Tree" mourns loses of the past: "This forest down by the blue-green water / That first separated us / Mother from son / Father from daughter / Sister from sister . . . I look across water / And cry for our trembling / Family tree," while the title poem, speaking of the present, cautions, "There are those who / Have brewed a / Bitter potion for / Children kissed long by the sun." The final offering, "Becoming the Tea," assures that "like the steeping brew / The longer I stand / The stronger I stay." Cooper's intimate paintings warmly reflect and extend the theme of the text. Steeped in tones of brown, rust, and gold, they are themselves a celebration of African American life.

CALVIN'S CHRISTMAS WISH

Calvin Miles. Illustrated by Dolores Johnson. (Viking, 1993) 32 pages. ISBN: 0-670-84295-8. Level: Ages 5-8.

While cutting a fresh tree, collecting holly, and gathering pine cones for decorations, Calvin and his sister imagine what Santa will bring, even though Calvin not only suspects there is no Santa but also thinks that his family cannot afford a bike. This first-person story about a memorable Christmas during the 1950s in rural North Carolina suggests that a strong sense of family can be more important than having things, no matter how much one wants a specific bicycle with all the extras. The author is inspirational in telling his own story of how he studied with Literacy Volunteers at age 39 to learn to read and write. Full-color paintings provide period and regional detail and bring the autobiographical African American characters to life in this 8½ by 10¼ in. picture book.

CLAMBAKE: A WAMPANOAG TRADITION

Russell M. Peters. Photographs by John Madama. (Lerner, 1992) 48 pages. ISBN: 0-8225-2651-4. Level: Ages 7-13.

One of the first titles in an excellent new series about the observance of tribal traditions by contemporary Native children features a Wampanoag boy in Plymouth, Massachusetts. Twelve-year-old Steven learns the traditions of the appanaug (clambake) from his grandfather who has been selected as the "bakemaster" for this special ceremony to honor an important person in the tribe. Both the text and the color photographs reinforce Steven's sense of pride in his heritage, his closeness to family and friends, and his great respect for his elders and the knowledge they share with him.

CLOUDS FOR DINNER

Lynne Rae Perkins. (Greenwillow, 1997) 32 pages. ISBN: 0-688-14903-0. Level: Ages 4-8.

Growing up in an unconventional family, Janet is certain her life would be better if her parents were ordinary, like her Aunt Peppy and Uncle Tim. When she spends the weekend at her cousins' house, she admires the predictable routine of their daily life, especially the fact that they all sit around a table to eat three square meals a day. Janet romanticizes every mundane detail of Aunt Peppy's household, from her constantly ringing telephone to her recliner chair, and she voices her desire to live with her all the time. "Kids always think that about their aunts," Aunt Peppy assures her. But when Janet witnesses a natural wonder early one morning while she's still at her aunt's house, she realizes that it is her poetic mother who will appreciate her account of it. Perkins's gentle story, grounded in psychological truth, is enlivened with touches of realistic humor in both the text and the detailed watercolor illustrations.

CYNTHIA GREGORY DANCES SWAN LAKE

Cynthia Gregory. Photographs by Martha Swope. (Simon and Schuster Books for Young Readers, 1990) 48 pages. ISBN: 0-671-68786-7. Level: Ages 5-11.

Readers literally peer backstage and beyond during one day of a working ballerina's career. In full-color photographs and Gregory's words, they glimpse her participating in a morning ballet class, meeting the wardrobe mistress for a final costume fitting, giving a telephone interview to a dance critic, rehearsing for the evening performance, taking advantage of opportunities to be home with her family, getting ready to go onstage, and celebrating the new American Ballet Theatre performance of "Swan Lake." Gregory's commentary brings readers down-to-earth elements of ballet dancers typically seen by audiences as "perfect creatures who seem to float and fly with no effort at all."

DEAR BEAR

Joanna Harrison. (Carolrhoda, 1994) 32 pages. ISBN: 0-87614-839-9. Level: Ages 4-8.

Katie is afraid of the bear she imagines living in the closet under the stairs, so her mom suggests she write him a letter telling him to go away. Thus begins an engaging correspondence between the two and, after a series of letters, Katie is no longer afraid. In fact, she is anxious to meet the bear, who turns out to be a lonely teddy. Perceptive readers will no doubt realize that Katie's parents are behind it all, helping to channel Katie's imagination along a more positive route. In any case, it all works, thanks to Harrison's adept use of illustrations to show Katie's mental images of the bear growing friendlier with each turn of the page.

DIGBY

Barbara Shook Hazen. Illustrated by Barbara J. Phillips-Duke. (An I Can Read Book) (HarperCollins, 1997) 32 pages. ISBN: 0-06-026253-2. Level: Ages 4-6.

A small brown-skinned boy learns from his older sister that even though their dog can't run and jump and play ball like she once did, Digby can still be a wonderful friend. This text depicts a warm sibling relationship and is perfect for beginning readers, with short, simple sentences and colorful illustrations that distinguish which child is speaking on each page.

DOLPHIN MAN: EXPLORING THE WORLD OF DOLPHINS

Laurence Pringle. Photographs by Randall S. Wells. (Atheneum, 1995) 41 pages. ISBN: 0-689-80299-4. Level: Ages 7-11.

The fifth volume in Pringle's series about contemporary biologists at work focuses on the life and work of Randy Wells, manager of the Marine Mammal Research Program based in Sarasota, Florida. Accompanied by color photographs, a concise text describes these scientists' day-to-day work, in addition to what their research has taught them about the free-ranging dolphin community.

DOWN THE ROAD

Alice Schertle. Illustrated by E. B. Lewis. (Browndeer / Harcourt Brace, 1995) 40 pages. ISBN: 0-15-276622-7. Level: Ages 4-7.

Hetty's first solo errand is to walk down the country road to the store to buy a dozen eggs and carry them safely back home. Solemn with responsibility, Hetty walks very carefully both ways and almost makes it home without breaking a single egg until she happens on an apple tree bearing ripe delicious fruit. This enchanting story of a contemporary African American rural family is well matched with Lewis's sun-dappled watercolor illustrations that brilliantly capture the determination of a young girl out to prove herself.

ELEANOR

Barbara Cooney. (Viking, 1996) 40 pages. ISBN: 0-670-86159-6. Level: Ages 7-10.

Powerful visual design and skillfully understated text combine to introduce young readers to Eleanor Roosevelt before she became one of the most influential women of the twentieth century. In paintings that brilliantly echo the emotional tenor of the story while capturing a sense of the time and place in which she lived and the economically privileged class to which she belonged, Eleanor is pictured as a small, almost incidental figure in many of the illustrations. It is the way she felt while growing up, but when she leaves her family and America to attend boarding school in England at the age of fifteen, Eleanor begins a transformation. Under the guidance of her headmistress and mentor, Mademoiselle Souvestre, and in the loving, supportive, challenging atmosphere that her school, Allenwood, provides, she gains assuredness and self-esteem. "Mlle. Souvestre had opened the world to Eleanor." And Eleanor had opened herself to the world, as Cooney's paintings reflect, carrying herself with dignity into whatever the future would bring.

ELEANOR ROOSEVELT: A LIFE OF DISCOVERY

Russell Freedman. (Clarion, 1993) 198 pages. ISBN: 0-89919-862-7. Level: Ages 9-14 and older.

Eleanor Roosevelt's biographers are challenged to unfold how her interests and opinions affected her husband's administration between 1932 and 1945 and how her example created a new image both of the First Lady and of women in general. They must show Eleanor's evolution from uncertain child into the woman whose public leadership became a force for justice and peace within the nation and beyond. They have to interpret the social dimensions of the times when Eleanor was young, during World War II, and while the United Nations was a fledgling organization. They have to picture some of the ways she exemplified and championed racial equity while segregation still dominated public and private life. Freedman met these challenges through skillful organization of an abundance of material, a thoughtful selection of personal details, and a compelling prose narrative. His account presents documented facts and emotional truths to bring this dynamic, principled woman to life. An abundance of black-and-white archival photographs, material about Eleanor's personal home at Val-Kill, and Freedman's well-developed bibliographic essay about materials written for adults also distinguish this splendid biography.

EMILY

Michael Bedard. Illustrated by Barbara Cooney. (Doubleday, 1992) 38 pages. ISBN: 0-385-30697-0. Level: Ages 5-8.

A small girl, fearful and yet fascinated by the reclusive woman who lives in the yellow house across the street from her, asks to go along with her mother when she is invited to come play the piano for "the Mystery." Although the shy hostess never shows herself during their visit, the child creeps up the stairs and encounters her sitting on a chair in the upstairs corridor. A lyrical story, based on an imagined meeting between Emily Dickinson and a neighbor child, is exquisitely illustrated with softly textured acrylic and pastel paintings on China silk.

FATHER AND SON

Denize Lauture. Illustrated by Jonathan Green. (Philomel, 1992) 32 pages. ISBN: 0-399-21867-X. Level: Ages 4-9.

A new understanding of a fundamental relationship springs from the brevity of one poem and its unity with oil paintings that illustrate each of its lines. Specificity of setting and race are balanced by the universal theme expressed in this elegant full-color picture book. The poet's dedication statement emphasizes the responsibility of "ever decent man" to the children of today: "The shadow of one / Touching / The shadow of the other." Lauture is a native of rural Haiti whose works appear in three languages; this book represents the first work for children by this poet and artist.

GEORGIA O'KEEFFE

Linda Lowery. Illustrated by Rochelle Draper. (Carolrhoda, 1996) 47 pages. ISBN: 0-87614-860-7. Level: Ages 6-8.

"Georgia O'Keeffe held the bone up high. She peered through the hole in the middle." Lowery's uncomplicated prose captures the spirit of O'Keeffe's life and art in this welcome biography for young readers. As an art student, O'Keeffe, who was born in Sun Prairie, Wisconsin, was skilled at pleasing others, but it wasn't until she decided to draw to please herself that her true talent and vision began to emerge. Color illustrations depicting O'Keeffe, her friends and companions, and her art appear on each double-page spread of this profile that emphasizes her fulfillment as an artist and her singular career.

GEORGIA O'KEEFFE

Robyn Montana Turner. (Little, Brown & Co., 1991) 32 pages. ISBN: 0-316-856495-7. Level: Ages 7-12.

Biographical details about O'Keeffe's childhood in Sun Prairie, Wisconsin, adolescence in Chatham, Virginia, and adulthood in New York City and New Mexico are woven into a fine introduction to her art. Turner stresses life events that influenced the development of O'Keeffe's distinctive style and unique vision, in addition to her struggles to prove herself as an artist in a world that did not welcome creative women. Several of O'Keeffe's most famous paintings are reproduced in full color to illustrate the range of her artistic ingenuity.

THE GIFT OF CHANGING WOMAN

Tryntje Van Ness Seymour. Illustrated by Apache artists. (Henry Holt, 1993) 38 pages. ISBN: 0-8050-2577-4. Level: Ages 9-14 and older.

A coming of age ritual that transforms Apache girls into women is the focus of an unusual book respectfully written by a non-Native woman with the permission, cooperation, and approval of Apache elders. Although the first two days of the ceremony are private and sacred (and are not described in the book for this reason), the last two days consist of a public celebration. First-person accounts by Apache women recalling details of their own ceremonies and explanations of ritual meaning by Apache medicine man Philip Cassadore are woven together with a straightforward narrative by the author who has been an invited guest at many of the ceremonies. Visual interpretations of the proceedings by ten Apache artists add another layer of authenticity.

GINGERBREAD DAYS

Joyce Carol Thomas. Illustrated by Floyd Cooper. (Joanna Cotler Books / HarperCollins, 1995) 32 pages. ISBN: 0-06-023469-5. Level: Ages 3-7.

From a "gingered" January to a firelit December, a boy experiences who he is: a beloved son and grandson, a unique individual, and a proud young man of African American heritage. In January, Grandma tells the boy that the gingerbread man looks just like him. During August, "Grandpa spreads a pallet / stitched with Buffalo Soldiers / for a bed / 'Oklahoma cowboys,' he says, / With a dark man at the head.'" And in December, Daddy's "chapped hands are brave / With work / Rough with knowing / How to keep a family from freezing / How to keep a young mind growing." Cooper's paintings and Thomas's poems form a picture-book companion to their earlier collection featuring a girl, BROWN HONEY IN BROOMWHEAT TEA (HarperCollins, 1993).

GREAT WOMEN IN THE STRUGGLE

Toyomi Igus, editor. (Just Us Books, 1991) 107 pages. ISBN: 0-940975-27-0. Level: Age 7 and older.

The accomplishments of eighty-four African and African American women from past centuries and present decades are chronicled in eighty-four inspiring, straight-forward paragraphs, each illustrated with a black-and-white photographic or hand-rendered portrait. Chapter headings convey the import and spirit of their achievements: Freedom Fighters—Breaking Down Barriers, Educators—Building Strong Foundations, Writers & Fine Artists—The Power of Creativity, Performing Artists—Bearing Witness Through Self-Expression, Athletes—The Spirit of Champions, Entrepreneurs—Taking Care of Business, Lawyers & Policy Makers—Forging Equal Justice, and Scientists & Healers—Exploring Without Boundaries. An African American historical chronology, a bibliography of related children's books, an index, and source notes for quoted material enrich this book for reading, reference, and reflection.

HAIRS / PELITOS

Sandra Cisneros. Illustrated by Terry Ybanez. (Apple Soup / Alfred A. Knopf, 1994) 32 pages. ISBN: 0-679-96171-2. Level: Ages 3-7.

A young Latino lyrically describes the hair of every member of her family, as each is distinctively unique.

She especially delights in her mama's hair, which has "the warm smell of bread before you bake it / . . . the smell when she makes room for you on her side of the bed." This eloquently spare celebration of differences within one close-knit, loving family first appeared as a short chapter in Cisneros' adult novella *House On Mango Street*. For this picture-book edition the text is printed in Spanish and English and the striking illustrations playfully extend the theme of individuality.

HATTIE AND THE WILD WAVES: A STORY FROM BROOKLYN

Barbara Cooney. (Viking, 1990) 40 pages. ISBN: 0-670-83056-9. Level: Ages 6-9.

Little Hattie always loved painting. Every experience gave her new images to put into her pictures. The specific details of a German-born family's increasing luxury on the East Coast a century ago are meticulously recorded in full-color paintings. Hattie's in-born vocation is expressed through her developing sense of independence and individuality as a privileged woman living in a time when sheer will is required to listen to one's heart … and to the wild waves which represent Hattie's inner turmoil.

HOW I WAS ADOPTED

Joanna Cole. Illustrated by Maxie Chambliss. (Morrow, 1995) 48 pages. ISBN: 0-688-11930-1. Level: Ages 3-7.

In what is undoubtedly one of the most upbeat and positive books for young children about adoption, an outgoing little girl named Samantha tells the straightforward story of how she was adopted. Cole's simple first-person text moves back and forth between general and specific, sometimes pausing to direct a question at the reader ("Do you know how old you were when you were adopted?"). Engaging watercolor illustrations suggest a biracial protagonist, as well as an interracial extended family. In a five-page "Note to Families" at the book's opening, the author gives general information about answering children's questions in addition to suggestions for extending the text to encourage family discussion about adoption.

HOW MY FAMILY LIVES IN AMERICA

Susan Kuklin. (Bradbury, 1992) 32 pages. ISBN: 0-02-751239-8. Level: Ages 4-7.

Three young children whose parents immigrated to the United States (from Senegal, Puerto Rico, and Taiwan) are featured in this appealing photo-essay that allows the children to speak for themselves about what they are learning from their parents and grandparents. In an author's note at the end of the book, Kuklin explains her intention: "To show how families impart a sense of identity to their young children." The book concludes with a simple recipe from each child's culture.

HOW YOU WERE BORN

Joanna Cole. Photographs by Margaret Miller. (Morrow, 1993) 48 pages. ISBN: 0-688-12060-1. Level: Ages 3-6.

"Before you were born, you grew in a special place inside your mother's body called her uterus, or womb." Written with simple, direct language, Cole's book for parents to share with children was designed to help answer the question "Where did I come from?" Cole explains the biological aspects of reproduction and fetal development with the help of simple drawings showing the union of an ovum and sperm and remarkable photographs taken inside the womb. The happiness and excitement parents feel over a child's birth is also discussed, accompanied by color photographs showing parents preparing for and then celebrating the arrival of a child. This newly revised and updated edition shows parents and babies of diverse racial backgrounds and firmly establishes the importance of the one special child with whom the book is being shared.

I AM A JESSE WHITE TUMBLER

Diane Schmidt. (Albert Whitman, 1990) 40 pages. ISBN: 0-8075-3444-7. Level: Ages 7-12.

Kenyon Conner tells about being a member of the Chicago-based tumbling team. The combination of personal discipline, tumbling expertise, team cooperation, and showmanship required of all Jesse White Tumblers is clear in thirty-four color photographs showing the internationally respected Tumblers performing at city neighborhood events as well as in metropolitan arenas. Kenyon's upbeat awareness of the far-reaching impact of team activity for his life and for others develops an important dimension of an absorbing $8\frac{1}{4}$ x 9 in. photodocumentary book.

I HAD A LOT OF WISHES

James Stevenson. (Greenwillow, 1995) 32 pages. ISBN: 0-688-13706-7. Level: Ages 10 and older.

Stevenson's gentle, perceptive recollections of childhood are brimming with the anticipation, disappointments, and satisfaction that all children know come with wishing for everything from the smallest of treasures to the biggest of hopes. Delicate watercolor illustrations enhance the intimacy of this autobiographical picture book that was preceded by earlier memoirs, also published by Greenwillow, including WHEN I WAS NINE (1986), HIGHER ON THE DOOR (1987), July (1990), DON'T YOU KNOW THERE'S A WAR ON? (1992), and FUN-NO FUN (1994).

I WANT TO BE

Thylias Moss. Illustrated by Jerry Pinkney. (Dial, 1993) 32 pages. ISBN: 0-8037-1287-1. Level: Ages 3-6.

A young African American girl ponders the answer to the question "What do you want to be?" and her imagination is alive with possibility: "I want to be big but not so big that a mountain or a mosque or a synagogue seems small. / I want to be strong but not so strong that a kite seems weak." Each stirring dream is expressed in Moss's exquisite, sensual writing that sends the child's strands of thought soaring into a realm where anything is possible, and then tethers them to concrete images that make what can only be imagined something tangible after all. Pinkney's illustrations, grounded in the writer's images, are filled with movement, color, and light.

I WAS A TEENAGE PROFESSIONAL WRESTLER

Ted Lewin. (Orchard, 1993) 128 pages. ISBN: 0-531-05477-2. Level: Ages 8-14.

Portrait of the Artist as a Young … pro wrestler? It's true! Before he ever signed a contract to illustrate a children's book, Lewin was a teenage professional wrestler. It was a profession he came by naturally; he had a wrestler's build and his two older brothers, Mark and Donn, were in the business, as was his brother-in-law, Dangerous Danny McShain. But between matches, in locker rooms, and at ringside, he was always sketching and painting pictures of the other wrestlers. With humor and understanding, Lewin gives us a first-hand look at the world of the professional wrestler back in the early 1950s. Numerous documentary black-and-white photographs and, of course, original sketches and oil paintings round out the portrait.

I'LL SEE YOU IN MY DREAMS

Mavis Jukes. Illustrated by Stacey Schuett. (Alfred A. Knopf, 1993) 32 pages. ISBN: 0-679-82690-4. Level: Ages 4-8.

A young girl contemplates how she will say goodbye to her dying uncle in this original, sensitive short fiction work about a child dealing with grief and loss. First, she imagines what she would do if she could: "If she were a skywriter … Across the face of the moon she'd write—in silver letters: 'I love you.' And then: 'I'll see you in my dreams.'" Later, she thinks about what it will really be like when she goes to see him: "She would fly across the country on an airliner with a vapor trail behind it—a 767 like her uncle used to fly." In a brilliantly styled and structured story, Jukes uses two simple sentences firmly stated ("She was not a skywriter. She was a little kid.") to connect the first and second parts of the story, like the fuselage connects the wings of a plane. Jukes uses conditionally stated action to place a slight temporal distance between the child and the overwhelming reality she is about to face, making a difficult, frightening experience less threatening. Soft, exquisitely colored full-page illustrations enhance the warmth of this unique book.

IMANI'S GIFT AT KWANZAA

Denise Burden-Patmon. Illustrated by Floyd Cooper. (Simon & Schuster, 1992) 23 pages. ISBN: 0-671-79841-3. Level: Ages 3-8.

While Imani's grandmother M'dear braids small red, black, and green beads into her hair, they talk about the seven-day African American December celebration they'll soon begin with family and friends. Imani looks forward to everything except being with Enna, a mean tease. How can Imani give formal Kwanzaa appreciation to Enna, one of the watoto (children) coming to their home tonight? M'dear tells Imani that Enna hasn't known much love: "She has had no one to believe in her . . . to tell her who she is and where she came from." Cooper's full-color illustrations show Kwanzaa details and complement this warm story created under the auspices of the Children's Museum in Boston. A glossary defines the fifteen Swahili words integrated within the English text. The Seven Principles are listed at the end of this durable paperback edition.

IN DADDY'S ARMS I AM TALL: AFRICAN AMERICANS CELEBRATING FATHERS

Javaka Steptoe, illustrator. (Lee & Low, 1997) 32 pages. ISBN: 1-880000-31-8. Level: Age 8 and older.

Thirteen African American writers explore and celebrate Black fathers in a collection that is illustrated with power and distinction by artist Javaka Steptoe. In poems that feel intensely personal at the same time they speak to broader cultural experiences, the poets write from the perspective of "child" in varying voices. Sometimes the choice is childlike and youthful and filled with pride and delight, as in the title poem, "in daddy's arms," by Folami Abiade or "Tickle Tickle" by Dakari Hru; and sometimes it speaks straight from adulthood or echoes adult understanding of a world in which Black men face great struggle, as in Davida Adedjoouma's "Artist to Artist" or "The Things in Black Men's Closets" by E. Ethelbert Miller. Collectively these works speak to dignity and grace, comfort and guidance, joy and heartbreak. The poems are paired with singular collage illustrations by Steptoe. His artwork takes each poem to heart and to mind, revealing insights into the words and extending the emotional experience on every two-page spread. Steptoe used a wide range of media to create the collages, from torn paper and paint to found objects such as sand, seeds, nails, and pennies. Like the words they accompany, the illustrations are connected to life in a way that is both immediate and revealing.

INSECTS ARE MY LIFE

Megan McDonald. Illustrated by Paul Brett Johnson. (Orchard, 1995) 32 pages. ISBN: 0-531-06874-9. Level: Ages 4-7.

Amanda Frankenstein is a sturdy little girl with glasses and a singular passion: "Insects are my life," she tells everyone she meets, and indeed they are. When she's not observing live bugs or collecting dead ones, she dreams of insects, and her obsessions sometimes makes life difficult. With gentle humor stemming from skillful use of exaggeration, McDonald celebrates the spirit of a young child bent on one particular interest while Johnson's sunny illustrations perfectly capture Amanda in her many moods.

JACQUES-HENRI LARTIGUE: BOY WITH A CAMERA

John Cech. (Four Winds Press, 1994) 32 pages. ISBN: 0-02-718136-7. Level: Ages 8-11.

Born in Paris in 1902, Jacques-Henri Lartigue got his first camera when he was seven. "I know that many, many things are going to ask me to have their pictures taken and I will take them all," he wrote in his diary. Young Lartigue's keen eye and innate sense of when to click the shutter resulted in photographs that suspend movement and transcend time. He captured his family and friends in the midst of action and forever froze the moment, creating images that are humorous, exciting, and sometimes even eerie. Lartigue's black-and-white photographs are the cornerstone of a wholly approachable and engaging text telling about his early life and the pictures he took.

KINAALDA: A NAVAJO GIRL GROWS UP

Monty Roessel. (Lerner, 1993) 48 pages. ISBN: 0-8225-2655-7. Level: Ages 7-11 and older.

Thirteen-year-old Celinda McKelvey is about to participate in her Kinaalda, a Navajo coming-of-age ceremony for girls. Over two days, with the support of her extended family and friends, she will run a race, prepare a corncake to be baked in the earth, and stay up through the night as traditional prayers are sung, all the while learning more about the Navajo culture. Celinda's preparations for and participation in this important event are recorded through documentary photographs and text that unite the history of the ceremony and the Navajo people with a girls' transition into womanhood.

KISSES FROM ROSA

Petra Mathers. (Apple Soup / Knopf, 1995) 40 pages. ISBN: 0-679-82686-6. Level: Ages 4-8.

When Rosa's mother gets sick, Rosa is sent to live with relatives she barely knows: her Aunt Mookie and Cousin Birgit who live on a farm in the Black Forest. Even though she misses her mother terribly, Rosa soon begins to feel at home on the farm as she gets to know the people and animals around her, and she has her weekly letters from Mami to look forward to. Mathers has based the story on her own childhood experiences; she was often sent away while her mother struggled with tuberculosis. Her stylized gouache paintings skillfully express a combination of nostalgia, homesickness, and a childlike excitement at first-time encounters.

LIVES OF THE ATHLETES: THRILLS, SPILLS (AND WHAT THE NEIGHBORS THOUGHT)

Kathleen Krull. Illustrated by Kathryn Hewitt. (Harcourt, Brace, 1997) 96 pages. ISBN: 0-15-200806-3. Level: Ages 11-14 and older.

Skater Sonja Henie found "a life without whirling was 'colorless' and 'pointless.'" To prepare Jackie Robinson for the racism and hostility he would face as the first black man to play in major league baseball, his team manager and others jeered and staged ugly scenes. When track-and-field superstar Wilma Rudolph first began speaking in public, "it scared her more than Olympic competition." These are just a few of the fascinating tidbits that Krull has compiled for the latest "Lives of" book, in which she once again teams with artist Kathryn Hewitt to provide offbeat looks at the lives of famous people. The short vignettes in this book profile twenty athletes from a variety of sports. Krull has a gift for digging up interesting facts and condensing them into a rapid-fire narrative that is guaranteed to hold the attention of young readers, regardless of their interest in sports.

LOVE LETTERS

Arnold Adoff. Illustrated by Lisa Dersimini. (Blue Sky/Scholastic, 1997) 32 pages. ISBN: 0-590-48478-8. Level: Ages 9-12.

Moving through the worlds of school, home, and neighborhood, twenty short poems from Adoff look at classroom crushes, playground romances, the essence of family relationships, and more with humor and touching sincerity. Each poem is structured as a love letter, complete with salutation and closure. "Dear Playground Snow Girl" begins one poem that is signed "Your Frozen Friend: / Frosty the Snow Boy." Another that starts "Dear Teacher" and is written in the voice of a shy student closes with "Yours As a Mouse." The poems focusing on families include "Dear Gram:" in which a boy who loves his grandmother's cookies concludes, "I am / even / full of love / when all your / jars are empty." With illustrations rendered in a variety of media, from torn paper and found-object collage to painting to photographs, Desimini has created a distinctive, clever work of art to accompany each amusing, appealing poem.

LOU GEHRIG: THE LUCKIEST MAN

David A. Adler. Illustrated by Terry Widener. (Gulliver/Harcourt Brace, 1997) 32 pages. ISBN: 0-15-200523-4. Level: Ages 7-11 and older.

Adler's picture-book biography deftly characterizes the hard work and uncomplicated integrity that made baseball player Lou Gehrig a man viewed with genuine respect and affection by his teammates and fans. As a child, Gehrig didn't miss a day of school in eight years. As an adult, "The boy who never missed a day of grade school became a man who never missed a game." Gehrig finally benched himself "for the good of the team" when his play suffered from the as-yet-undiagnosed amyotrophic lateral sclerosis, or ALS (today also known as Lou Gehrig's Disease). Adler also writes of the dignity with which Gehrig faced death. "We have much to be thankful for," he would write in cards to his friends at a time when the disease was rapidly progressing. Accompanying Adler's understated text are Widener's bold acrylic paintings. The stylized art perfectly captures a feeling of the past at the same time as it embraces Gehrig's humanity.

MAC & MARIE & THE TRAIN TOSS SURPRISE

Elizabeth Fitzgerald Howard. Illustrated by Gail Gordon Carter. (Four Winds, 1993) 32 pages. ISBN: 0-02-744640-9. Level: Ages 5-8.

Anticipation builds on a warm summer night long ago as Mac and Marie wait eagerly for the Florida train making its way north to rumble by the big house where they live near Baltimore. Uncle Clem has a job on the train and has promised to toss them a surprise as it passes! Big brother Mac isn't as fidgety as Marie, but even he has a hard time waiting. As the two children pass the time, Mac dreams of the day when he, too, will work on the railroad as a fireman or an engineer, traveling across the land. Skillfully paced text measures the waiting time perfectly, slowly building to the moment when the train finally approaches, and marking its passing in a rush of words that leaves the reader breathless. Afterwards, there is Mac and Marie's discovery of Uncle Clem's package. The beautiful shell inside is a solid reminder to Mac of the places he will someday see. Lovely colored pencil and watercolor illustrations by Carter illuminate the beauty and mystery of this midsummer night, and echo the warmth of the African American family's relationships depicted in the text.

MARY CASSATT

Robyn Montana Turner. (Little, Brown, 1992) 32 pages. ISBN: 0-316-85650-9. Level: Ages 7-12.

"I rejected conventional art. I began to live." These words by Mary Cassatt open a picture book biography about an American artist whose paintings and career broke new ground in the history of art and of women. Throughout her career, Cassatt encountered many barriers because she was female, but yet she preferred her art to the social life open to her through her family. Carefully reproduced full-color paintings, well-written appreciative comments, and an emphasis on life events influencing Cassatt's artistic development mark this and Turner's other excellent books about women artists published in 1991, *Rosa Bonheur* and *Georgia O'Keeffe*.

MEET DANITRA BROWN

Nikki Grimes. Illustrated by Floyd Cooper. (Lothrop, Lee and Shepard, 1994) 32 pages. ISBN: 0-688-12074-1. Level: Ages 7-10.

Thirteen poems tell about the friendship of two young African American girls living in a city neighborhood. Title character Danitra Brown has a strong sense of heritage, self, and self-respect, giving her a dynamic presence. Her best friend, Zuri Jackson, is shy and less confident, but it is her narrative voice that carries each poem, the themes of which extend from their friendship and families to growing up African American and female. Together, Grimes's free-verse text and Cooper's warm-toned paintings capture the moments of joy and moments of sadness that best friends share.

MINTY: THE STORY OF YOUNG HARRIET TUBMAN

Alan Schroeder. Illustrated by Jerry Pinkney. (Dial, 1996) 40 pages. ISBN: 0-8037-1889-6. Level: Ages 7-10.

"I'm gonna run away," the sad, angry Minty tells her mother after the Missus throws her rag doll into the fire. Later, after she is beaten by the overseer, the young girl who is a slave on a Maryland plantation tells her parents once again that she will flee. Realizing their daughter's determination, they subtly but deliberately begin to show her things she will need to know to survive: how to find her way north by moss on trees and one shining star, how to swim a river, how to find food in the forest. Schroeder's moving story never strays from what is possible in this fictional biography of the life of young Harriet Tubman. Pinkney's full-color paintings are rendered in pencil, colored pencil, and watercolor. Light and dark

dance across the pages of this 11¾ x 9¾ in. book as he skillfully and beautifully brings his vision of Minty's story to life.

MIRETTE ON THE HIGH WIRE

Emily Arnold McCully. (G. P. Putnam's Sons, 1992) 32 pages. ISBN: 0-399-22130-1. Level: Ages 6-9.

Mirette works daily in her mother's boardinghouse doing laundry, cleaning, assisting in the kitchen, and running errands. Most of the guests come from the entertainment world, so someone finally recognizes the man who had wanted to take his meals alone in his secluded room. After seeing him balance himself on the clothesline, Mirette begs the retired high-wire walker to teach her that skill. "Once you start, your feet are never happy again on the ground," he tells the child who then practices in secret. Nineteenth-century Paris is the setting for this full-color story about overcoming fear, taking risks, and establishing trust.

MOTHER GAVE A SHOUT: POEMS BY WOMEN AND GIRLS

Susanna Steele and Morag Styles, editors. Illustrated by Jane Ray. (Volcano Press, 1991) 126 pages. ISBN: 0-912078-90-1. Level: Ages 9-13 and older.

One hundred poems about identity, nature, women's work, dreaming, grandmothers, mothers, and daughters are gathered from a wide range of traditional and contemporary sources, featuring such poets as Maya Angelou, Nikki Giovanni, Judy Grahn, Grace Nichols, Sylvia Plath, Sappho, Alice Walker, and Charlotte Zolotow. Exquisite black-and-white vignettes reinforce the multicultural focus and enhance the celebratory tone.

MY BUDDY

Audrey Osofsky. Illustrated by Ted Rand. (Henry Holt, 1992) 32 pages. ISBN: 0-8050-1747-X. Level: Ages 4-9.

A wheelchair-mobile boy with muscular dystrophy feels excited about getting his first service dog, a golden retriever named Buddy. After he undergoes two weeks of training at a special camp that teaches him how to command Buddy, he's ready to take the dog home and adjust to the differences Buddy makes in his life around the house, in school, and out in the neighborhood. Realistic watercolor paintings illustrate this fine story about a spirited young boy and his trusted companion.

MY FELLOW AMERICANS: A FAMILY ALBUM

Alice Provensen. (Browndeer / Harcourt Brace, 1995) 61 pages. ISBN: 0-15-276642-1. Level: Ages 5-14 and older.

Provensen writes, "Like all families, my American family has its rich uncles and poor relations, its atheists and believers, its scoundrels and bigots, its gifted and compassionate. . . these relatives are individuals, idiosyncratic and exceptional . . . somehow larger than life and have come to represent our myths and legends, our fantasies and foibles." A detailed table of contents, end pages with portraiture, and a final written narrative further embellish the hundreds of images Provensen created using India ink and oil paint in this 11¾ x 11¾ in. text. The scope of her monumental approach to interpreting the American Experience can be seen in Provensen's provocative organization of her material. The first four titles of her twenty-three album themes demonstrate this: Free Spirits, Rebel Voices; Pilgrims and Puritans, Quakers and Shakers; Maverick Ministers, Guiding Lights; and Impassioned Fights for Freedom and Equal Rights. Sequoyah, "Native American Scholar," appears along with Anne Sullivan as guiding lights. Little Big Man is listed among the warriors and patriots. Margaret Sanger emerges with other radical reformers and humanitarians, while J. Edgar Hoover is pictured with villains and rogues, unnamed female moonshiners, and celebrity hoodlums. Lassie shares a page with Mae West and Jack Benny. Satchel Paige can be discovered, and so can Gertrude Stein, Jim Henson, and George Washington. Like all albums, this treasury is worth countless browsing hours by children of varying ages. Although they and their adults will have varying opinions on the comparative importance, inclusion, and/or exclusion of these "fellow Americans," all will be stimulated to think, find out more, and maybe even create their own categories and lists.

MY MAMA SINGS

Jeanne Whitehouse Peterson. Illustrated by Sandra Speidel. (HarperCollins, 1994) 32 pages. ISBN: 0-06-023859-3. Level: Ages 4-7.

"My mama sings me no new songs. We get along with used tunes from the radio, and hymns she learned with the Harmony Choir . . . She has one song for when daffodils are blooming, and winter is over, and everything's turning green, green, green—and one for hot, hot summer nights when I'm too sticky to sleep.

Then my mama sings me the same soft blues her mama taught her. Low and slow, the wavery tune smoothes the warm sheets in my tiny room." A poetic text describes the loving relationship between a young African American boy and his single-parent mother, and the special role that music plays in their lives. When the mother loses her job, she comes home too sad to sing, and in his need for reassurance the little boy imagines his own song to make his mother happy again. Speidel's warm, colorful paintings fill many of the two-page spreads. In some instances, the paintings make it difficult to read the words from a distance, but it will not detract from sharing this lyrically written picture book one on one.

MY NAME IS MARIA ISABEL

Alma Flor Ada. Illustrated by K. Dyble Thompson. (Atheneum, 1993) 57 pages. ISBN: 0-689-31517-1. Level: Ages 7-9.

"We already have two Marias in this class. Why don't we call you Mary instead?" So begins the first day at a new school for nine-year-old Maria Isabel Salazar Lopez, who is proud of her real name and the Puerto Rican family heritage it represents. Maria Isabel can't get used to the strange new name, Mary Lopez, but she is shy and doesn't know how to tell her teacher. If that weren't enough, her mother gets a job and is no longer at home when Maria Isabel finishes school each day. Maria Isabel's struggle to adapt to changes, and to find her voice, is at the center of this inviting story exploring important issues of identity and understanding.

NANA'S BIRTHDAY PARTY

Amy Hest. Illustrated by Amy Schwartz. (Morrow, 1993) 32 pages. ISBN: 0-688-07498-7. Level: Ages 4-8.

Every year just before her birthday, Nana posts a list for her children and grandchildren regarding the family celebration: "No gum. No jeans. No presents (except those you make yourself)." And every year Maggie and her cousin Brette compete with each other to see who can make the best gift. Maggie is good at writing stories and Brette is good at painting pictures, and just when the competition is becoming unbearable for both girls, they decide to collaborate and make the best present ever. Schwartz's watercolor paintings are filled with details of life within a close-knit extended family living in New York City.

NIGHT DRIVING

John Coy. Illustrated by Peter McCarty. (Henry Holt, 1996) 32 pages. ISBN: 0-8050-2931-1. Level: Ages 4-8.

A first-time author and a first-time illustrator make a promising debut in a gentle, realistic portrayal of a father-son relationship. The baseball-capped narrator describes a car trip with his dad in which the two drive all night to get to the mountains for a camping trip. Listening to a baseball game on the radio eats up the miles for a while but once they get out of the station's range, the two must work together to keep each other awake by telling stories, singing cowboy songs, and playing alphabet games. It's clear that they would enjoy each other's company at any time, but the night driving awakens a sense of adventure and heightens the closeness between them. McCarty's dramatic black-and-white pencil illustrations aptly depict scenes lit only by headlights and moonlight, echoing the intimate mood of the text.

THE OLD DOG

Charlotte Zolotow. Illustrated by James Ransome. (HarperCollins, 1995) 32 pages. ISBN: 0-06-024409-7. Level: Ages 3-8.

When Ben awakens one morning, he finds that his dog doesn't respond with the usual tail wagging when he pets her. He calls his father from the breakfast table to ask why. "She's dead," his father says. All day long Ben thinks of his dog and the things they used to do together. Zolotow's outstanding text explains and comforts simultaneously while Ransome's detailed oil paintings aptly show the sadness of a young African American boy grieving the death of a beloved pet.

OWEN

Kevin Henkes. (Greenwillow, 1993) 24 pages. ISBN: 0-688-11450-4. Level: Ages 3-8.

Owen the mouse and Fuzzy the blanket have been constant companions for a lifetime. "Fuzzy goes where I go," Owen asserts. And Fuzzy does with little fuss or bother until nosy Mrs. Tweezers from next-door comments that Owen is too old to cling to a security blanket. With their neighbor's helpful advice, Owen's parents try every trick in the book to separate the two, but Owen always manages to outsmart them. The situation seems hopeless until Owen's mother comes up

with a solution that makes everyone happy. Black pen and watercolor paintings add touches of humor to the marvelously plotted, skillfully worded story with universal appeal for the heroic little mouse in every child.

A PICTURE BOOK OF JESSE OWENS

David A. Adler. Illustrated by Robert Casilla. (Holiday House, 1992) 32 pages. ISBN: 0-8234-0966-X. Level: Ages 5-9.

An easy biography of the Olympic medal-winning sprinter and champion of the long jump recounts some of the childhood barriers overcome by this amazing African American athlete with "lucky legs." Jesse Owens' accomplishments at the 1936 Olympics in Berlin led to him being called the "World's Fastest Human" for many years. Adler's brief biography and page of notes point out racist and anti-Semitic occurrences during the 1936 Olympics, as well as the fact that this honored son of a former sharecropper faced prejudice afterward at home. Profusely illustrated with Casilla's watercolor paintings, the text also includes a brief chronology.

ROSA BONHEUR

Robyn Montana Turner. (Little, Brown & Co., 1991) 32 pages. ISBN: 0-316-85648-7. Level: Ages 7-12.

Known for her strikingly realistic paintings of animals and nature, Rosa Bonheur became the most celebrated member of an artistic family living in nineteenth century France. In the 1830s, painter Raymond Bonheur recognized that his young daughter Rosa was an enormously gifted artist. Throughout her childhood and adolescence, he saw to it that she received the formal art education generally denied to girls and women. By the time she was twenty-three years old, she had already achieved fame in the art world and was able to earn her living as an artist for the rest of her life. Turner's concise biography, generously illustrated with reproductions of the Bonheur family artwork, traces the life and work of a true visionary who overcame many barriers to pursue the work she loved best.

THE SECRET BOX

Gail Pearson. (Jean Karl/Atheneum, 1997) 119 pages. ISBN: 0-689-81379-1. Level: Ages 10-13 and older.

Five loosely connected short stories capture moments of revelation in the lives of their young protagonists. In "The Secret Box," twelve-year-old Taylor has a crush on her fifteen-year-old brother's best friend. When they invite her to an outing in San Francisco, however, she sees her brother and his friend in a new—and painful—light. Taylor's friend Lindsey gets a surprising new perspective on her own big brother, Eric, in the hilarious "Cousin Dolores" when a somber funeral for her aunt's dog (Cousin Dolores) turns into an outrageous embarrassment for Lindsey, until she is saved by Eric's unexpected kindness. In "The Year of the Pig" and "Teacher of the Year," Eric must deal with embarrassments of his own, trying to maintain his dignity and composure, first during a bout of serious, unrequited love, and later when dealing with the hurt and confusion that comes when an idolized teacher proves to be fallible. The final offering, "The Magic Box," picks up the strands of the opening story as Taylor longs for her brother's attention at the same time as she struggles to make sense of his growing anger. When he lashes out at a defenseless cat that Taylor has befriended, Taylor strikes back in a singular act of nonviolence that carries the weight of ritual and the momentary power of transformation. Pearson has created a set of wholly believable characters and relationships in this fine collection of stories.

SHORTCUT

Donald Crews. (Greenwillow, 1992) 32 pages. ISBN: 0-688-06436-1. Level: Ages 6-9.

In a companion book to BIGMAMA's (Greenwillow, 1991), Crews recounts a dramatic event remembered from a childhood summer on Bigmama's farm. As darkness falls one night, seven children decide to take a dangerous shortcut home along the train tracks to save time. When they hear the distant whistle of a freight train, they at first try to outrun the approaching train, but are finally forced to slide down the steep slope at the side of the tracks to avoid catastrophe. Five wordless double-page spreads of the passing train cars underscore the relief and the terror of the children who are humbled by their close brush with disaster. "We walked home without a word … We didn't tell anyone. We didn't talk about what happened for a very long time."

SKY PIONEER: A PHOTOBIOGRAPHY OF AMELIA EARHART

Corinne Szabo. Foreword by Linda Finch. (National Geographic Society, 1997) 62 pages. ISBN: 0-7922-3737-4. Level: Ages 7-11 and older.

Beautiful production distinguishes this photobiography of aviator Amelia Earhart. The stunning jacket, the embossed airplane on the cover of the bound book, and sky-blue endpapers all are an inviting starting point for a journey through Earhart's life. A wonderful graphic design has placed one or more large black-and-white photos, tinted a cloud-like shade of blue, on every two-page spread. The photos are sometimes accompanied by maps or quotes from Earhart, and always carefully captioned. The skillfully written text, like the photographs, documents Earhart's life from childhood to her final flight and disappearance and is especially suited to young readers with its engaging, appreciative tone. A chronology and sources are provided at the book's end, as well as an afterword that details theories about what happened to Earhart on her last flight and concludes that the real afterword to Earhart's story is not her disappearance but her legacy as a pioneering woman of the air.

THE SNOW LADY

Shirley Hughes. (Lothrop, Lee & Shepard, 1990) 24 pages. ISBN: 0-688-09874-6. Level: Ages 3-7.

Until Mum returns each day, Samantha spends the time after school with their next-door neighbor Mrs. Dean. Sam's dog Micawber is definitely not welcome near the clean, orderly home and neither are any other lively Trotter Street children or their pets. One afternoon before Christmas, Sam and her friend Barney create a snow lady and name it "Mrs. Mean." Sam later realizes that the labeled snow figure is hurtful and makes a valiant effort to keep Mrs. Dean from seeing it. The neighborhood community of ANGEL MAE (Lothrop, 1989) and BIG CONCRETE LORRY (Lothrop, 1990) is the locale for the small, ordinary incident from which Sam grows in a big way.

SUN & SPOON

Kevin Henkes. (Greenwillow, 1997) 135 pages. ISBN: 0-688-15232-5. Level: Ages 9-12.

Although the rest of his family seems to have adjusted to Gram's death, ten-year-old Spoon continues to grieve quietly two months later. His fear that he will begin to forget his grandmother becomes almost an obsession with him as he searches for the perfect memento, something private that will always remind him of her. He thinks he has found just the right thing when he takes her favorite deck of playing cards, the one with a picture of a sun on the back of each card, from the bottom drawer in her dining room cabinet. And, at first, things seem perfect: sleeping with the deck under his pillow inspires dreams of Gram and sharpens his memory. But when his grandfather announces that the deck is missing, Spoon is filled with remorse and worry. Henkes's eloquently spare novel shows his deep understanding of the inner life of the child, which comes through in his outstanding characterization of Spoon, who is both moody and thoughtful, a middle child who sees himself as nobody's favorite since his grandma died. Henkes enriches the narrative with subtle imagery relating to sunlight and shadow, changes in weather and in emotions, and the natural growth that results from it all.

TAKING FLIGHT: MY STORY

Vicki Van Meter with Dan Gutman. (Viking, 1995) 134 pages. ISBN: 0-670-86260-6. Level: Ages 10-12.

In 1993, at the age of twelve, Vicki Van Meter became the youngest girl at that time to pilot an airplane across the United States. One year later, she flew across the Atlantic Ocean. In a fresh, natural, engaging voice, Vicki describes her determination to become a pilot and chronicles each of her landmark flights. The text incorporates details that readers will love, from how Vicki felt as the only kid in flight school to technical details of planning a flight to her media appearances and dreams of becoming an astronaut.

TALKING WITH ARTISTS: CONVERSATIONS WITH VICTORIA CHESS, PAT CUMMINGS, LEO AND DIANE DILLON, RICHARD EGIELSKI, LOIS EHLERT, LISA CAMPBELL ERNST, TOM FEELINGS, STEVEN KELLOGG, JERRY PINKNEY, AMY SCHWARTZ, LANE SMITH, CHRIS VAN ALLSBURG AND DAVID WIESNER

Pat Cummings, compiler. (Bradbury, 1992) 96 pages. ISBN: 0-02-724245-5. Level: Ages 6-14 and older.

Fourteen picture-book artists each respond to the same frequently asked questions. Each artists tells about her/his childhood; this section features a childhood photograph (usually a school picture of the young artist) and a photograph of the artist today as well as one reproduction of childhood art and one or two representing their picture book art. Terrific organization and compelling subject matter make this unusual look at artists' lives and careers good for general browsing and difficult to put down.

TANYA AND EMILY IN A DANCE FOR TWO

Patricia Lee Gauch. (Philomel, 1994) 32 pages. ISBN: 0-399-22688-5. Level: Ages 3-7.

In this 11½ x 8¾ in. picture story about a small wiggly child who wants to be a ballet dancer, Tanya meets Emily, one of those kids with inborn coordination and grace. But Emily is also new to the class and always alone afterwards. The indomitable Tanya approaches Emily, demonstrating to "dance" an ostrich and a flamingo, even though it's difficult for Emily to do that when they are called a jete or an equilbire. Gauch and Ichikawa's best book yet shows the action, imagination, and fun of two children, each talented in different ways.

TOMÁS AND THE LIBRARY LADY

Pat Mora. Illustrated by Raul Colón. (Alfred A. Knopf, 1997) 32 pages. ISBN: 0-679-80401-3. Level: Ages 4-7.

When a family of migrant farm workers from Texas stops in Iowa to pick corn, Tomás's grandfather, Papá Grande, suggests that he spend part of each day at the public library because it is filled with stories he can read and then bring back to share with the family at night. While Tomás expects to find good books at the library, he doesn't expect to find a new friend—but he does. From the beginning, the librarian welcomes him. She shows him where the water fountain is, suggests books he might enjoy, and helps Tomás feel at home whenever he comes to the library. In return, Tomás teaches her some Spanish phrases and she is able to greet Papá Grande in Spanish when Tomás brings him to the library to meet his new friend. Based on an event that occurred in the childhood of national education leader Dr. Tomás Rivera, Mora brings the story to life through excellent characterization and natural-sounding dialogue. Colón's warm, earthtone illustrations give a strong sense of action occurring in the past.

TOTEM POLE

Diane Hoyt-Goldsmith. Photographs by Lawrence Migdale. (Holiday House, 1990) 32 pages. ISBN: 0-8234-0809-4. Level: Ages 5-10.

David is a Tsimshian boy whose pride in his father's artistry as a wood-carver and creator of a new totem pole provides the focus for a 10 x 10 in first-person narrative. The history and culture of David's paternal elders, the Eagle Clan from Metlakatla on Alaska's Annette Island, are described and shown in full-color photographs, as is a brief background of the Klallam Indians of the Northwest Coast. Written and visual explanations detail the steps David's father takes to find a straight, tall cedar tree and carve the Klallam Thunderbird, Raven, Whale, Bear, and other symbolic images into its trunk. The community's involvement in raising and celebrating the pole's placement on the Klallam Reservation is also pictured. David's maternal ancestors emigrated to the United States from Europe generations ago. The boy's Tsimshian heritage and Eagle Clan membership are interpreted in several ways, including the one-page retelling of the "Legend of the Eagle and the Young Child." A glossary concludes this unusual and absorbing photo documentary account.

A VISIT TO AMY-CLAIRE

Claudia Mills. Illustrated by Sheila Hamanaka. (Macmillan, 1992) 32 pages. ISBN: 0-02-766991-2. Level: Ages 4-7.

Five-year-old Rachel can't wait to get to her seven-year-old cousin's house. She is anxious to repeat all the fun she remembers having with her the previous summer—taking bubble baths, swinging on a tire swing, and playing school. But once she and her family get to Amy-Claire's house, Rachel is in for a major disappointment because all Amy-Claire wants to do is play with Rachel's two-year-old sister, Jessie. Hamanaka's bold, sun-dappled oil paintings depict Amy-Claire as Asian American while her cousins are biracial (Asian/white) in a realistic story about imaginary play and shifting family relationships.

WE CAN DO IT!

Laura Dwight. (Checkerboard Press, 1992) 32 pages. ISBN: 1-56288-301-1. Level: Ages 3-6.

Captioned color photographs introduce five preschoolers with disabilities, each of whom cites several things he or she likes to do. The brief, upbeat first-person statements focus on individual personalities and accomplishments.

WHEN JO LOUIS WON THE TITLE

Belinda Rochelle. Illustrated by Larry Johnson (Houghton Mifflin, 1994) 32 pages. ISBN: 0-395-614-7. Level: Ages 5-8.

Jo Louis is so tired of people making fun of her name that she dreads her first day in a new school. But her grandpa manages to raise her spirits by telling her the story behind her name, a story that begins when he was a young man and had just arrived in Harlem on the day of the fighter Joe Louis's great victory. Artist Larry Johnson is so skillful with a paint brush that he manages to pull feeling and drama from the stance of a listening child, and he aptly characterizes the grandfather and granddaughter with expressions of great mutual affection and respect.

WILMA MANKILLER

Linda Lowery. Illustrated by Janice Lee Porter. (Carolrhoda, 1996) 56 pages. ISBN: 0-87614-880-1. Level: Ages 6-8 and older.

The first woman chief to lead the Cherokee Nation did not have an easy path to her distinguished office. She endured displacement and racism as a child, as well as continued prejudice, including sexism, among her fellow Cherokee as she reached adulthood. But Mankiller learned to believe in herself and her ability to help her people. Lowery uses short, simple sentences to skillfully tell Mankiller's story, resulting in an inspiring biography for new readers. Porter's distinguished full-color artwork appears on each two-page spread.

WILMA UNLIMITED: HOW WILMA RUDOLPH BECAME THE WORLD'S FASTEST WOMAN

Kathleen Krull. Illustrated by David Diaz. (Harcourt Brace, 1996) 40 pages. ISBN: 0-15-201267-2. Level: Ages 5-10 and older.

Wilma Rudolph defied the odds to win three gold medals at the 1960 Summer Olympics in Rome, a record for American women. Rudolph's Olympic achievement resulted from incredible determination and in this strikingly illustrated picture book biography, she is profiled as an individual of remarkable energy and fortitude. Disabled by polio as a child, it was thought that Rudolph would never walk again, let alone run her way into the history books. With bold, full-color illustrations set against intriguing sepia-toned photographs that depict the text's background elements, artist Diaz captures Rudolph's spirit, power, and pride, as well as the loving, supportive African American family and community in which she was raised. Author Krull grounds the story with details of Rudolph's family life, her wishes and dreams, and the times in which she lived, so that the athlete's extraordinary accomplishments never overwhelm the human story that is at the heart of the book.

THE WINDOW

Michael Dorris. (Hyperion, 1997) 106 pages. ISBN: 0-7868-2240-6. Level: Ages 10-13 and older.

Rayona Taylor was first introduced at age fifteen in A YELLOW RAFT IN BLUE WATER (Henry Holt, 1987). This book describes earlier events in the fictional Rayona's life as the eleven-year-old biracial (American Indian/black) girl discovers that her family heritage is more complex than she knew. When Rayona's mother, with whom she lives, goes into treatment for alcoholism, her father places her at first in foster care, unable—or unwilling—to make the adjustments in his own life that taking care of Rayona would mean. When the foster placements don't work out, he takes Rayona to his family—relatives she's never known. It is on the flight to meet them that he reveals the secret he has kept from Rayona and her mother: he is half white, "Irish, actually." For Rayona, the news is stunning, all the more so because she senses there is something he isn't telling her about how her grandparents met and how his father—her African American grandfather—died. As Rayona gets to know her white grandmother, great-grandmother, and great-aunt, she sees how her father has, in one sense, rejected them, leaving a hole in their lives that she momentarily wonders if she can fill. But she feels loyalty to her own mother, too, and to her father, whose trust she wants to earn by keeping the secret he has guarded so long from her mother and others in his life. It is her feelings more than the facts that ultimately make a difference to Rayona in this portrait of a child at the center of complex family events.

WITH LOVE FROM KOKO

Faith McNulty. Illustrated by Annie Cannon. (Scholastic/Hardcover, 1990) 32 pages. ISBN: 0-590-42774-1. Level: Ages 8-10.

Raised by humans since she was six months old, Koko was the first gorilla taught to communicate using American Sign Language (ASL). Scientist Penny Patterson's history of teaching ASL to Koko and general information about gorilla behavior are interspersed with lively

anecdotes of Koko's interactions with the author during her visit with the gorilla. Koko is presented with respect and integrity, and a brief afterword discusses the human threat to gorilla habitats in Africa. Softly shaded, large illustrations are generously scattered throughout the text.

WOMEN WORKING A TO Z

Maria A. Kunstadter. Photographs by Shari Stanberry. (Highsmith Press, 1994) 32 pages. ISBN: 0-917846-25-7. Level: Ages 5-8.

"When you grow up, what do you want to be? A girl can be anything from A to Z. Look through this book and see the many things girls just like you have become. Then, think some more. Your opportunities are endless." Twenty-five women in traditional and nontraditional vocations such as airplane pilot, engineer, mother, postmaster, and zookeeper are briefly profiled in this text that includes two photos of each woman—one of her at work today, and one of her as a child. The entry for the letter Y is "You . . . When you grow up, just like the girls in this book, you can use your special talents to be anything you want to be."

A YOUNG PAINTER: THE LIFE AND PAINTINGS OF WANG YANI—CHINA'S EXTRAORDINARY YOUNG ARTIST

Zheng Zhensun and Alice Low. Photographs by Zheng Zhensun. (A Byron Preiss/New China Pictures Book, 1991) 80 pages. ISBN: 0-590-44906-0. Level: Age 8 and older.

The artistic genius of Wang Yani was recognized when she was only three years old, and just a year later she had her first major exhibition in Shanghai. Since that time she has created more than ten thousand paintings and has had exhibitions throughout Asia, Europe, and North America. At age sixteen, she began a successful transition from child prodigy to adult artist who works in the xieyi hua (free style) school of traditional Chinese painting. An absorbing photo-essay traces the growth and development of Wang Yani as an artist and as an extraordinary young woman dealing with the pressures of world attention, fame, and high expectations. Numerous color photographs of Yani at work and at home give young readers a close-up of her life in southern China. Fine, full-color reproductions of more than fifty of her paintings created from age two and one half to age sixteen show Yani's development as a gifted young artist.

ZORA HURSTON AND THE CHINABERRY TREE

William Miller. Illustrated by Cornelius Van Wright and Ying-Hwa Hu. (Lee & Low, 1994) 32 pages. ISBN: 1-880000-14-8. Level: Ages 6-9.

This picture-book account of the childhood of African American writer Zora Neale Hurston focuses on the influence of her mother, who told Hurston that all the world belonged to her, contrary to the messages she got from her father and society at large. When her mother died, young Zora, who liked climbing trees, wearing pants, and listening to old men spin their stories at the town store or around a night-time camp fire, promised herself that she would live up to her mother's expectations. Miller has chosen small, significant details to give a sense of Hurston's intellect and personality through his spare account of her childhood. Somber pencil and watercolor paintings provide the perfect match for the text and depict Hurston as a strong, active girl, even when she appears in the background as an observer.

Children's Trade Books with Individual Development and Identity as a Second Thematic Strand

The title index on pp. 173-180 lists the number of the page on which each book is annotated.

TITLE	AUTHOR	DATE	AGE LEVEL
Abuela's Weave	Omar S. Castaneda	1993	Ages 6-9
The Amazing Paper Cuttings of Hans Christian Andersen	Beth Wagner Brust	1994	Ages 8-12 and older
Apple Juice Tea	Martha Weston	1994	Ages 3-6
Betsy Ross: Patriot of Philadelphia	Judith St. George	1997	Ages 9-11 and older
A Boy Becomes a Man at Wounded Knee	Ted Wood and Wanbli Numpa Afraid of Hawk	1992	Ages 8-13 and older
Brothers & Sisters	Ellen B. Senisi	1993	Ages 3-6
Canto Familiar	Gary Soto	1995	Ages 9-12
Champions: Stories of Ten Remarkable Athletes	Bill Littlefield	1993	Ages 7-12
Chasing Redbird	Sharon Creech	1997	Ages 9-14 and older
Clean Your Room, Harvey Moon!	Pat Cummings	1991	Ages 3-6
Climbing Kansas Mountains	George Shannon	1993	Ages 4-8
Come Home with Me: A Multicultural Treasure Hunt	Aylette Jenness	1993	Ages 7-12 and older
Daddy and Me: A Photo Story of Arthur Ashe and His Daughter's Camera	Jeanne Moutoussamy-Ashe	1993	Ages 3-5
Drumbeat … Heartbeat: A Celebration of the Powwow (We Are Still Here)	Susan Braine	1995	Ages 7-11
Eagle	Judy Allen	1994	Ages 4-8
Eagle Song	Joseph Bruchae	1997	Ages 9-11 and older
Elijah's Angel: A Story for Chanukah and Christmas	Michael J. Rosen	1992	Ages 7-11
Flight: The Journey of Charles Lindbergh	Robert Burleigh	1991	Ages 5-10
Girls and Young Women Inventing: Twenty True Stories about Inventors, Plus How You Can Be One Yourself	Frances A. Karnes and Suzanne M. Bean	1995	Ages 10-14 and older
Grandaddy's Stars	Helen V. Griffith	1995	Ages 6-8
Grandfather's Journey	Allen Say	1993	Ages 8-12
Grandmother Bryant's Pocket	Jacqueline Briggs Martin	1996	Ages 5-7
Hoang Anh: A Vietnamese-American Boy	Diane Hoyt-Goldsmith	1992	Ages 8-12
Home Lovely	Lynne Rae Perkins	1995	Ages 4-7

Homeplace	Anne Shelby	1995	Ages 4-8 and older
A House by the River	William Miller	1997	Ages 5-8
I Thought My Soul Would Rise and Fly: The Diary of Patsy, a Freed Girl	Joyce Hansen	1997	Ages 10-13 and older
Indigo and Moonlight Gold	Jan Spivey Gilchrist	1993	Ages 5-8
L'chaim: The Story of a Russian Emigre Boy	Tricia Brown	1994	Ages 8-11
The Leaving Morning	Angela Johnson	1992	Ages 3-6
Let's Talk about Divorce	Kevin Henkes	1996	Ages 2-5
Lilly's Purple Plastic Purse	Fred Rogers	1996	Ages 4-8
Lion Dancer: Ernie Wan's Chinese New Year	Kate Waters and Madeline Slovenz-Low	1990	Ages 4-11
The Little Lama of Tibet	Lois Raimondo	1994	Ages 7-10
The Little Ships: The Heroic Rescue at Dunkirk in World War II	Louise Borden	1997	Ages 8-12 and older
Lives of the Musicians	Kathleen Krull	1993	Ages 7-14 and older
Ma Dear's Aprons	Patricia C. McKissack	1997	Ages 4-7
Mama Bear	Chyng Feng Sun	1994	Ages 4-8 and older
Mom Can't See Me	Sally Hobart Alexander	1990	Ages 6-11
Morning Milking	Linda Lowe Morris	1991	Ages 7-11
My Mama Had a Dancing Heart	Libba Moore Gray	1995	Ages 7-10 and older
My Painted House, My Friendly Chicken, and Me	Maya Angelou	1994	Ages 5-8
My Two Uncles	Judith Vigna	1995	Ages 4-8 and older
Neighborhood Odes	Gary Soto	1992	Age 8 and older
Nim and the War Effort	Milly Lee	1997	Ages 7-10 and older
One Nation, Many Tribes: How Kids Live in Milwaukee's Indian Community	Kathleen Krull	1995	Ages 8-12
Only a Pigeon	Jane and Christopher Kurtz	1997	Ages 4-8
Our People	Angela Shelf Medearis	1994	Ages 4-8
Pass It On; African-American Poetry for Children	Wade Hudson, selector	1993	Ages 4-9
The Real McCoy: The Life of an African-American Inventor	Wendy Towle	1993	Ages 7-10 and older
Red Dog, Blue Fly: Football Poems	Sharon Bell Mathis	1991	Ages 7-11

Run Away Home	Patricia C. McKissack	1997	Ages 10-12
Sam and the Lucky Money	Karen Chinn	1995	Ages 4-7
Sam Is My Half Brother	Lizi Boyd	1990	Ages 3-6
Seedfolks	Paul Fleischman	1997	Ages 9-13 and older
Serena Katz	Charlotte Pomerantz	1992	Ages 4-7
Shannon: An Ojibway Dancer	Sandra King	1993	Ages 7-11
Smoky Night	Eve Bunting	1994	Ages 6-10
Sofie's Role	Amy Heath	1992	Ages 4-8
Some of the Pieces	Melissa Madenski	1991	Ages 4-8
Songs from the Loom: A Navajo Girl Learns to Weave	Monty Roessel	1995	Ages 7-11
The Spirit of Tio Fernando: A Day of the Dead Story / El Espiritu de Tio Fernando: Una Historia del Dia de Los Muertos	Janice Levy	1995	Ages 6-9
Star of Fear, Star of Hope	Jo Hoestlandt	1995	Ages 7-10 and older
Stories from the Classical Ballet	Belinda Hollyer	1995	Ages 6-11 and older
The Sunday Outing	Pat Cummings, editor	1994	Ages 5-8
Talking with Artists	Gloria Jean Pinkney	1995	Ages 6-14 and older
This Land Is My Land	George Littlechild	1993	Ages 9-14 and older
The Two Mrs. Gibsons	Igus Toyomi	1996	Ages 3-7
Up North at the Cabin	Marsha Wilson Chall	1992	Ages 4-9
Vejigante Masquerader	Lulu Delacre	1993	Ages 5-9
Voices from the Fields: Children of Migrant Farmworkers Tell Their Stories	S. Beth Atkin	1993	Ages 9-14 and older
The Wall	Eve Bunting	1990	Ages 4-9 and older
Water Buffalo Days: Growing Up in Vietnam	Quang Nhuong Huyah	1997	Ages 9-11
What Instrument Is This?	Rosmarie Hausherr	1992	Ages 4-8
What Zeesie Saw on Delancey Street	Elsa Okon Rael	1996	Ages 5-8
Wheels	Shirley Hughes	1991	Ages 3-8
When I Go Camping with Grandma	Marion Dane Bauer	1995	Ages 3-6
Winter Rescue	W. D. Valgardson	1995	Ages 6-9
The Wright Brothers: How They Invented the Airplane	Russell Freedman	1991	Ages 9-14 and older

Children's Trade Books with Individual Development and Identity as a Third Thematic Strand

The title index on pp. 173-180 lists the number of the page on which each book is annotated.

Anastasia's Album	Hugh Brewster	1996	Ages 10-13 and older
Batboy: An Inside Look at Spring Training	Joan Anderson	1996	Ages 8-12
Calling the Doves / El Canto de las Palomas	Juan Felipe Herrera	1995	Ages 4-8
Celebrating Kwanzaa	Diane Hoyt-Goldsmith	1993	Ages 5-12
Coming Home: From the Life of Langston Hughes	Floyd Cooper	1994	Ages 4-12
Day of Delight: A Jewish Sabbath in Ethiopia	Maxine Rose Schur	1994	Ages 5-9
The Days before Now: An Autobiographical Note by Margaret Wise Brown	Joan W. Blos, Adapter	1994	Ages 3-9
Dick King-Smith's Animal Friends: Thirty-One True Life Stories	Dick King-Smith	1996	Ages 4-12
Farmer's Market	Paul Brett Johns	1997	Ages 4-7
Flood	Mary Calhoun	1997	Ages 5-8
A Forever Family	Roslyn Banish and Jennifer Jordan-Wong	1992	Ages 6-11
Hard to Be Six	Arnold Adoff	1991	Ages 4-6
Kids Making Quilts for Kids	ABC Quilts	1992	Ages 8-14
Laura Loves Horses	Joan Hewett	1990	Ages 4-9
Marven of the Great North Woods	Kathryn Lasky	1997	Ages 6-9 and older
Neve Shalom/Wahat Al-Salam: Oasis of Peace	Laurie Dolphin	1995	Ages 7-10
Orphan Train Rider: One Boy's True Story	Andrea Warren	1996	Ages 9-16 and older
Powwow	George Ancona	1993	Ages 5-11
Sitti's Secrets	Naomi Shihab Nye	1994	Ages 6-10
Treemonisha	Angela Shelf Medearis	1995	Ages 9-12 and older
Turtle Bay	Saviour Pirotta	1997	Ages 5-8
Twinnies	Eve Bimtomg	1997	Ages 4-7
Two Lands, One Heart: An American Boy's Journey to His Mother's Vietnam	Jeremy Schmidt and Ted Wood	1995	Ages 7-10
War Game	Michael Foreman	1994	Ages 8-12 and older

CHILDREN'S TRADE BOOKS WITH INDIVIDUALS, GROUPS, AND INSTITUTIONS AS THE MAJOR THEMATIC STRAND

A IS FOR AFRICA

Ifeoma Onyefulu. (Cobblehill, 1993) 28 pages. ISBN: 0-525-65147-0. Level: Ages 3-7.

A Nigerian photographer selected twenty-six photographs from her homeland to illustrate this introduction to Africa. Although the images she chose are specific to Nigeria, she states in an author's note that she attempted to capture what the people of Africa have in common: "traditional village life, warm family ties, and above all the hospitality for which Africans are famous." The color photographs were also chosen with the interests of young children in mind, as they show objects (drums, lamps, houses) and individuals (children) that will greatly appeal to them.

ALEF-BET: A HEBREW ALPHABET BOOK

Michelle Edwards. (Lothrop, Lee & Shepard, 1992) 32 pages. ISBN: 0-688-09724-3. Level: Ages 2-8.

A family composed of two adults and three children that might live in contemporary Jerusalem, Tel Aviv, New York, or Amsterdam introduces daily uses of modern Hebrew in a nearly wordless picture story. Signs of home-created entertainment, especially that involving the arts and play-acting, are everywhere, showing this to be a priority for the down-to-earth, energetic, affectionate household. Outside activities vary with the seasons while everyone has a visible role in sledding, leaf gathering, and night sky-watching. One of the three happily active children uses a wheelchair to move from place to place. A letter of the Hebrew alphabet appears in the upper left corner of each page, and Hebrew words with phonetic pronunciations are shown on the lower left of each page. Roman transliterations and English translations are also provided. Edwards succeeds in developing a fresh approach to the concept of family and to creating a book about a specific language.

APPLE JUICE TEA

Martha Weston. (Clarion, 1994) 32 pages. ISBN: 0-395-65480-7. Level: Ages 3-6.

Because her grandmother lives far away, Polly doesn't see her very often. When she does come to visit Polly and her mom and dada, she seems like a stranger and Polly is reluctant to include her in her life. But Gran is obviously an old pro with children and she knows just the right way to give Polly the time and space she needs to get acquainted. The muted tones of Weston's pen-and-ink and watercolor illustrations perfectly complement her understated story about the challenges of being a family together and apart.

BASEBALL SAVED US

Ken Mochizuki. Illustrated by Don Lee. (Lee & Low, 1993) 32 pages. ISBN: 1-880000-01-6. Level: Ages 7-11 and older.

The treatment of Japanese Americans during World War II is the subject of this remarkable picture book. "Shorty," a young Japanese American boy, has a hard time understanding why he and his family had to move out of their house and into a camp in the desert. "We weren't in a camp that was fun, like summer camp. Ours was in the middle of nowhere, and we were behind a barbed-wire fence. Soldiers with guns made sure we stayed there . . ." Everything at camp is different—and more difficult—than life back home; there are dust storms, the buildings have no privacy (even for going to the bathroom), and there is nothing for anyone to do. The day Shorty's dad decides they need a baseball diamond marks a turning point in camp life as, first building the field and later competing in the games themselves, adults and children finally have something for which to hope and work. Shorty, who has never been good at baseball, practices hard and eventually makes a game-winning hit in the camp championship. "But it wasn't as if everything was all fixed." Returning home after the war, he finds that he still must persevere against prejudice and his own fears to succeed. The straightforward narrative movingly captures a young boy's bewilderment over events that make no logical sense to adults, let alone to children. Sepia-toned color illustrations by Lee evoke a sense of a past that is washed in sadness.

BILLY AND BELLE

Sarah Garland. (Reinhardt/Viking, 1992) 32 pages. ISBN: 0-670-84396-2. Level: Ages 3-6.

School-aged Billy must take his preschool-aged sister Belle to class with him while Dad takes Mum to the hospital for the birth of a new baby. It's an exciting and extraordinary day for both of them—not just because they're getting a new brother or sister but because it's pet day at school. Even with just a last minute notice, Belle manages to muster up a pet of her own to take to school: a spider! The full-color illustrations set in a comic-strip format are filled with amusing details of a bustling home life and a refreshingly disorderly school. Billy and Belle (and baby Adam) are biracial: their mother is white and their dad is black.

THE BIRTHDAY SWAP

Loretta Lopez. (Lee & Low, 1997) 32 pages. ISBN: 1-880000-47-4. Level: Ages 5-8.

Six-year-old Lori lives in a border town between the United States and Mexico. She wants to give her older sister exactly the right birthday present, but what should it be? Lori and her mother visit Tia Sabina who is decorating a cake and go to the Mercado where even items in the curio shop won't do. On the day of her sister's birthday, the family attends church before going to a family gathering where Lori discovers a party planned for her. Her older sister has decided to exchange birthday seasons, so December-born Lori can have a summer pool party for a change. Tia Sabina's cake had been baked for her, and the Mercado trip gave her mother the idea Lori would enjoy a donkey piñata. Cultural elements abound in a richly detailed series of full-color illustrations created in gouache and colored pencil. A five-phrase glossary provides definitions.

BRASS BUTTON

Crescent Dragonwagon. Illustrated by Susan Paradise. (Atheneum, 1997) 40 pages. ISBN: 0-689-80582-9. Level: Ages 6-8 and older.

Ten brief chapters follow the chain of events that occur when Mrs. Moffatt unknowingly loses a shiny brass button off her new winter coat. It passes from person to person throughout the neighborhood and finally back to Mrs. Moffatt before she has even noticed it missing. The clever episodic story is lavishly illustrated with detailed gouache paintings.

BROTHERS & SISTERS

Ellen B. Senisi. (Scholastic, 1993) 32 pages. ISBN: 0-590-46419-1. Level: Ages 3-6.

The ups and downs of sibling relationships are explored in color photographs of sibling pairs that are accompanied by comments from the children on what it is like having a brother or sister who is younger than you, older than you, or even the same age. One brother/sister pair sums it up best: "Sometimes we're best friends. And sometimes we're worst enemies."

CALLING THE DOVES / EL CANTO DE LAS PALOMAS

Juan Felipe Herrera. Illustrated by Elly Simmons. (Children's Book Press, 1995) 32 pages. ISBN: 0-89239-132-4. Level: Ages 4-8.

In lyrical bilingual prose (Spanish/English), Chicano poet Herrera recalls his childhood growing up in a family of migrant farmworkers. "The road changed with the seasons," he observes, but some things stayed the same: his mother's love of poetry and music and his father's ability to whistle a tune that would attract doves. Colored pencil and acrylic paintings express the warmth and security felt by a child growing up in a loving household.

CELEBRATING FAMILIES

Rosmarie Hausherr. (Scholastic, 1997) 32 pages. ISBN: 0-590-48937-2. Level: Ages 4-9.

No two family structures are alike in this engaging portrait of fourteen American families. Christina lives with her older brother Sherron and their grandmother. Lindsay and her sister Masha live part of the time with their mother and part of the time with their father. Joseph lives on a farm with his parents, aunt and uncle, grandparents, and great-grandparents. Justin lives with his dad. Chris lives with his mom, and every Sunday they go visit Chris's dad in prison. Alexandra and Sarah live with their lesbian moms. Each double-page spread is devoted to an individual child and his or her family, depicted in a creatively compound family portrait that uses color photographs. On the facing page, a brief text describes the distinguishing characteristics of the living situation and tells one or two things that the family members enjoy doing together, using a black-and-white photograph as an illustration. No single family is presented as the norm here, and all are celebrated for their strength and diversity.

●

CHASING REDBIRD

Sharon Creech. (Joanna Cotler/HarperCollins, 1997) 261 pages. ISBN: 0-06-026987-1. Level: Ages 9-14 and older.

In the middle of a large and loving family, thirteen-year-old Zinny Taylor sometimes feels like an outsider. She is a quiet girl who often prefers the calm of her Aunt Jessie and Uncle Nate's house next door to the constant activity in her own family's home. The soothing quiet of the rural Kentucky countryside is also a source of solitude for her. The outdoors offers even greater solace for Zinny after Aunt Jessie dies unexpectedly. An old, overgrown trail on the edge of her family's farm provides Zinny with a focus for her grief, her energy, and her imagination as she determines to uncover the trail and follow it to its source. But Zinny unwittingly begins to unearth more than just the trail as she works. There are her confused feelings about Jake Boone, an older boy who has recently returned to Bybanks, not to mention her mixed-up feelings about her family. And there are also secrets—family secrets—that are rooted in an earlier family grief and are waiting for discovery. The further Zinny travels from home, the closer she comes to knowing just how much strength and love there is that binds her to her family. Creech has once again created a book of fine emotional tenor and quiet humor.

THE CHRISTMAS TREE / EL ÁRBOL DE NAVIDAD: A CHRISTMAS RHYME IN ENGLISH AND SPANISH

Alma Flor Ada. Illustrated by Terry Ybánez. (Hyperion, 1997) 32 pages. ISBN: 0-7868-2123-X. Level: Ages 2-5.

A cumulative bilingual (English/Spanish) story begins "Daddy brought a Christmas tree" followed by a wordless double-page spread showing him carrying the tree into the home. Brief declarative sentences encourage careful looks at each way the tree becomes decorated in turn by Grandma, Grandpa, Uncle Irineo, Brother Alfonzo, Aunt Mireya, and Mommy. The language in each new section is minimal, and the artwork, created in acrylic paint on black paper, is darkly hued, uncluttered, and cheerful. Ada's one-page note at the end tells about bombas, posadas, Papa Noel, Nochebuena, and the visit on January 5 of los Reyes Magos during her childhood in Cuba.

A CRACK IN THE WALL

Mary Elizabeth Haggerty. Illustrated by Ruben De Anda. (Lee & Low, 1993) 32 pages. ISBN: 1-880000-03-2. Level: Ages 4-8.

Until Carlos's mom finds another job, she can afford only a small, dingy apartment for the two of them. Carlos tries to brighten it up, first by painting leaves on a crack in the wall to make it look like a tree branch, then by placing shining stars made out of gum wrappers on the branch. But each day his mom returns from her job hunt so exhausted that she never notices Carlos's handiwork. This realistic story about one child's attempts to cheer up a discouraged parent in a time of stress has a wonderful surprise ending.

DADDY AND ME: A PHOTO STORY OF ARTHUR ASHE AND HIS DAUGHTER CAMERA

Jeanne Moutoussamy-Ashe. (Alfred A. Knopf, 1993) 40 pages. ISBN: 0-679-95096-6. Level: Ages 3-5.

Moutoussamy-Ashe's black-and-white photographs of her husband Arthur and her daughter Camera were taken in the years before Arthur died of AIDS in February 1993, when Camera was five. They capture a warm father/daughter relationship. Although Arthur's illness is a factor in their lives—sometimes draining his energy or hospitalizing him—it is never a factor in their love. Text accompanying the photographs is written in Camera's first person voice. She describes her life with her father this way: "Daddy has some bad days and lots of good days ... On good days we go to the tennis court ... Or we sit in the sun and sing ... On Daddy's bad days, I take care of him. I give him his pills. I take his temperature. I make him wait until the thermometer beeps, just like he does for me." This text provides a remarkable portrait of children's capacity for understanding, compassion, and love.

ELIJAH'S ANGEL: A STORY FOR CHANUKAH AND CHRISTMAS

Michael J. Rosen. Illustrated by Aminah Brenda Lynn Robinson. (Harcourt Brace Jovanovich, 1992) 32 pages. ISBN: 0-15-225394-7. Level: Ages 7-11.

A first-person narrator tells of the year he, a nine-year-old Jewish boy, regularly visited the shop of an eighty-four year old African American barber and woodcarver. His parents told their son that some of Elijah Pierce's carvings from the Bible represented what might be considered "graven images." The boy never spoke of this while he and Elijah shared "time together the way Chanukah and Christmas shared the same day that year." One December after Elijah gave him a polka-dotted guardian angel, the boy hid it. His parents helped him to cherish the gift as an angel of friendship; in that spirit, the boy gave Elijah a menorah he made at Hebrew school. Rosen based the moving personal story on the "character and vision" of Elijah Pierce (1892-1984), a woodcarver, lay minister, barber, and personal friend to many of his visitors. Robinson grew up in the same Columbus, Ohio, neighborhood and spent long hours in Elijah's barbershop modeling clay and quilting while he carved and varnished. Her full-color paintings were done in house paint on scrap rag.

FAMILIES; A CELEBRATION OF DIVERSITY, COMMITMENT AND LOVE

Aylette Jenness. (Houghton Mifflin, 1990) 48 pages. ISBN: 0-395-47038-2. Level: Ages 5-12.

Seventeen young people each briefly comment on the composition of their families in a photoessay that originated as an interactive exhibition at the Children's Museum in Boston. One strength of this unique book rests in its organizational pattern: no one type of family unit is presented as standard, or correct, or "other." Blended, adoptive, mixed-racial, biracial, two parent, one parent, gay and lesbian, collective, and extended families from diverse racial, ethnic, and economic backgrounds are pictured. Child-expressed definitions of "family" and a list of books for further reading are additional features of this important book.

A FOREVER FAMILY

Roslyn Banish and Jennifer Jordan-Wong. (HarperCollins, 1992) 44 pages. ISBN: 0-060-021674-3. Level: Ages 6-11.

An eight-year-old Amerasian girl briefly describes events leading up to her adoption the previous year by an interracial (Asian/white) couple. The first-person account, accompanied by black-and-white photographs, includes details of the court proceedings, as well as of her earlier life with her African American foster family and her current life with her new extended family.

GOOD NIGHT, STELLA

Kate McMullan. Illustrated by Emma Chichester Clark. (Candlewick Press, 1994) 24 pages. ISBN: 1-56402-065-7. Level: Ages 5-8.

With all sorts of questions running through her head (Can your eyeballs fall out? If a vampire bites you, will water spurt out your neck when you try to drink?), Stella just can't fall asleep. Even her dad's suggestion ("Try closing your eyes") doesn't help. And besides, she can't stop swallowing! Kate McMullan has perfectly characterized the mind-set of an imaginative, restless child who has more energy than anyone else in her household. Luckily, Stella has an equally imaginative dad who comes up with a solution that suits everyone. The amusing illustrations show a wide-eyed Stella whose brain stays switched on long after everyone else has gone to sleep.

GRANDADDY'S STARS

Helen V. Griffith. Illustrated by James Stevenson. (Greenwillow, 1995) 32 pages. ISBN: 0-688-13655-9. Level: Ages 6-8.

In the fourth volume in this series of easy chapter books, Grandaddy is traveling from Georgia to Baltimore to visit Janetta for a change. Janetta, true to form, worries constantly about the visit: What if Grandaddy misses the train? What if he sleeps through his stop? What if he finds everything Janetta plans to show him boring? And Grandaddy, true to form, arrives raring to go, with a repertoire of funny stories and wry observations that soon set Janetta's mind at ease. Griffith excels at creating distinctive, fully rounded characters through dialogue, while Stevenson's understated line drawings with watercolor washes provide the perfect complement.

GRANDMA'S BASEBALL

Gavin Curtis. (Crown, 1990) 32 pages. ISBN: 0-517-57389-X. Level: Ages 4-7.

A young grandson notices Grandma's grumpy manner now that she's moved from far away to live with him and his parents. There is oatmeal for breakfast, little after school leisure, and, above all, no slamming of the screen door. The autographed baseball from Grandpa's days on the Monarchs provides the first opportunity for the two to mutually enjoy each other. A contemporary African American family is pictured in the full-color illustrations.

HOME FIELD

David Spohn. (Lothrop, Lee & Shepard, 1993) 32 pages. ISBN: 0-688-11173-4. Level: Ages 3-7.

Bare spots in the grass serve as bases, maple trees behind home plate provide a backstop, and barn swallows are like fans in bleachers when young Matt and his dad get in a quick game of baseball before early morning farm chores. With his dad coaching him, Matt is perfecting his stance and his hitting this summer, but his real growth can probably be attributed to the fact that dad makes time for a little one-on-one baseball before the hectic pace of daily life takes over. Spohn's understated, gentle story of a father and son relationship in a rural, interracial family is itself a little solace in a busy world.

IN MY FAMILY / EN MI FAMILIA

Carmen Lomas Garza. Edited by David Schecter. Translated by Francisco X. Alarcon. (Children's Book Press, 1996) 32 pages. ISBN: 0-89239-138-3. Level: Age 5 and older.

Brilliantly colored oil, acrylic, and gouache paintings illustrate scenes from this Chicana artist's childhood in Kingsville, Texas, near the border with Mexico. She comments on growing up in her Mexican-American family in single-page narratives that accompany each work of art reproduced in the book. Children who cannot read yet can still see empañadas being made, a birthday celebration complete with a barbecue and a piñata, Easter egg decorations, a wedding blessing, and much more. The artist answers questions typically asked about her work in two pages at the end. The narrative passages are printed in Spanish and in English. A welcome continuation of her first book, FAMILY PICTURES / CUADROS DE FAMILIA, published in 1990.

L'CHAIM: THE STORY OF A RUSSIAN EMIGRE BOY

Tricia Brown. Photographs by Kenneth Kobre. (Henry Holt, 1994) 44 pages. ISBN: 0-8050-2354-2. Level: Ages 8-11.

Zev Tsukerman is a young émigré from the Ukraine whose family has settled in San Francisco. A narrative written in Zev's first-person voice and accompanied by lively full-color photographs depicts Zev's life in his new country, where he attends a Jewish day school, takes kung fu lessons, plays computer games, and learns about the religion he was never before able to practice.

LET'S TALK ABOUT DIVORCE

Fred Rogers. Photographs by Jim Judkis. (Putnam, 1996) 32 pages. ISBN: 0-399-22449-1. Level: Ages 2-5.

Preschoolers whose parents are divorcing will find reassurance in this photoessay that they will still have a family to help them feel safe, give them food, take care of them, and love them. Rogers's low-key statements articulate children's typical concerns with characteristic insight and suggest healthy ways to express the feelings most children experience. Color photographs show three families of differing racial heritages.

LILLY'S PURPLE PLASTIC PURSE

Kevin Henkes. (Greenwillow, 1996) 32 pages. ISBN: 0-688-12897-1. Level: Ages 4-8.

Lilly loves school—her "pointy pencils," the "squeaky chalk," the "clickety-clickety-clack" sounds her red cowgirl boots make in the halls, and "the privacy of her very own desk." Lilly especially loves her teacher, Mr. Slinger, who "is sharp as a tack," wears "a different colored tie each day of the week," and provides cheesy snacks. The normally loquacious Lilly is almost speechless when she tries to say why Mr. Slinger is such a good teacher: "Wow. That was just about all she could say. Wow." One day Lilly brings a new purple plastic purse, movie star sunglasses, and three shiny quarters to school. Her new possessions become such distractions to her that Mr. Slinger sets them on his desk during the day. Lilly's mean-spirited retaliation to such injustice soon makes her miserable. Her parents and Mr. Slinger help this basically warm-hearted, strong-willed child to move beyond the anxious episode. It's relatively easy for young children to forget that Lilly and the other characters are rodents, because author / artist Henkes has them behaving as most humans might under similar circumstances. It could be easy for adults to overlook Henkes's mastery of picture book narrative, splendid watercolor illustrations, and superb page designs because—like Mr. Slinger and Lilly's parents—he makes what he does so superbly look effortless. Wow.

THE LITTLE LAMA OF TIBET

Lois Raimondo. (Scholastic, 1994) 40 pages. ISBN: 0-590-46167-2. Level: Ages 7-10.

A child is recognized as the new incarnation of Ling Rinpoche, the late tutor of the Dalai Lama. He lives in exile in the mountains of Dharamsala, India, studying scriptures, reading religious stories, and otherwise preparing spiritually to pass on Buddhist teachings to his people. This young monk was six years old the year Raimondo was granted permission to interview and photograph him. Her photographs are reproduced in full color, providing unparalleled glimpses of his daily discipline and that of those who teach him. The Tibetan alphabet is reproduced on the endpapers.

LITTLE WHITE CABIN

Ferguson Plain. (Pemmican Publications, 1992) 24 pages. ISBN: 0-921827-26-1. Level: Ages 5-8.

Waaboozoons is an Ojibway boy who passes by a little white cabin nearly every day when he's out walking. Some days he sees an elder known as Ol' Danny sitting on the cabin's front porch, and when Waaboozoons sees him, the boy always calls out "Aniish naa?" (How are you?). He gets used to the fact that Ol' Danny never responds to his greeting. Much to the boy's surprise, however, one day the old man answers him, and from that day on the two become good friends, with Ol' Danny teaching Waaboozoons much about the old ways. This quiet picture story, illustrated in distinctive dark blue and white paintings by a self-taught Ojibway artist, shows the importance of respect for elders in the Native American value system.

MAYEROS: A YUCATEC MAYA FAMILY

George Ancona. (Lothrop, Lee & Shepard, 1997) 40 pages. ISBN: 0-688-13465-3. Level: Ages 7-11.

Photographer George Ancona returns to his roots, a small Mayan village in Yucatán, Mexico, to document the lives of one family who lives there, as seen through the eyes of their two young sons, Armando and Gaspár. The integration of traditional Mayan customs with contemporary Mexican life is evident in every aspect of their daily living, as Ancona explains in his cogent text. Throughout the book, his excellent color photographs are accompanied by reproductions of ancient Mayan artwork, showing Armando and Gaspár's ancestors engaged in exactly the same pursuit, from grinding spices with a metate, to carrying a heavy load with a tumpline, to sitting at a desk in school, writing.

MOM CAN'T SEE ME

Sally Hobart Alexander. Photographs by George Ancona (Macmillan, 1990) 48 pages. ISBN: 0-02-700401-5. Level: Ages 6-11.

Leslie, a nine-year-old girl, describes day-to-day life living with her mom who has been blind since age twenty-six. While Leslie describes how her family does things differently to accommodate her mom's special needs and speaks candidly about times her mom has embarrassed her, the overall focus of this photoessay is her mom's active life. She takes Leslie to dance and gymnastic classes, volunteers at her school, attends soccer games, and plays baseball with her kids.

MORNING, NOON, AND NIGHT: POEMS TO FILL YOUR DAY

Sharon Taberski. Illustrated by Nancy Doniger. (Mondo, 1996) 32 pages. ISBN: 1-57255-128-3. Level: Ages 5-8.

This energizing anthology of poems for young readers takes them through a day filled with cat kisses, shadows, missing socks, crayons, a fight with a friend, a bedtime story, and many other things. Lively, colorful collage illustrations are a celebration of each poetic moment that might be part of any school child's day.

MY MAMA HAD A DANCING HEART

Libba Moore Gray. Illustrated by Raul Colon. (Orchard, 1995) 32 pages. ISBN: 0-531-09470-7. Level: Ages 7-10.

"My mama had a dancing heart and she shared that heart with me." A young woman looks back on her mother's joyous embrace of life in a memory-rich picture book that recalls the many times in her childhood they danced together to celebrate the seasons. Gray's tender celebration of a warm and cherished mother-daughter relationship is movingly illustrated by Colon's graceful, deep-toned paintings that are burnished with plum and golden hues.

MYCCA'S BABY

Rinda M. Byers. Illustrated by David Tamura. (Orchard Books, 1990) 32 pages. ISBN: 0-531-05828-X. Level: Ages 4-7.

Mycca can hardly wait for the arrival of her Aunt Rose's new baby and, even though she's been assured that the baby will belong to her, too, she wonders just how much she'll be allowed to help out. The warmth and security of a loving extended family are captured in both the text and in the illustrations, the style and the palette of which are reminiscent of Mexican muralists.

NINE CANDLES

Maria Testa. Illustrated by Amanda Schaffer. (Carolrhoda, 1996) 32 pages. ISBN: 0-87614-940-9. Level: Ages 4-7.

While Raymond and his dad prepare for their weekly Sunday car trip to prison to visit his mother, the boy worries that she will forget that this is his seventh birthday—but she doesn't. Realistic emotions and circumstances surrounding visits to family members in correctional institutions are interspersed with the birthday story. Testa's note at the end distinguishes between the typical and the unusual in this story. From her background as an attorney with clinical experience in prison legal services, Testa suggests the importance of being a friend to someone with a parent in prison. Full-color paintings effectively illustrate this picture story.

OGBO: SHARING LIFE IN AN AFRICAN VILLAGE

Ifeoma Onyefulu. (U.S. edition: Gulliver/Harcourt, 1996) 24 pages. ISBN: 0-15-200498-X. Level: Ages 7-10.

This singular, shining book features Obioma, a six-year-old girl in eastern Nigeria who tells readers about ogbos, or age groups, in her community. From the time they are young, children of the same general age identify with their ogbos, which extend beyond family ties to embrace the community as a whole. Members of ogbos play and work together and help one another in time of need. It is a connection that lasts throughout their lives, regardless of where they later live. Through text accompanied by lively color photographs, Obioma tells about the ogbo to which each member of her immediate family belongs in this beautifully designed and realized book.

ORPHAN TRAIN RIDER: ONE BOY'S TRUE STORY

Andrea Warren. (Houghton Mifflin, 1996) 80 pages. ISBN: 0-395-69822-7. Level: Ages 9-16 and older.

Orphan trains were part of so-called "placing out" programs in New York City and other Eastern cities between 1854 and 1930, an effort to find homes for white children without parental support. Lee Nailling was one of these children. In 1926, Nailling rode with his younger brother on an "orphan train" to Texas. His story is skillfully interlaced with Warren's chilling overview of these social service programs. Because even today many survivors are unwilling to identify themselves as former "train kids," Nailling's witness offers a rare glimpse into the lifelong impact of his experiences. Black-and-white archival photos and Nailling family photos give human faces to information about the formal system that sent more than 200,000 children into homes where often they were expected to provide hard labor without receiving comfort or real family status in return.

RED DOG, BLUE FLY: FOOTBALL POEMS

Sharon Bell Mathis. Illustrated by Jan Spivey Gilchrist. (Viking, 1991) 32 pages. ISBN: 0-670-83623-0. Level: Ages 7-11.

The first-person voice of these thirteen poems is a seventy-pound quarterback who describes the ups and downs of a championship season. Some of the ecstasies of this youthful player are a touchdown, a playoff pizza, a coach's compliment, and, of course, winning the trophy. And some of the agonies are trying to keep the signals straight at practice, playing a game against his cousin's team, and catching a glimpse of the face of a player on the losing team: "His face/grab something/from/my win." The action-packed, full-color illustrations show all team members, coaches, and cheerleaders as African American.

REMEMBER THAT

Leslea Newman. Illustrated by Karen Ritz. (Clarion, 1996) 32 pages. ISBN: 0-395-66156-0. Level: Ages 4-8.

When this picture story begins, Bubbe lives in an apartment across the street from her family. "Everyone who wants to eat has to help out a little. Remember that," Bubbe says to her granddaughter while preparing their Sabbath dinner each Friday. "Always rest when you're tired. Remember that," Bubbe advises the girl when she herself doesn't feel well. As her health changes, Bubbe moves in with the family and then to a nursing home. Regardless of where she lives, Bubbe can be depended upon to celebrate Shhabbos, offer pithy wisdom based upon her life experience, and—best of all—tell her granddaughter she loves her. Most of all, remember that. This cheerful, gentle picture story about an aging elder contains watercolor illustrations.

SAM IS MY HALF BROTHER

Lizi Boyd. (Viking, 1990) 32 pages. ISBN: 0-670-83046-1. Level: Ages 3-6.

Now that baby Sam has joined the family, Hessie has trouble sharing parental attention with him when she goes to spend the summer with her father and stepmother. Distinctive full-color illustrations accompany this universal story of sibling rivalry with a contemporary twist.

SMOKY NIGHT

Eve Bunting. Illustrated by David Diaz. (Harcourt, Brace, 1994) 36 pages. ISBN: 0-15-269954-6. Level: Ages 6-10.

A young African American child describes a night of fear when rioting occurs in his city neighborhood. "Rioting can happen when people get angry," his mother explains to him. "They want to smash and destroy. They don't care anymore what's right and what's wrong." In the middle of the night, a fire forces the boy and his mother to flee their apartment building and take refuge in a shelter, where African American, Korean American, and Latino neighbors, some of whom are strangers to one another, have gathered in the confusion. Tensions between African American and Korean American residents of the neighborhood are specifically addressed. The child's anxiety is soothed but not extinguished by his mother's deliberate calm for the sake of her child, and these are the most powerful elements of the text. Diaz's explosive artwork is a powerful component—he sets his intense paintings against a multimedia backdrop that is suggested by elements of the text and created with items culled from everyday life.

SNOW DAY!

Barbara M. Joosse. Illustrated by Jennifer Plecas. (Clarion, 1995) 32 pages. ISBN: 0-395-66588-4. Level: Ages 3-6.

"The snow came at night, swirling and swishing. / It piled on the ground in big, whipped peaks. / In the morning, the plow could not get through. / Neither could the school bus." No school? Robby makes his own breakfast and runs outside to slide with Zippy, the dog. Louise begins the day by watching TV but is soon outside making snow angels with Robby. Heather is too grown-up to be excited, so she sleeps late, becoming involved with the snow fort that emerges after their parents shovel the walk. Everyone plays, and the family ends the day with cocoa and a warm fireplace. Joosse's cheerful prose recreates how a snow day becomes a time out of time. Executed in watercolor, gouache, colored pencil, and pastel, Plecas's light-hearted illustrations mesh perfectly with the brief text of this 9¼ x 8½ in. story.

THE SUNDAY OUTING

Gloria Jean Pinkney. Illustrated by Jerry Pinkney (Dial, 1994) 32 pages. ISBN: 0-8037-1198-0. Level: Ages 5-8.

A prequel to BACK HOME (Dial, 1992), this book shows the days and steps leading up to Ernestine's visit to her relatives' rural southern home. Both stories, set in the early twentieth century, provide a view of one middle-class African American family's means of keeping in touch and passing down family traditions to their children. In the story, the Pinkneys depict Ernestine's close relationship with her Aunt Odessa through their mutual interest in trains and adventure. A wise elder, Aunt Odessa knows exactly how to encourage Ernestine's budding sense of independence and assure that the child will be able to make the long train trip back home by herself.

TAXI! TAXI!

Cari Best. Illustrated by Dale Gottlieb. (Little, Brown, 1994) 32 pages. ISBN: 0-316-09259-2. Level: Ages 4-8.

Tina, a school-aged daughter of divorced parents, looks forward to the Sunday afternoons she spends with her papi, driver of the most yellow taxi in New York City. Each Sunday, Tina and Papi drive to the country to tend their flower and vegetable garden and to enjoy quiet times in each other's company. Spanish words and phrases are sprinkled throughout this realistic picture of life in a bilingual, divorced family. Boldly colored pastel paintings enhance the spirited account of a loving relationship between a father and daughter.

TEAMMATES

Peter Golenbock. Illustrated by Paul Bacon. (Harcourt Brace Jovanovich, 1990) 28 pages. ISBN: 0-15-200603-6. Level: Ages 5-10.

This brief 11¼ x 8¾ in. account of segregation, racism, humiliation, and personal courage takes place at a time in the United States "when automobiles were black and looked like tanks and the laundry was white and hung on clotheslines to dry." It features the former Negro Leagues, Brooklyn Dodgers General Manager Branch Rickey, Dodgers first baseman Jackie Robinson, and shortstop Pee Wee Reese. Archival photographs and full-color illustrations tell as much about the 1947 baseball season for Jackie Robinson, the first African American Major League player, as does the short text.

TWINNIES

Eve Bunting. Illustrated by Nancy Carpenter. (Harcourt Brace, 1997) 32 pages. ISBN: 0-15-291592-3. Level: Ages 4-7.

Twin baby sisters elicit a wide range of emotions in a young girl. She is frustrated by all the space they take up and jealous of the attention they receive from their parents, as well as from strangers. She is resigned to, and proud of, helping her mother out. ("She doesn't know what she'd do without me. I don't either. She'd be really truly overwhelmed.") And she is intrigued by the babies' play and accomplishments. ("Boo and Gwendolyn laugh even when nothing is funny. So we laugh with them.") Above all, however, she is fiercely protective, and "really, truly overwhelmed" by how much she loves them. Bunting hits the mark in this story that describes the ups and downs of big sisterhood in a warm and loving family. Carpenter's illustrations, rendered in oil, are especially effective in showing a contemporary family that is bound by the love expressed in everyday moments.

Ⓥ Ⓘⓥ

THE TWO MRS. GIBSONS

Toyomi Igus. Illustrated by Daryl Wells. (Children's Book Press, 1996) 32 pages. ISBN: 0-89239-135-9. Level: Ages 3-7.

The two Mrs. Gibsons don't seem to have much in common—one is tall, has dark skin, and was born in Tennessee, and the other is short, light-skinned, and was born in Japan. The narrator of this story describes the two by pointing out all their differences, but in the end, they have one important thing in common: "They both loved my daddy and they both loved me." This lyrical and unusually direct story of an interracial family focuses on the child's joyful acceptance of differences.

Ⓥ Ⓘⓥ Ⓘⓧ

WHAT ZEESIE SAW ON DELANCEY STREET

Elsa Okon Rael. Illustrated by Marjorie Priceman. (Simon & Schuster, 1996) 32 pages. ISBN: 0-689-80549-7. Level: Ages 5-8.

On her ninth birthday, Zeesie attends a package party with her parents, relatives, and neighbors. In the midst of all the excitement, she notices men taking turns going into a mysterious room. Her father tells her it's a money room where the heads of households can either leave or take money, according to their family's needs. Imagining that it must be filled with sparkling jewels and treasure, Zeesie sneaks in to take a peek, and what she sees inspires an act of great generosity on her part. Set in a thriving Jewish neighborhood in the 1930s, both the story and the lively illustrations are filled with ethnic and historical details.

Ⓥ Ⓘⓥ Ⓘ

WHAT'S IN AUNT MARY'S ROOM?

Elizabeth Fitzgerald Howard. Illustrated by Cedric Lucas. (Clarion, 1996) 32 pages. ISBN: 0-395-69845-6. Level: Ages 4-7.

The characters who first appeared in AUNT FLOSSIE'S HATS (AND CRAB CAKES LATER!) (Clarion, 1991) are back in an equally charming story about the relationship between two African American sisters and their great-great aunt. Here Susan and Sarah help Aunt Flossie open up a long-locked (and somewhat mysterious) room that had once belonged to their Aunt Mary to look for an old family Bible so the girls can add their own names to the family tree. Howard builds suspense through the girls' natural curiosity about what's in the room. Lucas's soft pastel illustrations complement the author's tone by getting across a sense of family intimacy in this original picture story dealing with African American heritage.

WHEN I AM OLD WITH YOU

Angela Johnson. Illustrated by David Soman. (Orchard Books, 1990) 32 pages. ISBN: 0-531-05884-0. Level: Ages 3-6.

A warm, tender relationship between a grandfather and his young grandson is recounted through the child's verbalized projections of all the things they'll do together when the child is as old as Grandaddy: "When I am old with you, Grandaddy, we will play cards all day underneath that old tree by the road. / We'll drink cool water from a jug and wave at all the cars that go by." Gentle, softly colored watercolor paintings show the African American grandfather and grandson doing today all the things they look forward to doing together in the future.

Ⓥ Ⓘ

THE WIDOW'S BROOM

Chris Van Allsburg. (Houghton Mifflin, 1992) 32 pages. ISBN: 0-395-64051-2. Level: Ages 6-11.

When a witch's broom loses its power mid-flight and falls, rider and all, into Widow Shaw's vegetable patch, the kindly widow swallows her own fear and takes the wounded witch into her farmhouse. The witch leaves as soon as she has healed herself, just as Widow Shaw expected, but leaves the useless broom behind. The broom soon proves itself to be far from useless—it feeds the chickens, chops wood, fetches water, and, of course, never tires of sweeping. In fact, it becomes something of a local celebrity until some of the townspeople feel that the broom is evil and demand that it be destroyed. This haunting tale appears to take place about two hundred years ago, although the theme of intolerance is especially pertinent to the late twentieth century. Van Allsburg's gritty, soft-edged black-and-white illustrations continually shift perspectives and perfectly capture contrasting responses to the unexpected—delight and fear. Meticulous attention to detail is evident on every page, right down to the physical shape of the book: tall and slender like a broom.

Children's Trade Books with Individuals, Groups, and Institutions as a Second Thematic Strand

The title index on pp. 173-180 lists the number of the page on which each book is annotated.

TITLE	AUTHOR	DATE	AGE LEVEL
Anthony Reynoso: Born to Rope	Ginger Gordon and Martha Cooper	1996	Ages 7-10
At the Beach	Huy Voun Lee	1994	Ages 6-10
Aunt Flossie's Hats (And Crab Cakes Later!)	Elizabeth Fitzgerald Howard	1991	Ages 4-9
Baseball in the Barrios	Henry Horenstein	1997	Ages 8-11
Batboy: An Inside Look at Spring Training	Joan Anderson	1996	Ages 8-12
Be Patient, Abdul	Dolores Sandoval	1996	Ages 5-7
Billy the Great	Rosa Guy	1992	Ages 6-10
Blessed Are You: Traditional Everyday Hebrew Prayers	Michelle Edwards	1993	Ages 3-6
Brown Angels: An Album of Pictures and Verse	Walter Dean Myers	1993	All ages
Brown Honey in Broomwheat Tea	Joyce Carol Thomas	1993	Ages 5-10
Camping in the Temple of the Sun	Deborah Gould	1992	Ages 3-7
The Carolers	Georgia Guback	1992	Ages 2-8
Christmas Counting	Lynn Reiser	1992	Ages 2-5
Cinnamon, Mint, & Mothballs: A Visit to Grandmother's House	Ruth Tiller	1993	Ages 4-8
A Day at Damp Camp	George Ella Lyon	1996	Ages 6-9
Dear Bear	Joanna Harrison	1994	Ages 4-8
Down the Road	Alice Schertle	1995	Ages 4-7
Eagle Drum: On the Powwow Trail with a Young Grass Dancer	Robert Crum	1994	Ages 7-11
Family Pictures/Cuadros de Familia	Carmen Lomas Garza	1990	Age 7 and older
Father and Son	Denize Lauture	1992	Ages 4-9
Flood	Mary Calhoun	1997	Ages 5-8
The Gift of Changing Woman	Tryntje Van Ness Seymour	1993	Ages 9-14
Giving Thanks: A Native American Good Morning Message	Chief Jake Swamp	1995	Ages 5-10
Glorious Angels: A Celebration of Children	Walter Dean Myers	1995	Age 3 and older

Going Home	Eve Bunting	1996	Ages 5-9
Grandaddy and Janetta	Helen V. Griffith	1993	Ages 4-8
Grandpappy	Nancy White Carlstrom	1990	Ages 5-8
Gus and Grandpa and the Christmas Cookies	Claudia Mills	1997	Ages 4-6
Habari Gani? / What's the News?: A Kwanzaa Story	Sundaira Morninghouse	1992	Ages 4-9
Hairs / Pelitos	Sandra Cisneros	1994	Ages 3-7
Halmoni and the Picnic	Sook Nyul Choi	1993	Ages 5-8
Hanukkah!	Roni Schotter	1990	Ages 4-6
Hard to Be Six	Arnold Adoff	1991	Ages 2-5
Her Stories: African American Folktales, Fairy Tales, and True Tales	Virginia Hamilton, reteller and author	1995	Ages 7-14 and older
How I Was Adopted	Joanna Cole	1995	Ages 3-7
In Daddy's Arms I Am Tall: African Americans Celebrating Fathers	Javaka Steptoe	1997	Age 8 and older
In for Winter, Out for Spring	Arnold Adolf	1991	Ages 5-8
Kwanzaa: A Family Affair	Mildred Pitts Walter	1995	Age 9 and older
Martha Calling	Susan Meddaugh	1994	Ages 4-8
Mary Cassatt	Robyn Montana Turner	1992	Ages 7-12
Me, Dad and Number 6	Dana Andrew Jennings	1997	Ages 6-8
Mimi's Tutu	Tynia Thomassie	1996	Ages 3-5
My First Kwanzaa Book	Deborah M. Newton Chocolate	1992	Ages 2-7
My Prairie Christmas	Brett Harvey	1990	Ages 4-8
Night on Neighborhood Street	Eloise Greenfield	1991	Ages 3-9
On Passover	Cathy Goldberg Fishman	1997	Ages 4-8
On Rosh Hashanah and Yom Kippur	Cathy Goldberg Fishman	1997	Ages 4-8
The Other Side: How Kids Live in a California Latino Neighborhood	Kathleen Krull	1994	Ages 7-11
Pablo Remembers: The Fiesta of The Day of The Dead	George Ancona	1993	Ages 5-9
Patrick Desjarlait: Conversations with a Native American Artist	Neva Williams	1995	Ages 8-14 and older

Potato: A Tale from the Great Depression	Kate Lied	1997	Ages 6-8 and older
Powwow	George Ancona	1993	Ages 5-11
Powwow Summer: A Family Celebrates the Circle of Life	Marcie R. Rendon	1996	Ages 7-11
The Seashore Book	Charlotte Zolotow	1992	Ages 3-8
Seven Days of Kwanzaa	Ella Grier	1997	Ages 3-8 and older
Starry Night	David Spohn	1992	Ages 3-7
Sun and Spoon	Kevin Herbes	1997	Ages 4-8
Take Me Out to the Ballgame	Jack Norworth	1992	Age 3 and older
The Tie Man's Miracle	Steven Schnur	1995	Ages 5-8
Tomorrow on Rocky Pond	Lynn Reiser	1993	Ages 3-6
Two Lands, One Heart: An American Boy's Journey to His Mother's Vietnam	Jeremy Schmidt and Ted Wood	1995	Ages 7-10
The Ugly Menorah	Marissa Moss	1996	Ages 5-8
Uncle Jed's Barbershop	Margaree King Mitchell	1993	Ages 5-9 and older
A Visit to Amy-Claire	Claudia Mills	1992	Ages 4-7
The Window	Michael Dorris	1997	Ages 10-13 and older
Working Cotton	Sherley Anne Williams	1992	Ages 6-9
The Year of No More Corn	Helen Ketteman	1993	Ages 4-8
Zora Hurston and the Chinaberry Tree	William Miller	1994	Ages 6-9

Children's Trade Books with Individuals, Groups, and Institutions as a Third Thematic Strand

The title index on pp. 173-180 lists the number of the page on which each book is annotated.

Abuelita's Paradise	Carmen Santiago Nodar	1992	Ages 4-7
All the Lights in the Night	Arthur A. Levine	1991	Ages 5-9
The Block	Langston Hughes	1995	Age 11 and older
Bloomers!	Rhoda Blumberg	1993	Ages 7-10 and older
Children of Clay: A Family of Pueblo Potters	Rina Swentzell	1992	Ages 7-13
The Children of Topaz: The Story of a Japanese-American Internment Camp, Based on a Classroom Diary	Michael O. Tunnell and George W. Chilcoat	1996	Ages 8-14 and older

Christmas Tree Memories	Aliki	1991	Ages 3-6
Come Back, Salmon: How a Group of Dedicated Kids Adopted Pigeon Creek and Brought It Back to Life	Molly Cone	1992	Ages 6-10
Dolphin Man: Exploring the World of Dolphins	Laurence Pringle	1995	Ages 7-11
Drumbeat … Heartbeat: A Celebration of the Powwow (We Are Still Here)	Susan Braine	1995	Ages 7-11
Emeka's Gift: An African Counting Story	Ifeoma Onyefulu	1995	Ages 4-7
Home Place	Crescent Dragonwagon	1990	Ages 7-10
Hopscotch around the World	Mary D. Lankford	1992	Ages 6-9
How My Family Lives in America	Susan Kuklin	1992	Ages 4-7
I Am a Jesse White Tumbler	Diane Schmidt	1990	Ages 7-12
Kinaalda: A Navajo Girl Grows Up	Monty Roessel	1993	Ages 7-11 and older
Mac & Marie & the Train Toss Surprise	Elizabeth Fitzgerald Howard	1993	Ages 5-8
The Magic Moonberry Jump Ropes	Dakari Hru	1996	Ages 4-7
My Daddy Was a Soldier: A World War II Story	Deborah Kogan Ray	1990	Ages 7-10
My Two Uncles	Judith Vigna	1995	Ages 4-8 and older
Seven Candles for Kwanzaa	Andrea Davis Pinkney	1993	Ages 3-9
Shannon: An Ojibway Dancer	Sandra King	1993	Ages 7-11
Six Words, Many Turtles, and Three Days in Hong Kong	Patricia McMahon	1997	Ages 8-11
Taking Flight: My Story	Vicki Van Meter with Dan Gutman	1995	Ages 10-12
Totem Pole	Diane Hoyt-Goldsmith	1990	Ages 5-10
Wheels	Shirley Hughes	1991	Ages 3-8

CHILDREN'S TRADE BOOKS WITH POWER, AUTHORITY, AND GOVERNANCE AS THE MAJOR THEMATIC STRAND

AIDA

Leontyne Price, reteller. Illustrated by Leo and Diane Dillon (Harcourt Brace Jovanovich, 1990) 32 pages. ISBN: 0-15-200405-X. Level: Ages 7-14 and older.

This handsome 11¼ x 10¼ in. volume provides readers with an internationally respected African American opera star's retelling of this opera narrative, which, she states, has given her "great inspiration onstage and off." In a storyteller's note at the end of the book, Price cites the qualities she admires in the Ethiopian Princess who "was my best friend operatically and was a natural for me because my skin was my costume." These qualities include Aida's "deep devotion and love for her country and people—her nobility, strength and courage." They are expressed in the Dillons' rich colors, dramatic costumings of characters, inventive stagings of action, and multiple uses of ancient Egyptian images. The tragic enslavement central to the opera is not romanticized, although the story contains romantic elements. Traditional typography combined with the elegance of contemporary book design and production complement the Dillons' contemporary illustrative style.

THE AMISTAD SLAVE REVOLT AND AMERICAN ABOLITION

Karen Zeinert. (Linnet Books, 1997) 101 pages. Pbk. ISBN: 0-208-02439-5. Level: Age 11 and older.

An account of this historic revolt on the ship *La Amistad* in 1839 led by the indomitable Mende man known both as Cinque and as Senge Pieh, and of abolitionist legal cases arising afterwards, was written from primary source materials at the Amistad Research Center and the New Haven Colony Historical Society. The intricacies of the court cases and the principal figures in all stages of this prolonged sequence of events are explained with clarity. Footnotes, two bibliographies, a map, archival visual material, and a summary of the aftermath for leading individuals add to the value of a compact report. The title contains a misnomer: "slave revolt." The thirty-five survivors of the tortuous trip from Sierra Leone, the subsequent revolt on the ship *La Amistad*, and various imprisonments were never enslaved.

ANASTASIA'S ALBUM

Hugh Brewster. (U.S. edition: Madison Press/Hyperion, 1996) 64 pages. ISBN: 0-7868-0292-8. Level: Ages 10-13 and older.

The inviting design and layout of this 10 x 10 in. biography of Anastasia Romanov, the youngest daughter of Tsar Nicholas II of Russia, features dozens of photographs of the young grand duchess and her family. Samplings of Anastasia's accomplished artistic efforts also grace many pages. Brewster writes of Anastasia and her family with an eye on the everyday aspects of these highly privileged individuals' lives, but does not ignore the political overtones that led to their ultimate tragedy. Excerpts from her letters to teachers and friends serve to bring this portrait of Anastasia into even sharper focus, while mention of the questions that still surround her death may send intrigued readers in search of additional information.

THE CHILDREN OF TOPAZ: THE STORY OF A JAPANESE-AMERICAN INTERNMENT CAMP, BASED ON A CLASSROOM DIARY

Michael O. Tunnell and George W. Chilcoat. (Holiday House, 1996) 74 pages. ISBN: 0-8234-1239-3. Level: Ages 8-14 and older.

Journal entries kept by Miss Hori's third grade class from March 8 to August 12, 1943, provide the springboard for an account of day-to-day life in the Topaz Relocation Center as it was experienced by Japanese American children. Their brief, upbeat entries describing camp life stand in stark contrast to the grim realities described in the text and shown in the accompanying black-and-white documentary photographs.

THE COPPER LADY

Alice Ross and Kent Ross. Illustrated by Leslie Bowman. (On My Own). (Carolrhoda, 1997) 48 pages. ISBN: 0-87614-934-4. Level: Ages 6-9.

Living in Paris in the 1880s, Andre, a nine-year-old who was taken in by a neighbor after his parents died, earns his keep by helping Mr. Malet deliver coal. On his rare breaks from work, he sneaks down the street to a shop where Mr. Bartholdi is supervising the construction of a gigantic lady made of copper. It is meant to be a gift from the people of France to the people of the United States, they tell him. Fascinated by the process, Andre returns day after day to watch and, as he watches, he develops a great curiosity about the place to which the completed statue will be delivered. When it is finally shipped to the United States, Andre decides to travel with it on the same ship—as a stowaway. Although Andre is a fictional character, the details about the building of the Statue of Liberty and its perilous journey overseas are based on facts. Children who are making the transition from beginning reading to longer chapter books will find a lot of drama and a surprising amount of depth in this extremely accessible story.

HIAWATHA: MESSENGER OF PEACE

Dennis Brindell Fradin. (McElderry Books, 1992) 40 pages. ISBN: 0-689-50519-1. Level: Ages 7-11 and older.

After briefly explaining the series of historical errors and misunderstandings that led to the fictional character of Longfellow's famous poem, the author provides a concise account of the life of the flesh-and-blood Hiawatha. Along with his Huron friend, Degandawida, Hiawatha convinced five warring tribes (Mohawk, Oneida, Onondaga, Cayuga, and Seneca) to lay down their weapons and form the Iroquois Federation, a representative system of government that is often credited with providing a model for American colonists three hundred years later. In addition to reproductions of historical prints by European and American artists, the text is illustrated with paintings by four contemporary Iroquois artists: John Fadden, Arnold Jacobs, Cleveland Sandy, and Ernest Smith.

A LONG WAY TO GO

Zibby Oneal. Illustrated by Michael Dooling. (Viking, 1990) 54 pages. ISBN: 0-670-82532-8. Level: Ages 7-10 and older.

Eight-year-old Lila is the pampered eldest daughter in an upper-class family living in New York City during World War I. Although she bristles under seemingly unreasonable rules about how she should behave, it has never occurred to her to question her father's authority until she finds out that her grandmother has been arrested at a Women's Suffrage demonstration. When her parents refuse to talk to her about it, Lila finds her own ways to learn more about her grandmother's political activity and even marches in a demonstration herself. This easy-to-

read fictional account of one girl's awakening political consciousness introduces the historical struggle for women's voting rights.

MAN AND MUSTANG

George Ancona. (Macmillan, 1992) 48 pages. ISBN: 0-02-700802-9. Level: Ages 8-13.

This photoessay with numerous black-and-white photographs describes the way in which the U.S. Bureau of Land Management (BLM) controls the mustang population in order to maintain an ecological balance in the Great Basin. After the wild horses are rounded up, they are turned over to penitentiaries where prisoners can volunteer to work with horses as part of job training. After a horse is gentled, it is ready to be adopted by a family as part of the BLM's Adopt-A-Horse project. Ancona goes through the step-by-step process of a complicated government program that will be of great interest to many young horse enthusiasts.

OFFICER BUCKLE AND GLORIA

Peggy Rathmann. (Putnam, 1995) 32 pages. ISBN: 0-399-22616-8. Level: Ages 3-7.

Whenever Officer Buckle visits elementary schools to give his lecture on personal safety, his audiences drift off to sleep. But once his trusty police dog Gloria begins to accompany him, suddenly his show is a hit! Little does Officer Buckle know, however, that his new-found popularity is actually due to Gloria's upstaging him behind his back—literally—as she enacts a dramatic interpretation of each of Officer Buckle's tips. Lively pen-and-ink drawings with watercolor washes add humor to this modern cautionary tale.

OUR JOURNEY FROM TIBET: BASED ON A TRUE STORY

Laurie Dolphin. Photographs by Nancy Jo Johnson. With a letter from His Holiness the Dalai Lama. Afterword by Rinchen K. Choegyal. (Dutton, 1997) 40 pages. ISBN: 0-525-45577-9. Level: Ages 9-12 and older.

Dolphin and Johnson recreate the journey of Sonam, a young girl who flees Tibet with her siblings to escape the oppression of Chinese rule. The text begins with a brief summary of the Chinese takeover of Tibet and the absence of religious, political, and educational freedom under the Chinese government. It goes on to describe

Tibetans' devotion to His Holiness the Dalai Lama, their exiled spiritual and political leader who advocates non-violence in the Tibetan quest for freedom. Sonam then recalls her journey with an older brother and two sisters from Tibet to Dharamsala, India, where free schools have been established for Tibetan refugee children. It is a decision that Sonam's parents make for their children's future, even though Sonam knows she may never see them again. The decision to write the entire text in Sonam's first-person voice makes the narrative feel a bit too contrived at times, but the facts and emotions it conveys are authentic. Likewise, the color photographs accompanying the description of Sonam's flight from her homeland appear to be documentary photographs of other children and other escapes from Tibet, but they are presented in a way that minimizes confusion and captures the courage and trepidation that any such journey involves. A letter from His Holiness the Fourteenth Dalai Lama that concludes the book assures readers that the oppression of Tibetans in their own country, and the journey of Sonam, her siblings, and so many other refugee children and families, is very real indeed.

PEACEBOUND TRAINS

Haemi Balgassi. Illustrated by Chris K. Soentpiet. (Clarion, 1996) 46 pages. ISBN: 0-395-72093-1. Level: Ages 8-12 and older.

During these years while her mother, or umma, is away in the U.S. Army, young Sumi lives with her grandmother, or harmuny. Sumi feels particularly lonesome for Umma one day, so Harmuny tells the girl what happened when Umma was a baby in Seoul, Korea, in 1951. Fleeing from Seoul and increasing dangers, Harmuny and Sumi's grandfather, or harabujy, took their children and the belongings they could carry and started walking toward far away Pusan. Finally Harabujy decided that the best chance his wife and their children might have for survival would be to ride with hundreds of other desperate refugees on top of the last train going south. The family made it safely, but they never saw Harabujy again. The story is based on actual experiences in the lives of Balgassi's mother and grandmother. Both she and Soentpiet were born in Seoul. Soentpiet's marvelous watercolors grace each page, expanding the contemporary and historical scenes and specifying cultural details. This compelling fictional account is divided into eight short sections.

PUBLIC DEFENDER: LAWYER FOR THE PEOPLE

Joan Hewett. Photographs by Richard Hewett. (Lodestar Books, 1991) 48 pages. ISBN: 0-525-67340-7. Level: Ages 9-14.

This photoessay describes typical activities in the worklife of Janice Fukai, an Asian American lawyer in Los Angeles County. Black-and-white photographs accompany the straightforward account of an individual public defender's work with clients who have been charged with serious crimes.

RED SCARF GIRL: A MEMOIR OF THE CULTURAL REVOLUTION

Ji-Li Jiang. Foreword by David Henry Hwang. (HarperCollins, 1997) 285 pages. ISBN: 0-06-027585-5. Level: Age 12 and older.

Readers won't need prior knowledge of the Chinese Cultural Revolution in the 1960s to be compelled by this gripping description of the revolution's impact on the life of twelve-year-old Ji-Li Jiang and her family, or to come away with an understanding of the ideas that fueled the revolution and the personal price paid by thousands as those ideas were carried out by Chairman Mao and his government. In the New China of the revolution, family connections are all it takes to condemn someone, even if the "sin" of the family took place many years ago. As a result, because her grandparents were landlords, Ji-Li and her family are suspect. Ji-Li, a bright and eager student before the revolution began, starts to dread going to school, where Party loyalty now means more than academic achievement. She is humiliated when her name appears in a da-zi-bao, a type of propaganda poster that raises suspicions about people's actions without any basis of truth. And she is frightened when her father is detained for weeks by the government for refusing to confess to a "crime" he did not commit; indeed, he does not even know what it is they want him to admit to. Initially, Ji-Li had been swept up in revolutionary fervor, eagerly identifying "four olds"—old ideas, old customs, old cultures, and old habits—to be destroyed. But now she is torn and confused. Her teachers tell her she is an "educable" child who can overcome her background if she denounces her family, but this, Ji-Li realizes, she is not prepared or willing to do. RED SCARF GIRL is Ji-Li Jiang's true story, not Orwellian fiction. Her voice is as real as the events it describes in this important, illuminating memoir.

STAR OF FEAR, STAR OF HOPE

Jo Hoestlandt. Illustrated by Johanna Kang. (Walker, 1995) 32 pages. ISBN: 0-8027-8373-2. Level: Ages 7-10 and older.

Helen looks back with regret and sadness on events in her childhood during the Nazi occupation of France. As a small girl, she was unable to comprehend the fear and injustice experienced by her best friend, Lydia, who was Jewish. To Helen, the yellow star was "pretty," and Lydia's decision to go home after a frightening event rather than spend the night for Helen's birthday was hurtful. The day after her birthday, Helen has forgiven Lydia for leaving, but it's too late. The Germans have come, and Lydia and her family are gone. Stark, full-page illustrations accompany a painful, somber story about the Holocaust.

TOUSSAINT L'OUVERTURE: THE FIGHT FOR HAITI'S FREEDOM

Walter Dean Myers. Illustrated by Jacob Lawrence. (Simon & Schuster, 1996) 40 pages. ISBN: 0-689-80126-2. Level: Ages 9-12.

Toussaint L'Ouverture dreamed of freedom for the people of African descent in Haiti, and when Blacks started to revolt against their French and Spanish oppressors in the late eighteenth century, he proved to be a brilliant military strategist whose leadership was invaluable and inspiring to his people. Lawrence created forty-one bold, harrowing paintings to tell the story of Toussaint and slavery and the struggle for freedom in Haiti. His dramatic, emotional art is balanced by Myers's skillful, measured narrative that serves to tell riveting story while pacing the runaway power of the images.

WHEN I LEFT MY VILLAGE

Maxine Rose Schur. Illustrated by Brian Pinkney. (Dial, 1996) 62 pages. ISBN: 0-8037-1562-5. Level: Ages 8-10 and older.

Young Menelik describes the dangerous journey he and his family make in an effort to flee Ethiopia, where they face intense oppression and scorn because they are Jewish. The forced flight of thousands of the Beta Israel, the Jews of Ethiopia, to Israel in the mid 1980s and early 1990s was the inspiration for this perilous story in which Menelik tells of his family's efforts to escape by foot down the mountains and across the plains. Fighting exhaustion and near starvation, Menelik and his family finally reach a border camp, where they wait and hope that Israel will come to their rescue. Menelik's story is grounded in cultural details, as well as the fervent hope for freedom. Menelik was introduced in an earlier story, DAY OF DELIGHT (Dial, 1994).

Children's Trade Books with Power, Authority, and Governance as a Second Thematic Strand

The title index on pp. 173-180 lists the number of the page on which each book is annotated.

TITLE	AUTHOR	YEAR	AGE LEVEL
The Ballot Box Battle	Emily Arnold McCully	1996	Ages 5-8
Baseball Saved Us	Ken Mochizuki	1993	Ages 7-11 and older
Big Annie of Calumet: A True Story of the Industrial Revolution	Jerry Stanley	1996	Ages 10-15 and older
Bloomers!	Rhoda Blumberg	1993	Ages 7-10 and older
The Boys' War: Confederate and Union Soldiers Talk about the Civil War	Jim Murphy	1990	Age 9 and older
The Day Gogo Went to Vote: South Africa, 1994	Elinor Batezat Sisulu	1996	Ages 7-10 and older
Eleanor Roosevelt: A Life of Discovery	Russell Freedman	1993	Ages 9-14 and older
The Feather-Bed Journey	Paula Kurzband Feder	1995	Ages 5-8 and older
A Forever Family	Roslyn Banish and Jennifer Jordan-Wong	1992	Ages 6-11
The Journey: Japanese Americans, Racism and Renewal	Sheila Hamanaka	1990	Age 9 and older
The Kid's Guide to Social Action: How to Solve the Social Problems You Choose—And Turn Creative Thinking into Positive Action	Barbara Lewis	1991	Age 8 and older
Places of Refuge: Our National Wildlife Refuge System	Dorothy Hinshaw Patent	1992	Ages 9-12 and older
A Separate Battle: Women and the Civil War	Ina Chang	1991	Age 9 and older
Tell Them We Remember: The Story of the Holocaust	Susan D. Baachrach	1994	Age 9 and older

Children's Trade Books with Power, Authority, and Governance as a Third Thematic Strand

The title index on pp. 173-180 lists the number of the page on which each book is annotated.

Antarctica: The Last Unspoiled Continent	Laurence Pringle	1992	Ages 8-12 and older
Here Comes the Mail	Gloria Skurzynski	1992	Ages 4-8
Many Thousand Gone: African Americans from Slavery to Freedom	Virginia Hamilton	1993	All ages
Martha Calling	Susan Meddaugh	1994	Ages 4-8
Oh, Freedom! Kids Talk about the Civil Rights Movement with the People Who Made It Happen	Casey King and Linda Barrett Osborn	1997	Ages 8-14

CHILDREN'S TRADE BOOKS WITH PRODUCTION, DISTRIBUTION, AND CONSUMPTION AS THE MAJOR THEMATIC STRAND

BATBOY: AN INSIDE LOOK AT SPRING TRAINING

Joan Anderson. Photographs by Matthew Cavanaugh. (Lodestar, 1996) 48 pages. ISBN: 0-525-67511-6. Level: Ages 8-12.
Kenny Garibaldi is a batboy for the San Francisco Giants during spring training in Scottsdale, Arizona. It's a lot of work for the thirteen-year-old, who must prepare uniforms and equipment before each game, be ready to predict and meet the needs of individual players, and help clean up the locker room at the end of each tiring day. But in return, Kenny gets to work side-by-side with some of the biggest names in major league baseball, and make friends with potential stars of the future, as he learns about the long, hard road to the major leagues. Text and color photographs put greater emphasis on the hard work involved and less on the glamour of life as a professional athlete.
Ⓥ Ⓥ Ⓘⓥ

BE PATIENT, ABDUL

Dolores Sandoval. (Margaret K. McElderry, 1996) 32 pages. ISBN: 0-689-50607-4. Level: Ages 5-7.
Abdul lives in Freetown, the capital of Sierra Leone. The seven-year-old sells oranges to earn money for his school fees, but when business is slow, he has a hard time being patient—he loves to learn and wants to be sure he'll be able to continue his education. The day that Momma marches in the big parade to celebrate the anniversary of Sierra Leone's independence, Abdul's worries come to an end, but not before he's learned to appreciate what patience can bring, and not before readers have learned a little about contemporary life for a child in this West African nation. This picture book features full-page, full-color acrylic illustrations and a text well-suited for emergent readers.
Ⓥ Ⓥ Ⓘ

BIG RIGS

Hope Irvin Marston. (Cobblehill, 1993) 48 pages. ISBN: 0-525-65123-3. Level: Ages 3-6.
Trucks, trucks, and more trucks, all of them BIG, are the subjects of this book filled with photographs and facts. From under the hood to inside the cab to the trailers that are pulled behind, color photographs, new to this revised edition, reveal the many makes, models, and uses of "big rigs." Brief text on each page provides an explanation of the truck pictured, including, when it has one, its nickname among truckers (a short trailer, for example, is called a "pup"). A glossary of some of the CB radio terms used by truckers when they're on the road is included in a section at the end of this book that will thrill young wheel enthusiasts.
Ⓥ Ⓥ

THE BOBBIN GIRL

Emily Arnold McCully. (Dial, 1996) 32 pages. ISBN: 0-8037-1828-4. Level: Ages 8-11 and older.
Ten-year-old Rebecca Putney has to stand on a box to reach the company ledger and sign her name after working all week with other girls and women in a New England textile mill in the 1830s. Rebecca is less naive than she might appear because innocence disappears quickly in a workplace replete with injustices, injuries, and twelve-hour workdays. Loosely basing the story on the well-documented childhood experiences of Harriet Hanson Robinson, McCully focuses on the mill workers' first strike in Lowell, Massachusetts. Watercolors and pastels illustrate each page of a picture book story full of written and visual historical details. A page of historical information concludes the book.
Ⓥ Ⓧ Ⓘ

BREAD IS FOR EATING

David Gershator and Phillis. Illustrated by Emma Shaw Smith. (Henry Holt, 1995) 28 pages. ISBN: 0-8050-3173-1. Level: Ages 4-8.
When her little boy leaves bread on his plate, Mamita says, "Bread is for eating." Gently she reminds him of the elements ripening the seeds and the people harvesting grain. She sings of these things, of millers and bakers, of family members working to earn money to buy bread, and "of people around the world, dreaming of bread." Readers are invited to think in new ways because of the warm, rich colors of the ink drawings on every page. Spanish and English words are provided along with

a musical notation for the short title song, the Spanish language refrain of which is part of the English language text. The book's restrained energy combined with the unusual perspectives and detailed borders of its art makes it one to re-read, sing, and remember.

EXTRA CHEESE, PLEASE! MOZZARELLA'S JOURNEY FROM COW TO PIZZA

Cris Peterson. Photographs by Alvis Upitis. (Boyds Mills Press, 1994) 32 pages. ISBN: 1-56397-177-1. Level: Ages 5-8.

Author Cris Peterson explains how the milk from her dairy farm in Grantsburg, Wisconsin, becomes cheese that tops the home-made pizza which is a Friday-night tradition in her home. The simple, appealing narrative, accompanied by full-color photographs, describes what happens from farm to factory in order to turn milk into cheese.

FARMERS' MARKET

Paul Brett Johnson. (Orchard, 1997) 32 pages. ISBN: 0-531-30014-5. Level: Ages 4-7.

On summer Saturdays, Laura and her family are up before sunrise to load their pick-up truck with the vegetables they will sell at the farmers' market in Lexington. It is still dark when they arrive at Vine Street to set up their stand and put out the vegetables: "We do it the same every week," she observes. As dawn breaks and customers start to file by, Laura helps out by keeping the vegetable baskets on display well stocked, as her brother and parents each have their own responsibilities with the stand. But just before noon, when things have started to slow down, Mom tells her that she's earned some free time and Laura runs off to find her "Saturday friend," a girl her age whose mother has a flower stand. Detailed acrylic paintings realistically portray a busy farmers' market from a child's point of view.

FATHER'S RUBBER SHOES

Yumi Heo. (Orchard, 1995) 32 pages. ISBN: 0-531-06873-0. Level: Ages 4-8.

Yungsu has difficulty adjusting to life in the United States after his family moves from Korea. Since they were all happy in Korea, he can't understand why they left. When his father tells him a story from his own childhood, it helps him to understand a parent's desire to provide a better life for the next generation. Heo combines oil paintings, pencil drawings, and collage to create her distinctive art style. Her innovative use of color and perspective reflects Yungsu's moods throughout the book.

FIRE AT THE TRIANGLE FACTORY

Holly Littlefield. Illustrated by Mary O'Keefe Young. (On My Own) (Carolrhoda, 1996) 48 pages. ISBN: 0-87614-868-2. Level: Ages 8-11 and older.

The circumstances of the Triangle Shirtwaist Company Fire of 1911 are related through the fictional experiences of Minnie Levine, a fourteen-year-old Jewish girl whose father was born in Poland, and Tesa Monnetti, her Catholic coworker from an Italian family. The girls' working conditions and experiences at the time of the fire are based on reports of survivors. Brief pages with historical background that are more challenging to read precede and follow the story. This extremely easy-to-read story introduces some of the prejudices of that time and situation. Full-color watercolor illustrations on every page further enliven this special format for finding out about a tragic event in U.S. history.

FIRE TRUCK NUTS AND BOLTS

Jerry Boucher. (Carolrhoda, 1993) 40 pages. ISBN: 0-87614-783-X. Level: Ages 5-10.

How is a fire truck built? Step by step and piece by piece. Simple text and large color photographs detail the production of one of these huge trucks, starting with the design process and ending with a shiny red pumper engine ready for the road.

GOOD-BYE, CURTIS

Kevin Henkes. Illustrated by Marisabina Russo. (Greenwillow, 1995) 24 pages. ISBN: 0-688-12828-9. Level: Ages 3-6.

Retiring after forty-two years as a mail carrier, Curtis's last day making his rounds is filled with memories, good wishes, and small gifts from an appreciative community. "We'll miss you, Curtis," they all tell him, and it is obvious that Curtis will miss his customers, too. Henkes's simple, patterned text will hook young listeners who are already tuned in to the comforting predictability of neighborhood routines. Russo's brightly colored gouache paintings bring the neighborhood filled with shops and houses, children and grownups, and cats and dogs to life.

GROWING UP IN COAL COUNTRY

Susan Campbell Bartoletti. (Houghton Mifflin, 1996) 127 pages. ISBN: 0-395-77847-6. Level: Ages 9-16.

This account of work and childhood chronicles the horrific circumstances in which children labored and lived in the coal mining towns of northeastern Pennsylvania during the late 1800s and early 1900s. Stimulated by hearing the personal stories of her late husband's grandparents, the author began to record many oral histories. She read old mining records, visited museums, and studied old photographs. She reports how women and children worked at home, how children's schooling and health suffered, and how the cycle was repeated from generation to generation. Bartoletti's masterfully developed narrative allows her human subjects to speak for themselves. The varied array of memorable black-and-white photos documents their experience.

THE HEART OF THE WOOD

Marguerite W. Davol. Illustrated by Sheila Hamanaka. (Simon & Schuster, 1992) 32 pages. ISBN: 0-671-74778-9. Level: Ages 3-8.

Illustrations created in oil paints on bark paper celebrate the artistry and multiple procedures leading to a joyous celebration complete with "music, now high, now low, / made by the fiddler with fingers and bow, / playing the fiddle created to find / the song in the heart of the wood, / shaped by the woodcarver with music in mind." The language pattern for THE HOUSE THAT JACK BUILT serves Davol's theme of creativity, while Hamanaka's inclusive vision of community embraces all in this celebratory full-color picture book.

IN THE STREET OF THE TEMPLE CLOTH PRINTERS

Dorothy Field. (Pacific Educational Press, 1996) 36 pages. (Paperback with perfect binding) ISBN: 1-895766-07-9. Level: Ages 9-14.

The families who create temple cloths live and work in one section of old Ahmedabad, India. Temple cloths are associated with the worship of the Hindu Mother Goddess whose image is in the center of each hand colored assemblage of block prints. Stories unfold on cloth as readers follow the exacting work of Vaghi, Otamben, Dilip, Jagadish, Babu, Kacharaji, and others whose families before them also created drawings and block prints for the temple cloths. Folkloristic and other cultural dimensions of textile printing are explained and then shown in a variety of photographs of people at work and reproduc-

tions of their designs. The modestly produced $8\frac{3}{8}$ x $10\frac{7}{8}$ in. book printed in two colors contains a wealth of accessible information about this art form.

JELLY BEANS FOR SALE

Bruce McMillan. (Scholastic, 1996) 32 pages. ISBN: 0-590-86584-6. Level: Ages 4-8.

A jelly bean stand staffed by two children provides the basis for an introduction to the monetary values of pennies, nickels, dimes, and quarters. With jelly beans that cost one cent apiece, McMillan is able to show the values of various coins by showing different coin combinations next to their exact value in jelly beans. Appealing full-color photographs on facing pages show the young customers enjoying their purchases. Added notes at the back include information on the history of jelly beans and a description of the seven-day manufacturing process used to make jelly beans today.

KIDS AT WORK: LEWIS HINE AND THE CRUSADE AGAINST CHILD LABOR

Russell Freedman. (Clarion, 1994) 104 pages. ISBN: 0-395-58703-4. Level: Ages 8-14 and older.

As an investigative reporter for the National Child Labor Committee during the early twentieth century, photographer Lewis Hine documented the fact that children were being exploited in factories, mills, mines, and fields across the nation. Just as Hine had found ways earlier to set up his camera quickly to record the faces of immigrant families in the harsh, poorly lit circumstances of Ellis Island, he brashly entered areas where he was unwelcome to document evidence of little boys and girls laboring. Fifty-nine of Hine's photographs are reproduced here with great technical skill. His works retain the power to astonish and anger, as does Freedman's account of the psychological and physical oppression of children used as beasts of burden. Freedman's written portrait of Hine at work is equally moving.

MAMA BEAR

Chyng Feng Sun. Illustrated by Lolly Robinson. (Houghton Mifflin, 1994) 32 pages. ISBN: 0-395-63412-1. Level: Ages 4-8.

From the moment she first saw it in the toy shop window, Mei-Mei has desperately wanted the huge stuffed bear, even though she knows her mama doesn't earn enough money in her job at the neighborhood Chinese restaurant to buy such extravagant luxuries. Mei-Mei manages to earn some money of her own with occasional odd jobs around the restaurant, but she still can't save enough to buy "the softest, warmest bear in the whole world." Luckily, Mei-Mei's mama is soft and warm and gives great bear hugs, and that is the most important thing of all. The warm, quiet tone of this refreshingly realistic story is echoed in the softly colored illustrations that accompany it.

THE MILKMAN'S BOY

Donald Hall. Illustrated by Greg Shed. (Walker, 1997) 32 pages. ISBN: 0-8027-8465-8. Level: Ages 5-9.

Paul's father delivers a route of bottled milk to individual doorsteps, an older brother delivers another route, and his mother manages the business end of the family's livelihood. Everyone washes bottles, and young Paul watches for cracks and chips. Farmer neighbors bring the milk during the early evening, and after the family fills the bottles at 4:00 a.m. Paul pushes paper caps into bottle tops. Hall describes a time when families kept cows in their backyards, when people depended on horse-drawn wagons, when small business owners knew their customers by name, and when a person would die from a high fever—occasionally. Later it became known that such a fever might have originated from drinking raw milk. Historic details about dairying fill a picture story about the Graves Family Dairy in Connecticut. Shed's paintings capture the feeling of the early twentieth century and are rendered in gouache on canvas. An endnote relates Hall's childhood connection to a family dairy and suggests additional changes affecting former family dairy businesses. James Cross Giblin's book MILK: THE FIGHT FOR PURITY (Crowell, 1986) provides substantial verification of this fictional account about a family dairy.

THE PAPERBOY

Dav Pilkey. (Orchard, 1996) 32 pages. ISBN: 0-531-09506-1. Level: Ages 3-7.

On the wordless opening double-page spreads, we see a truck leaving the loading dock of the Morning Star Gazette and traveling through residential streets to the house where the paperboy is just getting out of bed. The moon and stars shine brightly in the pitch black sky as the paperboy and his dog go through their early morning rituals of preparing for their route: moving quietly through the house, eating breakfast, and folding newspapers in the garage. The understated, poetic text brilliantly captures the rhythm of routine as Pilkey highlights small but evocative details, such as the snap of green rubber bands and the awkwardness of riding a bicycle while carrying a cloth bag filled with newspapers. As the paperboy and his dog make their rounds through the dark, familiar streets, the early morning sky gradually lightens. It is streaked with bright orange and pink hues by the time all the newspapers are delivered, and the paperboy must pull down his window shade to shut out the light when he returns to his own warm bed. Pilkey's expressive acrylic paintings playfully use light and dark contrasts to provide a delicious sense of being awake and active in a sleeping world. His paintings carry the mood through to the story's conclusion where we find the paperboy asleep and dreaming in the wide-awake world.

POTATO: A TALE FROM THE GREAT DEPRESSION

Kate Lied. Illustrated by Lisa Campbell Ernst. (National Geographic Society, 1997) 32 pages, ISBN: 0-7922-3521-5. Level: Ages 6-8 and older.

This picture story enveloped in brown involves a family who finds two weeks of work digging potatoes in Depression-era Idaho. "This is a story about my grandfather and my grandmother. It is also a story about the Great Depression and how hard things were," begins this story written when the author, now twelve, was eight years old. Written from the viewpoint of a very young girl and bordered in brown, the narrative moves the family from a round-the-clock two-week stint of potato digging in Idaho back home to Iowa where they trade potatoes for necessities and continue to work "very hard to live on what little they had."

THE SACRED HARVEST: OJIBWAY WILD RICE GATHERING

Gordon Regguinti. Photographs by Dale Kakkak. (Lerner, 1992) 48 pages. ISBN: 0-8225-2650-6. Level: Ages 7-13.

Narrative by an Ojibway writer and color photographs by a Menominee photographer recount eleven-year-old Glen Jackson's first time gathering wild rice with his father near their home on the Leech Lake Reservation in Minnesota. In addition to showing the harvest from start to finish, the author continually links the tradition to Glen's Ojibway heritage with the teachings of his elders, placing the harvest in a broader cultural context.

SOFIE'S ROLE

Amy Heath. Illustrated by Sheila Hamanaka. (Four Winds Press, 1992) 32 pages. ISBN: 0-02-743505-9. Level: Ages 4-8.

The family bakery will be extremely busy on December 24th. Before dawn, Sofie goes with her parents to help out. She fills pastry cases, bags orders, answers the phone, and even waits on a few customers "out front" once the shop opens. This spunky brown-skinned girl enjoys a one time stint in the busy bakery, especially when a girl from school is one of her customers. An appetite-whetting array of baked goods is pictured in Hamanaka's oil-on-canvas paintings reproduced in full color. The illustrations display bakery workers and customers from diverse backgrounds and enliven Heath's story about a child's foray into an adult world of work. Recipes for marzipan and cinnamon star cookies are included.

SUGARING SEASON: MAKING MAPLE SYRUP

Diane L. Burns. Photographs by Cheryl Walsh Bellville. (Carolrhoda, 1990) 48 pages. ISBN: 0-87614-422-9. Level: Ages 6-10.

Scenic and close-up color photographs, charts, and maps augment a ten-part explanation of a late twentieth century maple sap harvest: the trees, sap, sugar bush, preparations, tapping, run, cooking, grading, packaging, and the season's end. A glossary and author's note concerning the relative health and future of sugar maple trees in the United States and Canada add a helpful dimension.

UNCLE JED'S BARBERSHOP

Margaree King Mitchell. Illustrated by James Ransome. (Simon & Schuster, 1993) 32 pages. ISBN: 0-671-76969-3. Level: Ages 5-9 and older.

Mitchell's first-person narrative relates how her granddaddy's brother Jedediah Johnson, the only black barber in the county, was her favorite relative. She tells about his Wednesday night visits to her family, how he paid for the operation she needed to save her life, and how the Depression caused him to lose money he saved for a barbershop. This heartwarming story is the portrait of a generous, indomitable man whose personal dream is finally fulfilled when he is seventy-nine years old. The $11\frac{3}{4}$ by $9\frac{1}{4}$ in. picture story provides a straightforward account of segregation and its impact on one family during a crisis, and shows one man plying his trade to make a living. Ransome's dramatic illustrations created with oil paint on paper are reproduced in full color.

WORKING COTTON

Sherley Anne Williams. Illustrated by Carole Byard. (Harcourt Brace Jovanovich, 1992) 32 pages. ISBN: 0-15-299624-9. Level: Ages 6-9.

Sherlan, the next-to-the-youngest daughter in an African American family, describes a typical day working in the fields with her parents and three sisters. Although the author has fond memories of her family (most particularly her father), there is not the smallest hint of nostalgia in this reminiscence of her childhood spent as a migrant worker. Byard's expressive full-color paintings brilliantly evoke the summer heat, the immensity of the cotton fields, and the strain of hard work on both child and adult. In the midst of adversity, the strength of Sherlan's family comes through in both the lyrical language and the illustrations.

Children's Trade Books with Production, Distribution, and Consumption as a Second Thematic Strand

The title index on pp. 173-180 lists the number of the page on which each book is annotated.

TITLE	AUTHOR	DATE	AGE LEVEL
Chicken Soup Boots	Maria Kalman	1993	Ages 4-8
A Crack in the Wall	Mary Elizabeth Haggerty	1993	Ages 4-8
Cutters, Carvers & the Cathedral	George Ancona	1995	Ages 8-12
Cynthia Gregory Dances Swan Lake	Cynthia Gregory	1990	Ages 5-11
Day of Delight: A Jewish Sabbath in Ethiopia	Maxine Rose Schur	1994	Ages 5-9
The Great Migration: An American Story	Jacob Lawrence	1993	Ages 9 and older
Great-Grandma Tells of Threshing Day	Verda Cross	1992	Ages 5-8, or older for oral history purposes
Haystack	Bonnie Geisert and Arthur Geisert	1995	Ages 4-9
Look Alive: Behind the Scenes of an Animated Film	Elaine Scott	1992	Ages 7-11 and older
May'naise Sandwiches & Sunshine Tea	Sandra Belton	1994	Ages 5-8
My Mama Sings	Jeanne Whitehouse Peterson	1994	Ages 4-7
The Piñata Maker / El Piñatero	George Ancona	1994	Ages 8-10
Till Year's Good End: A Calendar of Medieval Labors	W. Nikola-Lisa	1997	Ages 7-11
Women Working A to Z	Maria A. Kunstadter	1994	Ages 5-8

Children's Trade Books with Production, Distribution, and Consumption as a Third Thematic Strand

The title index on pp. 173-180 lists the number of the page on which each book is annotated.

TITLE	AUTHOR	DATE	AGE LEVEL
Amelia's Road	Linda Jacobs Altman	1993	Ages 7-9
Big Annie of Calumet: A True Story of the Industrial Revolution	Jerry Stanley	1996	Ages 10-15 and older
Eagle Drum: On the Powwow Trail with a Young Grass Dancer	Robert Crum	1994	Ages 7-11
Gathering the Sun: An Alphabet in Spanish and English	Alma Flor Ada	1997	Ages 5-10
I've Got an Idea: The Story of Frederick McKinley Jones	Gloria M. Swanson and Margaret V. Ott	1994	Ages 9-11 and older
The Other Side: How Kids Live in a California Latino Neighborhood	Kathleen Krull	1994	Ages 7-11
Polar, The Titanic Bear	Daisy Corning Stone Spedden	1994	Ages 7-9 and older
The Return of the Buffaloes: A Plains Indian Story about Famine and Renewal of the Earth	Paul Goble, reteller and illustrator	1996	Ages 8-12
Rosa Bonheur	Robyn Montana Turner	1991	Ages 7-12
Voices from the Fields; Children of Migrant Farmworkers Tell Their Stories	S. Beth Atkin	1993	Ages 9-14 and older
Wake Up, City!	Alvin Tresselt	1990	Ages 3-7

▶ CHAPTER TWELVE

Children's Trade Books with Science, Technology, and Society as the Major Thematic Strand

ALMOST THE REAL THING: SIMULATION IN YOUR HIGH-TECH WORLD

Gloria Skurzynski. (Bradbury Press, 1991) 64 pages. ISBN: 0-02-778072-4. Level: Ages 9-12.

Physical and computer simulations, or "imitations of things that exist in the real world," are clearly described in this written text, and stunningly visualized in numerous, full-color photographs. Physical simulations discussed include uses of wind tunnels (both historical and contemporary), disaster simulations, and weightlessness. Some of the computer simulations covered are flight simulators, climate models, and molecular structure. Descriptions of forthcoming technology that will allow users to experience a "virtual reality" involving computer-generated images are thoroughly fascinating.

VIII

DEAR BENJAMIN BANNEKER

Andrea Davis Pinkney. Illustrated by Brian Pinkney. (Gulliver Books / Harcourt, Brace, 1994) 32 pages. ISBN: 0-15-200417-3. Level: Ages 5-9.

Beginning to teach himself mathematics and astronomy at age fifty-seven, Benjamin Banneker later became known for his scientifically developed predictions concerning the weather. He was the first black person to create a published almanac. Banneker can also be remembered for the forthright letter he wrote in 1791 to Secretary of State Thomas Jefferson concerning slavery and the need for equal opportunity for all people. This 11¼ x 8¼ in. picture biography created by a wife-and-husband team brings to life Banneker's early years and later accomplishments. The full-color illustrations were rendered using scratchboard colored with oil paint.

VIII II

FOLLOW THAT TRASH! ALL ABOUT RECYCLING

Francine Jacobs. Illustrated by Mavis Smith. (All Aboard Reading). (Grosset & Dunlap, 1996) 48 pages. ISBN: 0-448-41601-8. Level: Ages 5-7.

Many children may already be familiar with recycling in a general way if they sort cans, bottles, and paper at home or in school. This beginning reader describes why recycling is important and what happens after the recyclables are hauled away. Glass, paper, and plastic are followed to plants where they are processed. The text and simple color illustrations also highlight some of the products into which they are later transformed.

VIII X II

GIRLS AND YOUNG WOMEN INVENTING: TWENTY TRUE STORIES ABOUT INVENTORS, PLUS HOW YOU CAN BE ONE YOURSELF

Frances A. Karnes and Suzanne M. Bean. (Free Spirit, 1995) 168 pages. ISBN: 0-915793-89-X. Level: Ages 10-14 and older.

An engaging, inspiring profile of twenty girls and young women who are pioneers in the field of ideas demystifies the concept of "inventing" and affirms the ability of children to create. The young people in GIRLS AND YOUNG WOMEN INVENTING have designed and developed products that range from broom handles to paperweights to computer programs. Many of them have won prizes in Invent America! contests across the nation, and some of them even have patents. But their ideas most often come from their everyday lives. Each young inventor talks about how she got the idea for her invention and how she designed and developed a prototype. They also offer advice to other girls about inventing and following their dreams. A section on "How to Be an Inventor" takes readers through the invention process, from ways to come up with an idea to designing and, if desired, seeking a patent.

VIII IV I

HERE COMES THE MAIL

Gloria Skurzynski. (Bradbury, 1992) 32 pages. ISBN: 0-02-782916-2. Level: Ages 4-8.

Captioned color photographs trace a letter that young Stephanie mails in New Mexico to her cousin Kathy living in Utah. Because Stephanie painstakingly writes her cousin's name in the large lettering of a novice writer on the back of the envelope, it is quite easy to literally trace its journey through the U.S. postal system. Skurzynski provides an interesting look behind the scenes of a process we take for granted.

VIII III VI

I'VE GOT AN IDEA: THE STORY OF FREDERICK MCKINLEY JONES

Gloria M. Swanson and Margaret V. Ott. (Runestone Press / Lerner, 1994) 95 pages. ISBN: 0-8225-3174-7. Level: Ages 9-11 and older.

From the time he was a small child taking apart his father's watch, Frederick McKinley Jones showed a fascination and genius for things mechanical. By the time he was fourteen, the young African American was admired for his expertise with car engines. By the time he was seventeen, he was designing and building racing cars. Jones's inventive mind was never quiet, and over the course of his life from 1893 to 1961, he acquired over sixty patents for his ideas, which ranged from movie theater ticket machines and sound systems to mobile refrigeration units that enabled perishable food to be carried long distances. This is an appealing biography focusing on his personal and professional life and containing numerous black-and-white photos of Jones in his wide and varied creative pursuits.

LOOK ALIVE: BEHIND THE SCENES OF AN ANIMATED FILM

Elaine Scott. Photographs by Richard Hewett. (William Morrow, 1992) 68 pages. ISBN: 0-688-09936-X. Level: Ages 7-11 and older.

The making of *Ralph S. Mouse*, the animated film that won the first ALA Carnegie Medal for Excellence in Children's Video in 1991, is detailed in black-and-white photographs, diagrams, sketches, and movie stills. This account of the adaptation of Beverly Cleary's popular book RALPH S. MOUSE (William Morrow, 1982) even offers a first-hand example of animation via what one can see while quickly flipping the pages. Technical information and historical background are presented without dampening the high interest of the subject.

THE MOST BEAUTIFUL ROOF IN THE WORLD: EXPLORING THE RAINFOREST CANOPY

Kathryn Lasky. Photographs by Christopher G. Knight. (Gulliver Green/Harcourt, Brace, 1997) 46 pages. ISBN: 0-15-200893-4. Level: Ages 7-11 and older.

Since she was six years old, Meg Lowman has known that she wanted to be a scientist who studied the natural world. Inspired by the life work of two role models, Harriet Tubman (whom Lowman calls a "pioneer field naturalist") and scientist Rachel Carson, she has dedicated her life to exploring the unknown world of the rainforest canopy, unknown because it has been more inaccessible to scientists than the ocean floor. But Lowman doesn't let inaccessibility stand in her way. She uses technical rock climbing equipment to reach an elaborate system of platforms in order to gather specimens. The extremes to which she goes frequently pay off as she has been able to make firsthand observations of an ecosystem about which little is known. Lush photographs of the scientist at work accompany Lasky's eloquent text. Her account interweaves Lowman's field work, documentation and analysis, and her home life with two young sons who share their mother's passion for the rainforest.

POLAR, THE TITANIC BEAR

Daisy Corning Stone Spedden. Illustrated by Laurie McGaw. (Little, Brown, 1994) 64 pages. ISBN: 0-316-80625-0. Level: Ages 7-9 and older.

Once upon a time, a little American boy's mother, Daisy Spedden, created a book for him, a book about his Steiff bear, a story about a boy whose stuffed animal had traveled with him on the *Titanic* and survived. Created in 1913, the book was discovered decades later in Daisy's trunk. That homemade volume became the core of POLAR, an astonishing record of the disaster as well as a social history. POLAR can be understood on one or more levels. Most children will read it from the perspective of a child passenger on the *Titanic*. Some may see POLAR as an example of the economic privilege of the few who could afford that voyage. Older readers will notice the epilogue that foreshadows the transience of such leisure. Archival photos of toys from the era, family pictures, entries from Daisy Spedden's diaries, and facts about the *Titanic* are successfully integrated within this intriguing volume. Because the juvenile appearing jacket art does not do justice to the content, the children who can appreciate it the most will probably not notice the book on their own.

RADIO BOY

Sharon Phillips Denslow. Illustrated by Alec Gillman. (Simon & Schuster, 1995) 32 pages. ISBN: 0-689-80295-1. Level: Ages 7-10 and older.

Nathan B. Stubblefield, inventor of the radio, sensed the future even as a boy. Growing up in the small town of Murray, Kentucky, in the 1870s, Nathan was forever tinkering and experimenting with coils, wires, and other "electricals." A fictionalized account of Nathan's boyhood passion for invention is enhanced by illustrations rendered in pen-and-ink and watercolor that provide a warm sense of this singular figure in his small town's life.

THE REAL MCCOY: THE LIFE OF AN AFRICAN-AMERICAN INVENTOR

Wendy Towle. (Scholastic, 1993) 32 pages. ISBN: 0-590-43596-5. Level: Ages 7-10 and older.

Born in Canada in 1844, Elijah McCoy, the son of former slaves, patented more than fifty inventions throughout his life. This simply told history of an African American inventor focuses on McCoy's achievements without minimizing the barriers he faced because he was black. Full-page illustrations by Clay show a man wholly dedicated to his work and his dreams. A role model for many African Americans while he was alive, McCoy is once again a source of pride and inspiration.

ROCKET! HOW A TOY LAUNCHED THE SPACE AGE

Richard Maurer. (Crown, 1995) 64 pages. ISBN: 0-517-59628-8. Level: Ages 8-12.

A concise, generously illustrated history of rockets begins with their invention one thousand years ago in China when they were initially constructed as toys for children before being adapted for warfare. Since they were never very accurate, they were not considered a very useful weapon, however, and it was not until the early twentieth century that true rocket science was born as a means to shoot astronauts into space. Much of this history focuses on the life work of Robert Goddard who, as a boy, was inspired to dream by the nineteenth century science fiction of Jules Verne and H. G. Wells.

RUTH LAW THRILLS A NATION

Don Brown. (Ticknor & Fields, 1993) 32 pages. ISBN: 0-395-66404-7. Level: Ages 4-8 and older.

"On November 19, 1916, Ruth Law tried to fly from Chicago to New York City in one day. It had never been done before." She had practiced for the cold by sleeping on the roof of a hotel. Although she wore woolen and leather pant suits while flying, in public she covered these flying garments with a skirt because of conventions dictating what women should wear. Even though she set a record that day by flying a five-hundred mile nonstop lap, neither Ruth Law nor that feat is well known today because darkness came while New York City was still two hours away. Brown's pen-and-ink and watercolor illustrations reproduced in full color provide a strong sense of the woman and the flight. His first published book reads aloud with grace and its 8¼ by 10⅜ in. size invites hands-on interest.

SAMUEL TODD'S BOOK OF GREAT INVENTIONS

E. L. Konigsburg. (Atheneum Publishers, 1991) 32 pages. ISBN: 0-689-31680-1. Level: Ages 3-6.

Samuel Todd, who was first introduced in SAMUEL TODD'S BOOK OF GREAT COLORS (Atheneum, 1990), is back, this time to extol the virtues of his favorite inventions. Unlike his parents, who think that the telephone and television are the greatest inventions, Samuel Todd appreciates belt loops, backpacks, step stools, birthday-cake candles, training wheels, and security blankets. His comments on the necessity and usefulness of each invention are amusingly direct and childlike: "Halloween was invented so that no one has to go trick-or-treating as his or her same old self."

THE THIRD PLANET: EXPLORING THE EARTH FROM SPACE

Sally Ride and Tam O'Shaughnessy. (Crown, 1994) 48 pages. ISBN: 0-517-59361-0. Level: Ages 7-11.

Using color photographs from NASA, physicist and astronaut Sally Ride introduces the scientific methods used when studying Earth from afar, and describes what data have revealed about the atmosphere, water, and land that make up our biosphere.

TUNNELS, TRACKS, AND TRAINS: BUILDING A SUBWAY

Joan Hewett. Photographs by Richard Hewett. (Lodestar, 1995) 48 pages. ISBN: 0-525-67466-7. Level: Ages 7-10.

There is abundant activity both above and below the ground as work on the Los Angeles subway continues: crews dig trenches for equipment, miners bore a tunnel in the ground, archeologists excavate ruins at a station site, and artists plan artwork for station and tunnel walls. In a fascinating documentary, Hewett describes the many aspects of work involved in building the Los Angeles subway system as she introduces readers to some of the people who are doing the many and varied jobs required. Color photographs capture the work-in-progress, from deep within the newly dug tunnels to a supervisor's office high above the ground.

THE WRIGHT BROTHERS: HOW THEY INVENTED THE AIRPLANE

Russell Freedman. (Holiday House, 1991) 129 pages. ISBN: 0-8234-0875-2. Level: Ages 9-14 and older.

Orville and Wilbur Wright diligently photographed each phase of their experiments in order to learn from their mistakes as well as keep a pictorial record of their progress. Because of their almost obsessive attention to detail, an amazing record of their accomplishments still exists. Freedman's incorporation of some of this archival material brings a dynamic visual dimension to previous accounts about the two brothers' efforts to create a machine that could be flown. The author's skillful use of unfamiliar details about the lives of two siblings who worked, lived, and even "thought together" makes for compelling reading. His lucid explanation of the physics of flight rounds out this interpretation of an important technological milestone achieved by two very human beings.

Children's Trade Books with Science, Technology, and Society as a Second Thematic Strand

The title index on pp. 173 lists the number of the page on which each book is annotated.

TITLE	AUTHOR	DATE	AGE LEVEL
Alphabet City	Stephen T. Johnson	1995	Ages 3-6
Big Rigs	Hope Irvin Marston	1993	Ages 3-6
Come Back, Salmon: How a Group of Dedicated Kids Adopted Pigeon Creek and Brought It Back to Life	Molly Cone	1992	Ages 6-10
Fire Truck Nuts and Bolts	Jerry Boucher	1993	Ages 5-10
Jacques-Henri Lartigue: Boy with a Camera	John Cech	1994	Ages 8-11
Kids at Work: Lewis Hine and the Crusade against Child Labor	Russell Freedman	1994	Ages 8-14 and older
Kids Making Quilts for Kids	ABC Quilts	1992	Ages 8-14
The Milkman's Boy	Donald Hall	1997	Ages 5-9
On Board the Titanic	Shelley Tanaka	1996	Ages 8-14
Raptor Rescue! An Eagle Flies Free	Sylvia A. Johnson	1995	Ages 7-11
Sugaring Season; Making Maple Syrup	Diane L. Burns	1990	Ages 6-10
Taking Flight: My Story	Vicki Van Meter with Dan Gutman	1995	Ages 10-12
We Can Do It!	Laura Dwight	1992	Ages 3-6

Children's Trade Books with Science, Technology, and Society as a Third Thematic Strand

The title index on pp. 173 lists the number of the page on which each book is annotated.

Cutters, Carvers & the Cathedral	George Ancona	1995	Ages 8-12
Extra Cheese, Please! Mozzarella's Journey from Cow to Pizza	Cris Peterson	1994	Ages 5-8
Fire at the Triangle Factory	Holly Littlefield	1996	Ages 8-11 and older
Frozen Man	David Getz	1994	Ages 8-16 and older
The Golden Lion Tamarin Comes Home	George Ancona	1994	Ages 7-11
Haystack	Bonnie Geisert and Arthur Geisert	1995	Ages 4-9
My Buddy	Audrey Osofsky	1992	Ages 4-9
Sky Pioneer: A Photobiography of Amelia Earhart	Corine Szabo	1997	Ages 7-11 and older
What Instrument Is This?	Rosmarie Hausherr	1992	Ages 4-8

CHAPTER THIRTEEN

CHILDREN'S TRADE BOOKS WITH GLOBAL CONNECTIONS AS THE MAJOR THEMATIC STRAND

AANI AND THE TREE HUGGERS

Jeannine Atkins. Illustrated by Venantius J. Pinto. (Lee & Low, 1995) 32 pages. ISBN: 1-880000-24-5. Level: Ages 4-9.

This fictionalized picture story, told from the point of view of young Aani, recounts the origins of the Chipko Andolan (Hug the Tree) Movement in northern India in the 1970s. When men from the city came into rural areas to cut down trees, women villagers successfully stopped them by embracing individual trees. Indian artist Venantius J. Pinto explains in a note at the end how and why his pictures for this book were influenced by five different styles of traditional miniature painting that were used in northern India in the seventeenth century.

THE BIG BOOK FOR PEACE

Ann Durell and Marilyn Sachs, editors. (Dutton, 1990) 120 pages. ISBN: 0-525-44605-2. Level: All ages.

This unique family anthology offers pieces by thirty-one contemporary children's book creators, including writers Mildred Pitts Walter and Yoshiko Uchida; reteller John Bierhorst; and artists Leo and Diane Dillon, Jerry Pinkney, and Allen Say. Walter's powerful short account concerning a nonviolent African American civil rights demonstration in Washington, D.C., and Uchida's epistolary fictional narrative originating in a Japanese American internment camp extend the concept of peace to embrace social justice issues. Jacket art by Maurice Sendak introduces the compilation, which intends to offer alternate resolutions to various barriers to understanding and justice.

COCOA ICE

Diana Applebaum. Illustrated by Holly Meade. (Orchard, 1997) 44 pages. ISBN: 0-531-30040-4. Level: Ages 5-9.

More than one hundred years ago, ice was harvested in Maine, and cocoa was harvested in Santo Domingo, Dominican Republic. What do the two have in common? The former cocoa ice trade. In the 1870s, "Yankee trading schooners brought ice, manufactured goods, and refined sugar to Santo Domingo to trade for cocoa and coffee beans … children in Santo Domingo and children

in Maine could eat chocolate ices on lazy summer afternoons, just as they do in this story." Cut paper pictures unfold a connected, parallel picture story involving two girls who never meet yet have one specific thing in common despite many differences.

COMMON GROUND: THE WATER, EARTH, AND AIR WE SHARE

Molly Bang. (Blue Sky/Scholastic, 1997) 32 pages. ISBN: 0-590-10056-4. Level: Ages 5-8 and older.

Our common ground is the earth we all share. Bang's introduction to environmental issues gives young readers a simple, accessible means for understanding the difference between reckless consumption and careful use and conservation of the earth's natural resources. Looking at fish, trees, fossil fuels, and water, Bang explains how consuming them for short-term benefits such as more fish to sell, more money to make, and more products to buy only hurts all living things in the long run. Unlike the village common of long ago, when those who didn't want to share the land could find someplace else to go, there is no place else to go for the people of our planet. That is why, Bang tells readers, we must all work together to protect the earth's resources. Bang has illustrated her short text with bright, colorful art that is both intimate and grand in scale and feeling—just like the message she conveys in this small (9 x 6¼ in.) and heartfelt book.

DIA'S STORY CLOTH: THE HMONG PEOPLE'S JOURNEY TO FREEDOM

Dia Cha. Story cloth stitched by Chue and Nhia Thao Cha. (Denver Museum of Natural History/Lee & Low, 1996) 24 pages. ISBN: 0-880000-34-2. Level: Ages 8-11 and older.

From a refugee camp in Thailand, Dia Cha's aunt and uncle, Chue and Nhia Thao Cha, sent her the story cloth that is the inspiration and the centerpiece for this important 11 x 8 in. book about the Hmong. The cloth they stitched depicts the history of the Hmong, whose culture reaches back thousands of years to China, and stretches from Asia to North America, where more than

100,000 Hmong have settled in the years since the Vietnam War (including many in Wisconsin). Hmong means "free people," Cha writes in her introduction. "This story cloth will tell you about our life." In the text, Cha simply and skillfully threads her own story into that of the Hmong people as she tells about farming with her family as a child in Laos, and then the violent upheaval of the Vietnam War that caused the death or displacement of thousands of Hmong in Southeast Asia. This book includes a discussion of Hmong history, culture, and artistic traditions by the curator of ethnology at the Denver Museum of Natural History.

DIEZ DEDITOS / TEN LITTLE FINGERS, AND OTHER PLAY RHYMES AND ACTION SONGS FROM LATIN AMERICA

José-Luis Orozco. Illustrated by Elisa Kleven. (Dutton, 1997) 56 pages. ISBN: 0-525-45736-4. Level: Babies-age 8, adults.

Thirty-four traditional and original action songs are abundantly illustrated with Kleven's trademark collage assemblages filled with happy children, interacting families, and people with individual faces and skin colors. The finger games are graphically represented with brief written directions and clear diagrams. Music notations suggest the tunes and can be played on a guitar or recorder by older children and adults quite new to these instruments. A bilingual subject index cites entries under Animals, Body Parts (8), Call-and-Response (2), Clapping (7), Counting (4), Dances (5), Family (3), Farewell (2), Finger Play (8), Food (4), Friendship (3), Greetings (3), Group Play (5), Musical Instruments (2), Professions (1), Self-Esteem (5), Sorrow (1), Special Celebrations (3), Tickling (2), Time (1), Transportation (1), Vowel Sounds (1), and Weather (2). Everything about this cheerful book is child friendly. It's Spanish-language friendly, too—with Spanish words under the music and nearest to the graphic finger games, the English translations are secondary.

EARTH, FIRE, WATER, AIR

Mary Hoffman. Illustrated by Jane Ray. (Viking, 1995) 68 pages. ISBN: 0-525-45420-9. Level: Ages 8-14.

Hoffman looks at how earth, fire, water, and air have been essential elements as well as fuel for human imagination throughout time. Exploring history, folklore, and customs of cultures around the world, as well as scientific and environmental perspectives, she looks at each of the elements in turn, acknowledging their innate

power and celebrating the ideas they have inspired. Her narrative is set against Ray's exquisite illustrations: burnished, beautifully detailed expressions of nature's power and the creativity of the human mind.

GLOBAL WARMING

Laurence Pringle. (Arcade/Little, Brown, 1990) 46 pages. ISBN: 1-55970-012-2. Level: Ages 7-10.

In this concise, clearly written text, Pringle describes global warming, the factors contributing to it, and possible solutions to the worldwide problem. Color photographs and diagrams illustrate this readable account, and a glossary defines scientific terms used.

GLORIOUS ANGELS: A CELEBRATION OF CHILDREN

Walter Dean Myers. (HarperCollins, 1995) 40 pages. ISBN: 0-06-024822-X. Level: Age 3 and older.

Myers, a distinguished author of novels and biographies for teen readers and stories for young children, is also a poet and collector of antique photographic portraits. In the sepia-toned portraits in this work, most children will be able to find at least one old photo close to their own heritage. Myers's first photo-poetry album, BROWN ANGELS (HarperCollins, 1993), celebrated African American children who lived almost a century ago. The elegant bookmaking of each volume underscores Myers's respect for all children of yesterday, along with his hopes for all children of tomorrow. His photos and poems are reminders that angels are in front of us today.

THE GOLDEN LION TAMARIN COMES HOME

George Ancona. (Macmillan, 1994) 40 pages. ISBN: 0-02-700905-X. Level: Ages 7-11.

The coastal rain forest in southeastern Brazil is the only known natural habitat of the mico, or golden lion tamarin, a small monkey about the size of a squirrel. With 98 percent of the Brazilian rain forest depleted, wild micos are becoming scarce. But thanks to the tireless efforts of Andreia Martins and other Brazilian conservationists, micos born in captivity in zoos are slowly and successfully being introduced back into the wild. This lively text and color photographs document the painstaking work of Martins, in addition to describing the habits of the mico and the reasoning behind human efforts to protect its native home.

HOPSCOTCH AROUND THE WORLD

Mary D. Lankford. Illustrated by Karen Milone. (William Morrow, 1992) 47 pages. ISBN: 0-688-08420-6. Level: Ages 6-9.

Hopscotch has a long history worldwide, and children in most parts of the world still play it today. Directions for nineteen hopscotch variants played in sixteen nations follow brief notes that place each of the variants in its historical and geographical contexts. Each description is illustrated with a full-page, full-color illustration of contemporary children playing the game.

THE MAGIC MOONBERRY JUMP ROPE

Dakari Hru. Illustrated by E. B. Lewis. (Dial, 1996) 32 pages. ISBN: 0-8037-1755-5. Level: Ages 4-7.

Sisters Erica and April want to jump Double Dutch but they can't get any of their friends to join them, and their little sister Carmen is too small to twirl the ropes. When Uncle Zambezi returns from Tanzania, he brings them some magic moonberry ropes, claiming they will grant them a wish. Of course, the girls wish for a third jumper and, of course, their wish comes true when a new family moves in next door. But are the ropes really magic? Hru's gentle, humorous tale of the endless days of summer and the seriousness of child's play is aptly illustrated with Lewis's sun-dappled watercolor paintings. Jump in!

ON THE WINGS OF PEACE: WRITERS AND ILLUSTRATORS SPEAK OUT FOR PEACE IN MEMORY OF HIROSHIMA AND NAGASAKI

Sheila Hamanaka, coordinator. (Clarion, 1995) 144 pages. ISBN: 0-395-72619-0. Level: Age 8 and older.

Writing and art from sixty authors and artists forms a stunning anthology concerning the 1945 bombings of Hiroshima and Nagasaki and visions of peace. Handsome full-color art created in a variety of media accompanies history, poetry, short stories, and memoirs. This important assemblage can be read a bit at a time, in any order, in any year. As a whole, the volume energizes, rather than assessing blame or creating melancholy. A reliable resource list for children and adults suggests further reading. Brief biographical information placed next to tiny black and white photos marks the credentials of contributors. They include Marjorie Agosin, Joseph Bruchac, Ashley Bryan, Omar S. Castaneda, Peter Catalanotto, Peter E. Clarke, Edwidge Danticat, Jean Durandisse, Tom Feelings, Shinya Fukatsu, Nikki Grimes, Hushang Moradi Kermani, Marie G. Lee, George Littlechild, Ana Maria Machado, Kam Mak, Milton Meltzer, Wendell Minor,

Kyoko Mori, Junko Morimoto, Walter Dean Myers, Keiko Narahashi, Katherine Paterson, Jerry Pinkney, James E. Ransome, Enrique O. Sanchez, Virginia Driving Hawk Sneve, Rigoberta Menchu Tum, Martin Waddell, Yoko Kawashima Watkins, and Ed Young. Royalties from sales of ON THE WINGS OF PEACE are designated for three organizations devoted to these issues.

QUILTED LANDSCAPE: CONVERSATIONS WITH YOUNG IMMIGRANTS

Yale Strom. (Simon & Schuster, 1996) 80 pages. ISBN: 0-689-80074-6. Level: Ages 11-14 and older.

Writer and photographer Strom turns a keen and understanding eye on children and young adults who are recent immigrants to the United States. Twenty-six young people who range in age from eleven to seventeen discuss when, how, and why they came to the United States; what their life is like here; who and what they left behind; and their plans and hopes for the future. Though the children come from twenty-six countries all over the world, and from diverse social and economic backgrounds, their experiences in this country are often similar as they confront the challenges of culture and language barriers, discrimination, and prejudice, and deal with the conflicts that can arise when family and cultural expectations clash with a new way of life. Each profile includes black-and-white photographs of the child and a brief summary of facts about the country from which he or she came. This important book encourages readers to consider what it means to be a newcomer and what sustains us as a nation.

SADAKO

Eleanor Coerr. Illustrated by Ed Young. (Putnam, 1993) 48 pages. ISBN: 0-399-21771-1. Level: Ages 8-11.

Sadako Sasaki is the child honored by the monument of a girl holding a large origami crane in the Hiroshima Peace Park. The monument is a strong call for peace, representing the many who perished in Japan as a result of the atomic bombs dropped on Hiroshima and Nagasaki in 1945. As she suffered from radiation sickness, Sadako and her friends are reported to have folded origami cranes, in accordance with the Japanese legend that if a sick person folds one thousand cranes, the gods will restore her health. The same author who wrote the moving short fiction book SADAKO AND THE THOUSAND PAPER CRANES (Putnam, 1977) presents this adaptation of the script for a film of the same name. The striking 9¼ by 11¼ in. book includes a selection of the almost three hundred images artist Ed Young created for the film using pastels, many of which reflect images of origami cranes or those from nature.

SITTI'S SECRETS

Naomi Shihab Nye. Illustrated by Nancy Carpenter. (Four Winds Press, 1994) 32 pages. ISBN: 0-02-768460-1. Level: Ages 6-10.

Mona's grandmother, Sitti, lives "on the other side of the earth" in a Palestinian village on the West Bank. Despite their uncommon language, Mona and her grandmother share daily life and special moments together when Mona and her father take a trip to visit Sitti. Upon her return to the United States, Mona writes a letter to the president: "If the people of the United States could meet Sitti, they'd like her for sure. You'd like her, too." Paired with Carpenter's sun-drenched illustrations, Nye's poetic text explores a child's feelings and fears about a grandparent living far away in a part of the world that most children in the United States know only one dimensionally, if at all, through reports in the news.

SIX WORDS, MANY TURTLES, AND THREE DAYS IN HONG KONG

Patricia McMahon. Photographs by Susan G. Drinker. (Houghton Mifflin, 1997) 45 pages. ISBN: 0-395-68621-0. Level: Ages 8-11.

Tsz Yan is an eight-year-old Chinese girl living in Hong Kong. Many facets of her life are similar to those of children in the United States: she rides the bus to and from school, goes to a neighbor's house for daycare, and both her parents work. And like many U.S. children, Tsz Yan eagerly looks forward to the weekend, and definitely does not like making homework part of her weekend plans. On this particular weekend, Tsz Yan's assignment is to learn how to write and understand six new words in English; happy, hungry, friend, scared, family, and noisy. Over the course of three days (Friday evening, Saturday, and Sunday), Tsz Yan finds ways to apply the six words she must learn to her weekend activities, from spending time with her parents (which makes her HAPPY), to feeding the HUNGRY turtles near her apartment building (which was SCARY), to seeing her extended FAMILY. The author works many details of life in contemporary Hong-Kong into the text, which is accompanied by numerous full-color photographs of Tsz Yan, her family, and the city in which she lives.

THE TALKING CLOTH

Rhonda Mitchell. (Orchard, 1997) 32 pages. ISBN: 0-531-30004-8. Level: Ages 4-7.

Amber likes to visit her Aunt Phoebe who owns "things and things and things." She calls it her "collection of life," but Amber's father calls it "junk." Aunt Phoebe can tell the history of everything she owns. Much of it comes from the African continent and is part of her family heritage. Amber is especially intrigued with Aunt Phoebe's "talking cloth"—adinkra cloth from Ghana—because every color and every symbol has a meaning. Sharp oil paintings reflect the pride that Amber feels in her heritage and the enthusiasm for it that she shares with her aunt.

TURTLE BAY

Saviour Pirotta. Illustrated by Nilesh Mistry. U.S. edition. (Farrar, Straus and Giroux, 1997) 28 pages. ISBN: 0-374-37888-6. Level: Ages 5-8.

An elderly Japanese man shares his secrets of the natural world with two young Japanese children in a story that blends their growing appreciation of nature with their deepening understanding of another human being. Taro has always liked Jiro-san, but his sister, Yuko, thinks the old man is weird. Taro thinks Yuko might be right after all when he arrives at the beach and finds Jiro-san sweeping the sand in preparation for the arrival of his "friends." But Jiro-san's friends turn out to be endangered giant loggerhead turtles, and the children are thrilled to witness their arrival on the beach, the laying of their eggs, and later the hatching of the babies. This charming story that appreciates the mysteries of human nature and the larger world is illustrated with quiet, full-color paintings that span each two-page spread.

V FOR VANISHING: AN ALPHABET OF ENDANGERED ANIMALS

Patricia Mullins. (HarperCollins, 1994) 32 pages. ISBN: 0-06-023556-X. Level: Ages 5-10.

Mullins' incredibly detailed collage artwork highlights animals that are in danger of becoming extinct in this alphabet book with an environmental twist. From A (Pink Fairy Armadillo) to Z (Cape Mountain Zebra), each page is alive with natural color and form. Information provided for the animals includes their common and scientific names and the countries or regions in which they are found—for now.

Children's Trade Books with Global Connections as a Second Thematic Strand

The title index on pp. 173-180 lists the number of the page on which each book is annotated.

TITLE	AUTHOR	YEAR	AGE LEVEL
Alef-Bet: A Hebrew Alphabet Book	Michelle Edwards	1992	Ages 2-8
Antarctica: The Last Unspoiled Continent	Laurence Pringle	1992	Ages 8-12 and older
The Copper Lady	Alice and Kent Ross	1997	Ages 6-9
Everglades	Jean Craighead George	1995	Ages 7-10 and older
Father's Rubber Shoes	Yumi Heo	1995	Ages 4-8
The Hunterman and the Crocodile: A West African Folktale	Baba Wague DiakitJ	1997	Ages 5-9
Jackal Woman: Exploring the World of Jackals	Laurence Pringle	1993	Ages 7-13
The Living Earth	Eleonore Schmid	1994	Ages 4-8
The Moon Was the Best	Charlotte Zolotow	1993	Ages 3-5
My Daddy Was a Soldier: A World War II Story	Deborah Kogan Ray	1990	Ages 7-10
Popcorn at the Palace	Emily Arnold McCully	1997	Ages 6-9
Save the Earth: An Action Handbook for Kids	Betty Miles	1991	Ages 8-12
Seven Candles for Kwanzaa	Andrea Davis Pinkney	1993	Ages 3-9
Silent Night: The Song from Heaven	Linda Granfield	1997	Age 7 and older
Spill! The Story of the Exxon Valdez	Terry Carr	1991	Ages 9-14 and older
Wake Up, City!	Alvin Tresselt	1990	Ages 3-7
War Game	Michael Foreman	1994	Ages 8-12 and older
What a Wonderful World	Ashley Bryan, illustrator	1995	Ages 2-8

Children's Trade Books with Global Connections as a Third Thematic Strand

The title index on pp. 173-180 lists the number of the page on which each book is annotated.

A Blue Butterfly: A Story about Claude Monet	Bijou Le Tord	1995	Ages 5-8
The Feather-Bed Journey	Paula Kurzband Feder	1995	Ages 5-8 and older
Going Home	Eve Bunting	1996	Ages 5-9
Halmoni and the Picnic	Sook Nyul Choi	1993	Ages 5-8
In My Family / En Mi Familia	Carmen Garza Lomas with Harriet Rohmer	1996	Age 5 and older
My First Kwanzaa Book	Deborah M. Newton	1992	Ages 2-7
My Place	Nadia Wheatley and Donna Rawlins	1990	Ages 6-12 and older
The Piñata Maker / El Piñatero	George Ancona	1994	Ages 8-10
Seedfolks	Paul Fleischman	1997	Ages 9-13 and older
Street Music: City Poems	Arnold Adoff	1995	Ages 7-11
Tell Them We Remember: The Story of the Holocaust	Susan D. Baachrach	1994	Age 9 and older
The Two Mrs. Gibsons	Toyomi Igus	1996	Ages 3-7
Water Buffalo Days: Growing Up in Vietnam	Quang Nhuong Huynh	1997	Ages 9-11
When I Left My Village	Maxine Rose Schur	1996	Ages 8-10 and older
The Whispering Cloth	Pegi Deitz Shea	1995	Ages 7-11

CHILDREN'S TRADE BOOKS WITH CIVIC IDEALS AND PRACTICES AS THE MAJOR THEMATIC STRAND

AUNT HARRIET'S UNDERGROUND RAILROAD IN THE SKY

Faith Ringgold. (Crown, 1992) 32 pages. ISBN: 0-517-58767-X. Level: Ages 6-11.

Cassie Lightfoot, the eight-year-old who shared the glories of flying with little brother Be Be in TAR BEACH (Crown, 1991), is at it again. This time she and Be Be take a dream journey to the past where they travel through history on the Underground Railroad with Harriet Tubman herself. Details about the harsh realities of slavery and the dangers fugitives faced are balanced (but never trivialized) by Ringgold's stunning oil paintings that show Cassie's childlike, whimsical interpretations of Aunt Harriet's oral account of history; she pictures the Underground Railroad, for example, as a real train and Harriet Tubman dressed in a conductor's hat and apron. A two-page note at the book's end offers biographical information about Tubman as well as a list of resources.

THE BALLOT BOX BATTLE

Emily Arnold McCully. (Alfred A. Knopf, 1996) 32 pages. ISBN: 0-679-87938-2. Level: Ages 5-8.

Cordelia, the heroine of this picture story, which takes place in 1880, loves horses so much that she willingly volunteers to help her elderly neighbor Mrs. Stanton care for her horse in exchange for daily riding lessons. More than anything, Cordelia would like to learn to jump a four-foot fence, although she can't imagine the old woman teaching her to do something quite so daring. But Mrs. Stanton, it seems, is quite a dare-devil in her own right. In a smoothly executed flashback sequence, the woman recounts some events from her early nineteenth century childhood when she broke a social taboo by attending a boys' academy where she became one of the school's best pupils. This childhood experience set her on her life-long struggle for women's rights. Mrs. Stanton, of course, is Elizabeth Cady Stanton, shown here as both a child and as a mature woman who tried—unsuccessfully—to cast a ballot whenever there was an election. Through the eyes of young Cordelia, perceptive readers will see that Mrs. Stanton was every bit as courageous as those who jump four-foot fences. McCully's style, both verbal and visual, is understated but her message about equal rights is clear. Most of today's young readers will no doubt be amazed that the right to vote was something women fought long and hard to attain.

BIG ANNIE OF CALUMET: A TRUE STORY OF THE INDUSTRIAL REVOLUTION

Jerry Stanley. (Crown, 1996) 102 pages. ISBN: 0-517-70097-2. Level: Ages 10-15 and older.

A strike became inevitable in 1913 after Copper Country mine owners refused a hearing to Upper Michigan miners organized to improve their wages and working conditions. Seven days a week for more than five months, twenty-five year-old Annie Clemenc marched carrying an American flag at the head of a protest parade. As a hospital worker, this woman had seen first-hand the injuries typically suffered by miners in cave-ins. As the wife and daughter of miners, she knew much about the dangers and deaths. In the early twentieth century, U.S. workers had few legal rights to organize for safe working conditions and higher wages. Thousands of people ultimately became involved on both sides. The strike and ongoing parades led to bitter economic repercussions for women and men engaged in the protest. Violence and bloodshed became common. While mining families were gathered for a Christmas party, a false fire alarm caused eighty children to die in the surge of people fleeing the building. By highlighting the basic rights for which Annie and the protesters struggled, Stanley underscores the relationship between workers' rights and human rights. By focusing the narrative on a previously unsung labor leader, he captures the strength and importance of women in the labor movement. The abundant archival black-and-white photographs contribute an important dimension to the compelling, fast-moving narrative. Informed adult readers might wish the author had found a way to acknowledge the unsalaried domestic roles of the women protesters, and they might debate Stanley's generous version of Henry Ford's role. This important book brings to life an appalling, heartbreaking segment of U.S. labor history rarely detailed for young readers.

COME BACK, SALMON: HOW A GROUP OF DEDICATED KIDS ADOPTED PIGEON CREEK AND BROUGHT IT BACK TO LIFE

Molly Cone. Photographs by Sidnee Wheelwright. (Sierra Club Books for Children, 1992) 48 pages. ISBN: 0-87156-572-2. Level: Ages 6-10.

Beginning in 1984, a complex combination of activities in an Everett, Washington, elementary school (i.e., an interactive, interdisciplinary science curriculum involving classroom experiments, firsthand observations, art activities, and community activism) led to a stream restoration project. Everyone deemed the project successful when the salmon raised in the classroom from eyed eggs and released two years earlier returned to Pigeon Creek. Detailed with color photographs, background information, and dialogue-laced narratives based on taped interviews with the participating children and teachers, this exemplary project offers information, encouragement, and hope.

THE DAY GOGO WENT TO VOTE: SOUTH AFRICA, APRIL 1994

Elinor Batezat Sisulu. Illustrated by Sharon Wilson. (U.S. edition: Little, Brown, 1996) 32 pages. ISBN: 0-316-70267-6. Level: Ages 7-10 and older.

A six-year-old black child tells how her one-hundred year-old gogo (grandmother) is determined to vote in the first general election in South Africa. Gogo has not left home for years, not even to attend church. The family is incredulous. "Do you want me to die not having voted?" Gogo asks her astonished relatives, and so she goes to the polls. The child's-eye view of the historic election is an effective device for including information in context about voting procedures in the unprecedented 1994 election. Sisulu was born in Zimbabwe and now lives in Capetown, South Africa. Wilson visited South Africa before creating the artwork for this inspiring picture book story with pastels on sanded board.

EAGLE SONG

Joseph Bruchac. Illustrations by Dan Andreasen. (Dial, 1997) 80 pages. ISBN: 0-8037-1918-3. Level: Ages 9-11 and older.

"Chief." "Hiawatha." Danny hates that his classmates tease him with these names. But ever since his family moved away from the Mohawk reservation so that his mother could take a job as a social worker in Manhattan,

his life at school has been miserable. Outside of the fourth grade, things aren't always easy either. His father works fifty stories up in the air on the iron beams of skyscrapers under construction, a dangerous job that takes him away from home for weeks at a time. No matter how much his parents love him and one another, and no matter how much they encourage Danny to trust the Iroquois way of life that says "if you believe in peace … an enemy can become a friend," Danny can't find a way to feel at home in the world away from his own home and people. In Bruchac's welcome novel about a contemporary American Indian child and family, a young boy's struggle with the stereotypes and prejudice of his peers begins to turn around when he finds the strength inside himself to extend a hand in friendship.

GUS AND GRANDPA AND THE CHRISTMAS COOKIES

Claudia Mills. Illustrated by Catherine Stock. (Farrar, Straus and Giroux, 1997) 47 pages. ISBN: 0-374-32823-4. Level: Ages 4-6.

Gus spends the day at Grandpa's helping him roll out, bake, and decorate six dozen cutout cookies. Neighbors who assume Grandpa doesn't bake stop by to share their home-baked cookies with him. During a trip with Grandpa to buy sprinkles, Gus overhears a man dressed as Santa saying, "God bless you" to people putting coins into a red kettle. Gus learns that children in a homeless shelter don't have enough food or warm clothes, not to mention cookies, which gives him and Grandpa a solution to their cookie surplus. Mills's four brief, easy-to-read chapters establish the warm relationship between Gus and Grandpa and show an understated but credible introduction to two ways of giving. Stock's full color illustrations expand the story.

HANNA'S COLD WINTER

Trish Marx. Illustrated by Barbara Knutson. (Carolrhoda, 1993) 32 pages. ISBN: 0-87614-772-4. Level: Ages 6-9 and older.

This first-person story describes family outings to the zoo to watch the hippo Hanna devour pitchforks of hay on the Sundays before the war, before the twin towns of Buda and Pest were occupied by soldiers fighting each other, and before food for both people and zoo creatures became scarce. The text is based on an incident that took place during World War II in Budapest, Hungary, when the coldest winter on record froze the river between the two towns. According to the story told to the author, Papa, Mama, and their three children took a straw doormat and an old pair of straw slippers to the zoo, broke them up with a pitchfork, and encouraged the starving hippos to eat. They ate, and by the time winter ended, more than nine thousand hats, mats, and slippers had been given to the zoo to help the hippos survive the winter and the war. Full-color illustrations on every page of a 10¼ by 8¼ in. volume provide historical and regional details along with impressive pictures of Hanna and her prodigious appetite in action.

HAPPY BIRTHDAY, MARTIN LUTHER KING

Jean Marzollo. Illustrated by J. Brian Pinkney. (Scholastic, 1993) 32 pages. ISBN: 0-590-44065-9. Level: Ages 3-8.

This 11½ by 8½ in. picture-book biography offers fresh and vibrant images of King's life and accomplishments. An excellent selection of biographical details to interest young children makes very brief information about King's life and contributions accessible and appealing. Pinkney's lively illustrations created on scratchboard with oil pastels showcase young Martin as well as the mature leader. An author's note at the beginning explains the reason for devoting a page in a book for such young children to the assassination of the Nobel Peace Prize-winning African American leader.

I HAVE A DREAM

Martin Luther King, Jr. Foreword by Coretta Scott King. Illustrated by fifteen Coretta Scott King Award and Honor Book Artists. (Scholastic, 1997) 40 pages. ISBN: 0-590-20516-1. Level: Age 5 and older.

An illustrated edition of Martin Luther King, Jr.'s, famous speech during the March on Washington in 1963 has been divided into fifteen sections, each one illustrated by award-winning artists. Artists' statements about their tributes following the speech offer insights about their art and their sense of this particular history. Their comments vary widely, as do their visual interpretations of each section of text. The artists are Ashley Bryan, Carole Byard, Wil Clay, Floyd Cooper, Pat Cummings, Diane and Leo Dillon, Tom Feelings, George Ford, Jan Spivey Gilchrist, Brian Pinkney, Jerry Pinkney, James E. Ransome, Teréa Shaffer, and Kathleen Atkins Wilson.

THE KID'S GUIDE TO SOCIAL ACTION: HOW TO SOLVE THE SOCIAL PROBLEMS YOU CHOOSE—AND TURN CREATIVE THINKING INTO POSITIVE ACTION

Barbara Lewis. (Free Spirit Publishing, 1991) 185 pages. ISBN: 0-915793-29-6. Level: Age 8 and older.

A well-organized, attractively designed, and accessible handbook offers a wealth of information for young people who want to change things. Written by a Salt Lake City elementary school teacher whose students have effected impressive changes at local, state, and national levels, the step-by-step guide moves logically from the simplest forms of action, such as writing a letter to the editor or circulating a student petition, to the more sophisticated—for instance, lobbying federal government. Lewis illustrates each model of social action with a true story of a child activist who successfully used the method to make a change. She also presents a realistic picture of the hard work involved, outlining the steps from identifying a problem and developing an action plan to gathering information, fund-raising, and getting publicity.

KIDS MAKING QUILTS FOR KIDS

ABC Quilts. (Quilt Digest Press, 1992) 43 pages. ISBN: Paperback: 0-913327-36-0. Level: Ages 8-14.

In many parts of the United States, youngsters in Scout troops, Sunday School classes, 4-H clubs, and other youth organizations are gathering together to make quilts to send to children who are HIV positive as part of the ABC Quilt Project. Basic information about getting started, as well as step-by-step instructions for four types of quilt faces, are included in an attractive paperback illustrated with color photographs of kids working on quilts and finished quilts. Facts about AIDS and suggestions for adult-led discussion starters are appended.

THE LILY CUPBOARD

Shulamith Levey Oppenheim. Illustrated by Ronald Himler. (A Charlotte Zolotow Book/HarperCollins, 1992) 32 pages. ISBN: 0-06-024669-3. Level: Ages 5-8.

The heroism of ordinary rural Dutch people unfolds in a first person fictional narrative about a child named Miriam, "hidden" with a non-Jewish family during the World War II German occupation of Holland. Paintings rendered in watercolor and gouache illustrate the spare text of a picture-book glimpse into the bravery and sacrifice of Jewish parents who entrusted their children's lives to strangers within whose homes children like Miriam lived amidst constant danger.

THE LITTLE SHIPS: THE HEROIC RESCUE AT DUNKIRK IN WORLD WAR II

Louise Borden. Illustrated by Michael Foreman. (Margaret K. McElderry, 1997) 32 pages. ISBN: 0-689-80827-5. Level: Ages 8-12 and older.

"In 1940, I lived with my father in the town of Deal, on the Kent coast of England, safe from the thunder of the Germans' guns in France. Some days in May I could hear it, rolling in big booms across the English Channel. Some days I could feel it, rattling the glass in the windows on our street." So writes a girl who climbed into her brother's clothes and then—unbidden—onto her father's fishing boat to become part of the "motley group of ships," an armada crossing the Channel to rescue the British soldiers trapped on the sandy beaches of France. Thousands of soldiers were saved by that now legendary civilian armada. Fright, drama, and simple heroics are described almost poetically by a girl looking all the while for her brother John but seeing, instead, the horrific details of an army in retreat. Foreman's watercolors vividly expand the first person narrative, while the overall design of the volume adds urgency. An author's note provides facts about this historic effort and an excerpt from Winston Churchill's June 4 speech to Parliament—welcome reality from pages otherwise too amazing to be believed.

MARTHA CALLING

Susan Meddaugh. (Houghton Mifflin, 1994) 32 pages. ISBN: 0-395-69825-1. Level: Ages 4-8.

The dog who suddenly began speaking after a bowl of alphabet soup went to her brain instead of her stomach in MARTHA SPEAKS (Houghton, 1992) is back again. This time she's learning that there's a downside to communication. Not all words are pleasing, and three in particular are downright rude: "No dogs allowed." When Martha wins a vacation to a seaside resort in a telephone contest, she must suffer the ultimate indignity of being disguised as a human. Once again, Meddaugh combines understatement, dialogue balloons, and humorously expressive illustrations to allow Martha to speak for herself.

NEVE SHALOM / WAHAT AL-SALAM; OASIS OF PEACE

Laurie Dolphin. Photographs by Ben Dolphin. (Scholastic, 1993) 48 pages. ISBN: 0-590-45799-3. Level: Ages 7-10.

Shlomo Franklin and Muhammad Jabar both live in Israel. Shlomo, who is Jewish, lives in the village of Nataf with other Jewish families and has never had any Arab friends. Muhammad, who is a Palestinian Moslem, lives in Abu Gosh, an old Arab village, and has never had any Jewish friends. The parents of each of these ten-year-old boys have decided to send their sons to a remarkable school in a remarkable village called Neve Shalom (Hebrew) / Wahat al-Salam (Arabic), or Oasis of Peace. At the school, Arab and Jewish teachers together teach Arab and Jewish children, who learn about the customs, history, and language of both cultures in a curriculum designed to foster friendship rather than fear. Text and photographs depicting first the separateness of Shlomo's and Muhammad's lives, and then their meeting and burgeoning friendship, build understanding of the current tenor of Arab and Israeli relations and hope for a peaceful future.

NIM AND THE WAR EFFORT

Milly Lee. Illustrated by Yangsook Choi. (Frances Foster/Farrar, Straus and Giroux, 1997) 36 pages. ISBN: 0-374-35523-1. Level: Ages 7-10 and older.

The story concerns a typical World War II school project, a newspaper drive with a contest to see which child can collect the most paper. During a last minute scramble, Chinese American Nim confronts a white male classmate who claims an "American" will win the contest. Nim wins, but according to her family's values, she also loses. The paper drive is only one of the ways Nim and her public school friends in San Francisco aid the war effort during World War II. Her family is also part of the war effort, but they do not want to be mistaken as Japanese. Nim learns Cantonese at home, practices calligraphy lessons, and attends Chinese school in the late afternoons. The homefront is carefully detailed within a Chinese American context in a relatively long illustrated narrative filled with smoothly incorporated historical and cultural details. Lee raises several issues regarding patriotism, national pride, and culture.

OH, FREEDOM! KIDS TALK ABOUT THE CIVIL RIGHTS MOVEMENT WITH THE PEOPLE WHO MADE IT HAPPEN

Casey King and Linda Barrett Osborne. Foreword by Rosa Parks. Illustrated with photographs. (Alfred A. Knopf, 1997) 137 pages. ISBN: 0-679-85856-3; pbk: 0-679-89005-X. Level: Ages 8-14 and older.

Brief interviews were conducted by thirty-four middle school students with thirty-four adults who lived through the U.S. civil rights movement. Some of the adults were active in the movement, others describe what life was like when segregation was legal, and one former KKK member talks candidly about his own racist views prior to his religious conversion while in prison for bombing the home of a Jewish civil rights leader in Meridian, Mississippi. Each interview is accompanied by a photographic portrait of the interviewer with his or her subject, along with documentary photographs of the activists at marches and sit-ins, revealing that many of them were middle school students themselves when they got involved in the movement. The conversational tone of the interviews will make them accessible and appealing to young readers and because the interviewers are children, they often ask their subjects to explain things adults take for granted: how a sit-in worked, for example, or what "rhetoric" means. The interviews are organized into three sections: life under segregation, the movement to end legalized segregation, and the struggle to end poverty and discrimination. Each of these three sections opens with a cogent overview that provides a context for the interviews that will follow. The third section includes some remarkable interviews with people who were active in the Black Nationalist Movement and the Black Panthers, a side of U.S. history and politics rarely seen in children's books.

Ⓧ Ⓘ Ⓥ

SAMI AND THE TIME OF THE TROUBLES

Florence Parry Heide and Judith Heide Gilliland. Illustrated by Ted Lewin. (Clarion, 1992) 32 pages. ISBN: 0-395-55964-2. Level: Ages 8-11.

Ten-year-old Sami and his family live in contemporary Beirut, Lebanon. Sometimes the family picnics on a beach and goes to the market. Too often gunfire fills the streets, requiring family members to stay in a basement shelter where they try to remember sunsets, peach orchards, and happier times. After the shooting stops, Sami and his friend Amir help clean up rubble in the streets and then play in their makeshift fort. "We run, we hide, we pre-

tend to shoot, we pretend to die. I see my mother at a stall buying flowers, and she frowns at me. She does not like for me to play this game." Expressing the ambiguity of Sami's life and of a childhood in which maturity means using guns to fight a civil war, this full-color picture story illuminates an experience transferable to other places in the world. Gilliland's firsthand experience in Beirut contributes a valuable dimension to the provocative book.

SAVE THE EARTH: AN ACTION HANDBOOK FOR KIDS

Betty Miles. Illustrated by Nelle Davis. (Alfred A. Knopf, 1991) 118 pages. ISBN: 0-679-81731-X. Level: Ages 8-12.

Accessible information about environmental issues and activities is well-organized in seven chapters titled "Land," "Atmosphere," "Water," "Energy," "Plants & Animals," "People," and "Getting to Work." The first six chapters focus on the named subject by providing factual background information, accounts of relevant youth efforts currently taking place, detailed projects appropriate to the book's audience, and a "checklist" of simple activities anyone can attempt. The final chapter outlines helpful procedures applicable to a variety of issues, including finding information in the library, joining environmental groups, writing letters, speaking, and holding press conferences. A glossary, reading list, and addresses of several environmental groups are included. Interested readers will appreciate the book's "do-able," action-oriented approach.

Ⓧ ⒾⓍ

SEEDFOLKS

Paul Fleischman. (Joanna Cotler/HarperCollins, 1997) 69 pages. ISBN: 0-06-027471-9. Level: Ages 9-13 and older.

A young Vietnamese girl plants six lima bean seedlings in an overgrown, garbage-strewn, inner-city lot in Cleveland. An elderly longtime resident of the neighborhood watches the child from a third-story apartment window, unsure of what the girl is doing all alone in that abandoned lot, but suspicious. Life in the neighborhood has taught the woman to be distrustful of people, even of children, but when she discovers the girl has planted beans, she is startled and moved by the tender act. Realizing it is far too early in the spring for such young plantings to survive, she calls upon a friend to help her secretly tend them so the child's small garden will grow. From these small acts, a neighborhood begins to change. Where once there was an old, abandoned lot, a garden emerges. Where once there were disconnected lives, a fragile sense of community begins to grow. *Seedfolks* takes place in an economically disadvantaged urban neighborhood comprising individuals from diverse racial and ethnic backgrounds, a neighborhood in which some of the residents are relative newcomers to the United States while others have lived on those very city blocks for most or all of their lives. Fleischman gives them voice, writing each chapter from the point of view of a different individual in the neighborhood who gets involved in the garden. There are conflicts as well as connections that result from the garden's growth in *Seedfolks*, but ultimately there is hope, and a flowering of the human spirit.

Children's Trade Books with Civic Ideals and Practices as a Second Thematic Strand

The title index on pp. 173-180 lists the number of the page on which each book is annotated.

TITLE	AUTHOR	DATE	AGE LEVEL
Aani and the Tree Huggers	Jeannine Atkins	1995	Ages 4-9
The Bobbin Girl	Emily Arnold McCully	1996	Ages 8-11 and older
Celebrating Kwanzaa	Diane Hoyt-Goldsmith	1993	Ages 5-12
Common Ground: The Water, Earth, and Air We Share	Molly Bang	1997	Ages 5-8 and older
Follow That Trash! All about Recycling	Francine Jacobs	1996	Ages 5-7
The Gardener	Sarah Stewart	1997	Ages 5-9
Kwanzaa	A. P. Porter	1991	Ages 5-9
Lift Ev'ry Voice and Sing	James Weldon Johnson	1995	Age 3-adult
Officer Buckle and Gloria	Peggy Rathmann	1995	Ages 3-7
Public Defender: Lawyer for the People	Joan Hewett	1991	Ages 9-14
The Snow Walker	Margaret K. Wetterer and Charles M. Wetterer	1996	Ages 7-10
Toussaint L'Ouverture: The Fight for Haiti's Freedom	Walter Dean Myers	1996	Ages 9-12

Children's Trade Books with Civic Ideals and Practices as a Third Thematic Strand

The title index on pp. 173-180 lists the number of the page on which each book is annotated.

Christmas Counting	Lynn Reiser	1992	Ages 2-5
Fire at the Triangle Factory	Holly Littlefield	1996	Ages 8-11
Great-Grandma Tells of Threshing Day	Verda Cross	1992	Ages 5-8, or older for oral history purposes
Growing Up in Coal Country	Susan Campbell Bartoletti	1996	Ages 9-16
Habari Gani? / What's the News?: A Kwanzaa Story	Sundaira Morninghouse	1992	Ages 4-9
Imani's Gift at Kwanzaa	Denise Burden-Patmon	1992	Ages 3-8
Sam and the Lucky Money	Karen Chinn	1995	Ages 4-7
Winter Rescue	W. D. Valgardson	1995	Ages 6-9

How to Use the Index

Complete annotations for each children's book recommended in this publication can be found listed alphabetically under each book's Major Thematic Strand (as identified in Chapter Three). For example, *A Is for Africa* can be found under ❺ (Individuals, Groups, and Institutions), on page 125.

► SUBJECT INDEX

Social studies disciplines are not listed in this index, and readers interested in identifying books suitable for a particular discipline should refer to the chapter dealing with the appropriate strand of the social studies standards. For example, for books with historical themes, the reader should consult chapter 6, which deals with the strand of Time, Continuity, and Change.

DeAn M. Krey began her career as an elementary school teacher of the sixth and then the second grades. Since 1969, she has been a Professor of Elementary Social Studies in the Department of Teacher Education at the University of Wisconsin—River Falls. She is team leader of a methods block which integrates social studies, language arts and science. She also teaches children's literature and a graduate level social studies course. She has received the Distinguished Teacher Award from the University of Wisconsin-River Falls and the Outstanding Faculty Award from the College of Education.

Dr. Krey is a Past President of the Wisconsin Council for the Social Studies (WCSS). She has served as the Chairperson for the Nominations Committee and the Sexism and Social Justice Committee of National Council for the Social Studies (NCSS). Dr. Krey has made numerous presentations at both WCSS and NCSS, has served as consultant to public school systems and has authored and co-authored a wide variety of journal articles.

For the past three years, Dr. Krey has served on the national selection committee for "Notable Children's Trade Books in the Field of Social Studies," sponsored by the Children's Book Council and NCSS and is the 1999 Chairperson of that committee.